BANKING: HISTORY, LAW AND PRACTICE

Banking: History, Law and Practice

Lalit Lilothia

CYBER TECH PUBLICATIONS
4264/3, Ansari Road, Daryaganj, New Delhi-110002 (India)
Ph.: 011-23244078. Fax: 011-23280028
E-Mail: cyberpublicationsdelhi@yahoo.com

BANKING: HISTORY, LAW AND PRACTICE

Lalit Lilothia

First Edition 2009

Published by :

G.S. Rawat for **Cyber Tech Publications**
4264/3, Ansari Road, Daryaganj, New Delhi-110002 (India)
Ph.: 011-23244078. Fax: 011-23280028
E-Mail: cyberpublicationsdelhi@yahoo.com

Printed at : Asian Offset Printers

Preface

The changing economic environment has a significant impact on banks and thrifts as they struggle to effectively manage their interest rate spread in the face of low rates on loans, rate competition for deposits and the general market changes, industry trends and economic fluctuations. It has been a challenge for banks to effectively set their growth strategies with the recent economic market. A rising interest rate environment may seem to help financial institutions, but the effect of the changes on consumers and businesses is not predictable and the challenge remains for banks to grow and effectively manage the spread to generate a return to their shareholders.

The management of the banks' asset portfolios also remains a challenge in today's economic environment. Loans are a bank's primary asset category and when loan quality becomes suspect, the foundation of a bank is shaken to the core. While always an issue for banks, declining asset quality has become a big problem for financial institutions. There are several reasons for this, one of which is the lax attitude some banks have adopted because of the years of "good times."

This book deals all with the history, law and banking practices. Undersigned is confident enough that this work of him would be beneficial to the readers those who are keen to know more about bank and its operation methods.

—Author

CONTENTS

1

Introduction

A banker or bank is a financial institution that acts as a payment agent for customers, and borrows and lends money. In some countries such as Germany and Japan banks are the primary owners of industrial corporations while in other countries such as the United States banks are prohibited from owning non-financial companies.

The first modern bank was founded in Italy at Genoa in 1406, its name was Banco di San Giorgio (Bank of St. George).

Banks act as payment agents by conducting checking or current accounts for customers, paying cheques drawn by customers on the bank, and collecting cheques deposited to customers' current accounts. Banks also enable customer payments via other payment methods such as telegraphic transfer, EFTPOS, and ATM.

Banks borrow money by accepting funds deposited on current account, accepting term deposits and by issuing debt securities such as banknotes and bonds. Banks lend money by making advances to customers on current account, by making installment loans, and by investing in marketable debt securities and other forms of lending.

Banks provide almost all payment services, and a bank account is considered indispensable by most businesses, individuals and governments. Non-banks that provide payment services such as remittance companies are not normally considered an adequate substitute for having a bank account.

Banks borrow most funds borrowed from households and non-financial businesses, and lend most funds lent to households and non-financial businesses, but non-bank lenders provide a significant and in many cases adequate substitute for bank loans, and money market funds, cash management trusts and other non-bank financial institutions in many cases provide an adequate substitute to banks for lending savings to.

DEFINITION

The definition of a bank varies from country to country.

Under English law, a bank is defined as a person who carries on the business of banking, which is specified as:

- conducting current accounts for customers
- paying cheques drawn on a given person, and
- collecting cheques for their customers.

In most English common law jurisdictions there is a Bills of Exchange Act that codifies the law in relation to negotiable instruments, including cheques, and this Act contains a statutory definition of the term banker: banker includes a body of persons, whether incorporated or not, who carry on the business of banking' (Section 2, Interpretation). Although this definition seems circular, it is actually functional, because it ensures that the legal basis for bank transactions such as cheques do not depend on how the bank is organised or regulated.

The business of banking is in many English common law countries not defined by statute but by common law, the definition above. In other English common law jurisdictions there are statutory definitions of the business of banking or banking business. When looking at these definitions it is important to keep in mind that they are defining the business of banking for the purposes of the legislation, and not necessarily in general.

In particular, most of the definitions are from legislation that has the purposes of entry regulating and supervising banks rather than regulating the actual business of banking. However, in many cases the statutory definition closely mirrors the common law one. Examples of statutory definitions:

- "banking business" means the business of receiving money on current or deposit account, paying and collecting cheques drawn by or paid in by customers, the making of advances to customers, and includes such other business as the Authority may prescribe for the purposes of this Act; (Banking Act (Singapore), Section 2, Interpretation).

- "banking business" means the business of either or both of the following:
  1. receiving from the general public money on current, deposit, savings or other similar account repayable on demand or within less than [3 months]... or with a period of call or notice of less than that period;
  2. paying or collecting cheques drawn by or paid in by customers

Since the advent of EFTPOS (Electronic Funds Transfer at Point Of Sale), direct credit, direct debit and internet banking, the cheque has lost its primacy in most banking systems as a payment instrument. This has lead legal theorists to suggest that the cheque based definition should be broadened to include financial institutions that conduct current accounts for customers and enable customers to pay and be paid by third parties, even if they do not pay and collect cheques.

WIDER COMMERCIAL ROLE

However the commercial role of banks is wider than banking, and includes:

- issue of banknotes (promissory notes issued by a banker and payable to bearer on demand)
- processing of payments by way of telegraphic transfer, EFTPOS, internet banking or other means
- issuing bank drafts and bank cheques
- accepting money on term deposit
- lending money by way of overdraft, installment loan or otherwise
- providing documentary and standby letters of credit, guarantees, performance bonds, securities underwriting commitments and other forms of off balance sheet exposures
- safekeeping of documents and other items in safe deposit boxes
- currency exchange

sale, distribution or brokerage, with or without advice, of insurance, unit trusts and similar financial products as a 'financial supermarket'

ECONOMIC FUNCTIONS

The economic functions of banks include:

1. issue of money, in the form of banknotes and current accounts subject to cheque or payment at the customer's order. These claims on banks can act as money because they are negotiable and/or repayable on demand, and hence valued at par and effectively transferable by mere delivery in the case of banknotes, or by drawing a cheque, delivering it to the payee to bank or cash.
2. netting and settlement of payments--banks act both as collection agent and paying agents for customers, and participate in inter-bank clearing and settlement systems to collect, present, be presented with, and pay payment instruments. This enables banks to economise on reserves held for settlement of payments, since inward and outward payments offset each other. It also enables payment flows between geographical areas to offset, reducing the cost of settling payments between geographical areas.
3. credit intermediation--banks borrow and lend back-to-back on their own account as middle men
4. credit quality improvement--banks lend money to ordinary commercial and personal borrowers (ordinary credit quality), but are high quality borrowers. The improvement comes from diversification of the bank's assets and the bank's own capital which provides a buffer to absorb losses without defaulting on its own obligations. However, since banknotes and deposits are generally unsecured, if the bank gets into difficulty and pledges assets as security to try to get the funding it needs to continue to operate, this puts the note holders and depositors in an economically subordinated position.
5. maturity transformation--banks borrow more on demand debt and short term debt, but provide more long term loans. Bank can do this because they can aggregate issues (e.g. accepting deposits and issuing banknotes)

and redemptions (e.g. withdrawals and redemptions of banknotes), maintain reserves of cash, invest in marketable securities that can be readily converted to cash if needed, and raise replacement funding as needed from various sources (e.g. wholesale cash markets and securities markets) because they have a high and more well known credit quality than most other borrowers.

LAW OF BANKING

Banking law is based on a contractual analysis of the relationship between the bank and the customer. The definition of bank is given above, and the definition of customer is any person for whom the bank agrees to conduct an account.

The law implies rights and obligations into this relationship as follows:

1. The bank account balance is the financial position between the bank and the customer, when the account is in credit, the bank owes the balance to the customer, when the account is overdrawn, the customer owes the balance to the bank.
2. The bank engages to pay the customer's cheques up to the amount standing to the credit of the customer's account, plus any agreed overdraft limit.
3. The bank may not pay from the customer's account without a mandate from the customer, e.g. a cheque drawn by the customer.
4. The bank engages to promptly collect the cheques deposited to the customer's account as the customer's agent, and to credit the proceeds to the customer's account.
5. The bank has a right to combine the customer's accounts, since each account is just an aspect of the same credit relationship.
6. The bank has a lien on cheques deposited to the customer's account, to the extent that the customer is indebted to the bank.
7. The bank must not disclose the details of the transactions going through the customer's account unless the customer consents, there is a public duty to disclose, the bank's interests require it, or under compulsion of law.

8. The bank must not close a customer's account without reasonable notice to the customer, because cheques are outstanding in the ordinary course of business for several days.

These implied contractual terms may be modified by express agreement between the customer and the bank. The statutes and regulations in force in the jurisdiction may also modify the above terms and/or create new rights, obligations or limitations relevant to the bank-customer relationship.

ENTRY REGULATION

Currently in most jurisdictions commercial banks are regulated by government entities and require a special bank licence to operate.

Usually the definition of the business of banking for the purposes of regulation is extended to include acceptance of deposits, even if they are not repayable to the customer's order, however money lending, by itself, is generally not included in the definition.

Unlike most other regulated industries, the regulator is typically also a participant in the market, i.e. government owned bank (a central bank). Central banks also typically have a monopoly on the business of issuing banknotes. However, in some countries this is not the case, e.g. in the UK the Financial Services Authority licences banks and some commercial banks, such as the Bank of Scotland, issue their own banknotes in competition with the Bank of England, the UK government's central bank.

Some types of entity may be partly or wholly exempt from bank licence requirements and are regulated by separate regulators, e.g. building societies and credit unions.

The requirements for the issue of a bank licence vary between jurisdictions but typically incude:

1. Minimum capital
2. Minimum capital ratio
3. 'Fit and Proper' requirements for the bank's controllers, owners, directors, and/or senior officers
4. Approval of the bank's business plan as being sufficiently prudent and plausible.

POLITICS AND HISTORY

Banks have influenced economies and politics for centuries. Historically, the primary purpose of a bank was to provide loans to trading companies. Banks provided funds to allow businesses to purchase inventory, and collected those funds back with interest when the goods were sold. For centuries, the banking industry only dealt with businesses, not consumers. Commercial lending today is a very intense activity, with banks carefully analysing the financial condition of their business clients to determine the level of risk in each loan transaction. Banking services have expanded to include services directed at individuals, and risk in these much smaller transactions are pooled.

ORIGIN OF THE WORD

The name bank derives from the Italian word banco "desk/ bench", used during the Renaissance by Florentines bankers, who used to make their transactions above a desk covered by a green tablecloth. However, there are traces of banking activity even in ancient times.

In fact, the word traces its origins back to the Ancient Roman Empire, where moneylenders would set up their stalls in the middle of enclosed courtyards called macella on a long bench called a bancu, from which the words banco and bank are derived. As a moneychanger, the merchant at the bancu did not so much invest money as merely convert the foreign currency into the only legal tender in Rome-that of the Imperial Mint.

Banking Channels

Banks offer many different channels to access their banking and other services:

- A branch, banking centre or financial centre is a retail location where a bank or financial institution offers a wide array of face to face service to its customers
- ATM is a computerised telecommunications device that provides a financial institution's customers a method of financial transactions in a public space without the need for a human clerk or bank teller. Most banks now have more ATMs than branches, and ATMs are providing

a wider range of services to a wider range of users. For example in Hong Kong, most ATMs enable anyone to deposit cash to any customer of the bank's account by feeding in the notes and entering the account number to be credited. Also, most ATMs enable card holders from other banks to get their account balance and withdraw cash, even if the card is issued by a foreign bank.

- Mail is part of the postal system which itself is a system wherein written documents typically enclosed in envelopes, and also small packages containing other matter, are delivered to destinations around the world. This can be used to deposit cheques and to send orders to the bank to pay money to third parties. Banks also normally use mail to deliver periodic account statements to customers.
- Telephone banking is a service provided by a financial institution which allows its customers to perform transactions over the telephone. This normally includes bill payments for bills from major billers (e.g. for electricity).
- Online banking is a term used for performing transactions, payments etc. over the Internet through a bank, credit union or building society's secure website

TYPES OF BANKS

Banks' activities can be divided into retail banking, dealing directly with individuals and small businesses; business banking, providing services to mid-market business; corporate banking, directed at large business entities; private banking, providing wealth management services to High Net Worth Individuals and families; and investment banking, relating to activities on the financial markets. Most banks are profit-making, private enterprises. However, some are owned by government, or are non-profits.

Central banks are normally government owned banks, often charged with quasi-regulatory responsibilities, e.g. supervising commercial banks, or controlling the cash interest rate. They generally provide liquidity to the banking system and act as Lender of last resort in event of a crisis.

Types of Retail Banks

- Commercial bank: the term used for a normal bank to distinguish it from an investment bank. After the Great Depression, the U.S. Congress required that banks only engage in banking activities, whereas investment banks were limited to capital market activities. Since the two no longer have to be under separate ownership, some use the term "commercial bank" to refer to a bank or a division of a bank that mostly deals with deposits and loans from corporations or large businesses.
- Community Banks: locally operated financial institutions that empower employees to make local decisions to serve their customers and the partners
- Community development banks: regulated banks that provide financial services and credit to underserved markets or populations.
- Postal savings banks: savings banks associated with national postal systems.
- Private banks: manage the assets of high net worth individuals.
- Offshore banks: banks located in jurisdictions with low taxation and regulation. Many offshore banks are essentially private banks.
- Savings bank: in Europe, savings banks take their roots in the 19th or sometimes even 18th century. Their original objective was to provide easily accessible savings products to all strata of the population. In some countries, savings banks were created on public initiative, while in others socially committed individuals created foundations to put in place the necessary infrastructure. Nowadays, European savings banks have kept their focus on retail banking: payments, savings products, credits and insurances for individuals or small and medium-sized enterprises. Apart from this retail focus, they also differ from commercial banks by their broadly decentralised distribution network, providing local and regional outreach and by their socially responsible approach to business and society.

- Building societies and Landesbanks: conduct retail banking.
- Ethical banks: banks that prioritize the transparency of all operations and make only what they consider to be socially-responsible investments.
- Islamic banks: Banks that transact according to Islamic principles.

Types of Investment Banks

- Investment banks "underwrite" (guarantee the sale of) stock and bond issues, trade for their own accounts, make markets, and advise corporations on capital markets activities such as mergers and acquisitions.
- Merchant banks were traditionally banks which engaged in trade financing. The modern definition, however, refers to banks which provide capital to firms in the form of shares rather than loans. Unlike Venture capital firms, they tend not to invest in new companies.

Both Combined

- Universal banks, more commonly known as a financial services company, engage in several of these activities. For example, First Bank (a very large bank) is involved in commercial and retail lending, and its subsidiaries in tax-havens offer offshore banking services to customers in other countries. Other large financial institutions are similarly diversified and engage in multiple activities. In Europe and Asia, big banks are very diversified groups that, among other services, also distribute insurance, hence the term bancassurance is the term used to describe the sale of insurance products in a bank. The word is a combination of "banque or bank" and "assurance" signifying that both banking and insurance are provided by the same corporate entity.

OTHER TYPES OF BANKS

Islamic Banking

- Islamic banks adhere to the concepts of Islamic law. Islamic banking revolves around several well established concepts which are based on Islamic canons. Since the concept of interest is forbidden in Islam, all banking activities must avoid interest. Instead of interest, the bank earns profit (mark-up) and fees on financing facilities that it extends to the customers.

Banks in the Economy

Size of Global Banking Industry

Worldwide assets of the largest 1,000 banks grew 15.5% in 2005 to reach a record $60.5 trillion. This follows a 19.3% increase in the previous year. EU banks held the largest share, 50% at the end of 2005, up from 38% a decade earlier. The growth in Europe's share was mostly at the expense of Japanese banks whose share more than halved during this period from 33% to 13%. The share of US banks also rose, from 10% to 14%. Most of the remainder was from other Asian and European countries.

The US had by far the most banks (7,540 at end-2005) and branches (75,000) in the world. The large number of banks in the US is an indicator of its geography and regulatory structure, resulting in a large number of small to medium sized institutions in its banking system. Japan had 129 banks and 12,000 branches. In 2004, Germany, France, and Italy had more than 30,000 branches each-more than double the 15,000 branches in the UK.

Bank Crisis

Banks are susceptible to many forms of risk which have triggered occasional systemic crises. Risks include liquidity risk (the risk that many depositors will request withdrawals beyond available funds), credit risk (the risk that those who owe money to the bank will not repay), and interest rate risk (the risk that the bank will become unprofitable if rising interest rates force it to pay relatively more on its deposits than it receives on its loans), among others.

Banking crises have developed many times throughout history when one or more risks materialize for a banking sector as a whole. Prominent examples include the U.S. Savings and Loan crisis in 1980s and early 1990s the Japanese banking crisis during the 1990s, the bank run that occurred during the Great Depression, and the recent liquidation by the central Bank of Nigeria, where about 25 banks were liquidated.

Challenges within the Banking Industry

The banking industry is a highly regulated industry with detailed and focused regulators. All banks with FDIC-insured deposits have the FDIC as a regulator; however, for examinations, the Federal Reserve is the primary federal regulator for Fed-member state banks; the Office of the Comptroller of the Currency ("OCC") is the primary federal regulator for national banks; and the Office of Thrift Supervision, or OTS, is the primary federal regulator for thrifts. State non-member banks are examined by the state agencies as well as the FDIC. National banks have one primary regulator-the OCC.

Each regulatory agency has their own set of rules and regulations to which banks and thrifts must adhere.

The Federal Financial Institutions Examination Council (FFIEC) was established in 1979 as a formal interagency body empowered to prescribe uniform principles, standards, and report forms for the federal examination of financial institutions. Although the FFIEC has resulted in a greater degree of regulatory consistency between the agencies, the rules and regulations are constantly changing.

In addition to changing regulations, changes in the industry have led to consolidations within the Federal Reserve, FDIC, OTS and OCC. Offices have been closed, supervisory regions have been merged, staff levels have been reduced and budgets have been cut. The remaining regulators face an increased burden with increased workload and more banks per regulator. While banks struggle to keep up with the changes in the regulatory environment, regulators struggle to manage their workload and effectively regulate their banks. The impact of these changes is that banks are receiving less hands-on assessment by the regulators, less time spent with each institution, and the potential for more problems slipping through the cracks, potentially resulting in an overall increase in bank failures across the United States.

The changing economic environment has a significant impact on banks and thrifts as they struggle to effectively manage their interest rate spread in the face of low rates on loans, rate competition for deposits and the general market changes, industry trends and economic fluctuations. It has been a challenge for banks to effectively set their growth strategies with the recent economic market. A rising interest rate environment may seem to help financial institutions, but the effect of the changes on consumers and businesses is not predictable and the challenge remains for banks to grow and effectively manage the spread to generate a return to their shareholders.

The management of the banks' asset portfolios also remains a challenge in today's economic environment. Loans are a bank's primary asset category and when loan quality becomes suspect, the foundation of a bank is shaken to the core. While always an issue for banks, declining asset quality has become a big problem for financial institutions. There are several reasons for this, one of which is the lax attitude some banks have adopted because of the years of "good times." The potential for this is exacerbated by the reduction in the regulatory oversight of banks and in some cases depth of management. Problems are more likely to go undetected, resulting in a significant impact on the bank when they are recognized. In addition, banks, like any business, struggle to cut costs and have consequently eliminated certain expenses, such as adequate employee training programs.

Banks also face a host of other challenges such as aging ownership groups. Across the country, many banks' management teams and board of directors are aging. Banks also face ongoing pressure by shareholders, both public and private, to achieve earnings and growth projections. Regulators place added pressure on banks to manage the various categories of risk. Banking is also an extremely competitive industry. Competing in the financial services industry has become tougher with the entrance of such players as insurance agencies, credit unions, check cashing services, credit card companies, etc.

Profitability

A bank generates a profit from the differential between the level of interest it pays for deposits and other sources of funds, and the level of interest it charges in its lending activities. This difference is referred to as the spread between the cost of funds and the loan interest rate. Historically, profitability from lending activities has been cyclical and dependent on the needs and strengths of loan customers. In recent history, investors have demanded a more stable revenue stream and banks have therefore placed more emphasis on transaction fees, primarily loan fees but also including service charges on an array of deposit activities and ancillary services (international banking, foreign exchange, insurance, investments, wire transfers, etc.). Lending activities, however, still provide the bulk of a commercial bank's income.

In the past 10 years American banks have taken many measures to ensure that they remain profitable while responding to increasingly changing market conditions. First, this includes the Gramm-Leach-Bliley Act, which allows banks again to merge with investment and insurance houses. Merging banking, investment, and insurance functions allows traditional banks to respond to increasing consumer demands for "one-stop shopping" by enabling cross-selling of products (which, the banks hope, will also increase profitability). Second, they have expanded the use of risk-based pricing from business lending to consumer lending, which means charging higher interest rates to those customers that are considered to be a higher credit risk and thus increased chance of default on loans.

This helps to offset the losses from bad loans, lowers the price of loans to those who have better credit histories, and offers credit products to high risk customers who would otherwise been denied credit. Third, they have sought to increase the methods of payment processing available to the general public and business clients.

These products include debit cards, pre-paid cards, smart-cards, and credit cards. These products make it easier for consumers to conveniently make transactions and smooth their consumption over time (in some countries with under-developed financial systems, it is still common to deal strictly in cash, including carrying suitcases filled with cash to purchase a home). However, with convenience there is also increased risk that consumers will mismanage their financial resources and accumulate excessive debt. Banks make money from card products through interest payments and fees charged to consumers and transaction fees to companies that accept the cards.

The banking industry's main obstacles to increasing profits are existing regulatory burdens, new government regulation, and increasing competition from non-traditional financial institutions.

Bank Size Information

Top ten banking groups in the world ranked by shareholder equity ($m)

The 2006 bank atlas was compiled from commercial banks' annual reports and financial statements for 2006 and 2005.[9] Figures in U.S. dollars

Rank	Country	Company	Shareholder equity ($m)
1	United States	Bank of America	138510 $mln
2	United States	Citigroup	127113 $mln
3	United Kingdom	HSBC	108352 $mln
4	Japan	Mitsubishi UFJ Financial Group	93913 $mln
5	France	Credit Agricole Group	65137 $mln
6	United Kingdom	Royal Bank of Scotland Group	64453 $mln
7	France	BNP Paribas	56610 $mln
8	Spain	Banco Santander	53640 $mln
9	Japan	Mizuho Financial Group	52243 $mln

Top ten banking groups in the world ranked by assets

Figures in U.S. dollars, and as at end-2004[10]

Rank	Country	Company	Assets (US $)
1	United Kingdom	HSBC Holdings	1,861 billion
2	Switzerland	UBS	1,533 billion
3	United States	Citigroup	1,400 billion
4	Japan	Mizuho Financial Group	1,296 billion
5	France	Credit Agricole Group	1,243 billion
6	France	BNP Paribas	1,234 billion
7	United States	JPMorgan Chase & Co.	1,157 billion
8	Germany	Deutsche Bank	1,144 billion
9	United Kingdom	Royal Bank of Scotland	1,119 billion
10	United States	Bank of America	1,110 billion

Top ten banks in the world ranked by market capitalization

Figures in Euros, and as at 22 November 2007.

Rank	Country	Company	Market Capitalisation (Eur)
1	China	Industrial and Commercial Bank of China	230.880 billion
2	China	China Construction Bank	154.295 billion
3	China	Bank of China	141.466 billion
4	UK	HSBC Holdings	137.869 billion
5	US	Bank of America	128.430 billion
6	US	Citigroup	105.820 billion
7	US	JPMorgan Chase	94.609 billion
8	Spain	Banco Santander	92.438 billion
9	Italy	UniCredit	72.558 billion
10	US	Wells Fargo	69.036 billion

Top ten banking groups in the world ranked by Tier 1 capital

Figures in U.S. dollars, and as at end-2005

Rank	Country	Company	Tier 1 Capital (US $)
1	UK	HSBC	79 billion
2	US	Citigroup	75 billion
3	US	Bank of America	73 billion
4	US	JP Morgan Chase	72 billion
5	Japan	Mitsubishi UFJ Financial Group	64 billion
6	France	Credit Agricole Group	60 billion
7	UK	Royal Bank of Scotland	48 billion
8	Japan	Sumitomo Mitsui Financial Group	40 billion
9	Japan	Mizuho Financial Group	39 billion
10	Spain	Banco Santander	38 billion

2

History of Banking

EARLIEST BANKS

The first banks were probably the religious temples of the ancient world, and were probably established sometime during the 3rd millennium B.C. Banks probably predated the invention of money. Deposits initially consisted of grain and later other goods including cattle, agricultural implements, and eventually precious metals such as gold, in the form of easy-to-carry compressed plates. Temples and palaces were the safest places to store gold as they were constantly attended and well built. As sacred places, temples presented an extra deterrent to would-be thieves. There are extant records of loans from the 18th century BC in Babylon that were made by temple priests to merchants. By the time of Hammurabi's Code, banking was well enough developed to justify the promulgation of laws governing banking operations.

Ancient Greece holds further evidence of banking. Greek temples, as well as private and civic entities, conducted financial transactions such as loans, deposits, currency exchange, and validation of coinage. There is evidence too of credit, whereby in return for a payment from a client, a moneylender in one Greek port would write a credit note for the client who could "cash" the note in another city, saving the client the danger of carting coinage with him on his journey. Pythius, who operated as a merchant banker throughout Asia Minor at the beginning of the 5th century B.C., is the first individual banker of whom we have records. Many of the early bankers in Greek city-states were "metics" or foreign residents. Around 371 B.C., Pasion, a slave, became the wealthiest and most famous Greek banker, gaining his freedom and Athenian citizenship in the process.

The fourth century B.C. saw increased use of credit-based banking in the Mediterranean world. In Egypt, from early times, grain had been used as a form of money in addition to precious metals, and state granaries functioned as banks. When Egypt fell under the rule of a Greek dynasty, the Ptolemies (330-323 B.C.), the numerous scattered government granaries were transformed into a network of grain banks, centralized in Alexandria where the main accounts from all the state granary banks were recorded. This banking network functioned as a trade credit system in which payments were effected by transfer from one account to another without money passing.

In the late third century B.C., the barren Aegean island of Delos, known for its magnificent harbor and famous temple of Apollo, became a prominent banking center. As in Egypt, cash transactions were replaced by real credit receipts and payments were made based on simple instructions with accounts kept for each client. With the defeat of its main rivals, Carthage and Corinth, by the Romans, the importance of Delos increased. Consequently it was natural that the bank of Delos should become the model most closely imitated by the banks of Rome.

Ancient Rome perfected the administrative aspect of banking and saw greater regulation of financial institutions and financial practices. Charging interest on loans and paying interest on deposits became more highly developed and competitive. The development of Roman banks was limited, however, by the Roman preference for cash transactions. During the reign of the Roman emperor Gallienus (260-268 CE), there was a temporary breakdown of the Roman banking system after the banks rejected the flakes of copper produced by his mints. With the ascent of Christianity, banking became subject to additional restrictions, as the charging of interest was seen as immoral. After the fall of Rome, banking was abandoned in western Europe and did not revive until the time of the crusades.

RELIGIOUS RESTRICTIONS ON INTEREST

Most early religious systems in the ancient Near East, and the secular codes arising from them, did not forbid usury. These societies regarded inanimate matter as alive, like plants, animals and people, and capable of reproducing itself. Hence if you lent 'food money', or monetary tokens of any kind, it was legitimate to charge interest. Food money in the shape of olives, dates, seeds or animals was lent out as early as c. 5000 BC, if not earlier. Among the Mesopotamians, Hittites, Phoenicians and Egyptians, interest was legal and often fixed by the state. But the Jews took a different view of the matter.

The Torah and later sections of the Hebrew Bible criticize interest-taking, but interpretations of the Biblical prohibition vary. One common understanding is that Jews are forbidden to charge interest upon loans made to other Jews, but allowed to charge interest on transactions with non-Jews, or Gentiles. However, the Hebrew Bible itself gives numerous examples where this provision was evaded. Johnson holds that the Hebrew Bible treats the lending as philanthropy in a poor community whose aim was collective survival, but which is not obliged to be charitable towards outsiders.

DURING LATE ANTIQUITY AND MIDDLE AGES

Jews were ostracized from most professions by local rulers, the Church and the guilds and so were pushed into marginal occupations considered socially inferior, such as tax and rent collecting and moneylending, while the provision of financial services was increasingly demanded by the expansion of European trade and commerce.

Medieval trade fairs, such as the one in Hamburg, contributed to the growth of banking in a curious way: moneychangers issued documents redeemable at other fairs, in exchange for hard currency. These documents could be cashed at another fair in a different country or at a future fair in the same location. If redeemable at a future date, they would often be discounted by an amount comparable to a rate of interest. Eventually, these documents evolved into bills of exchange, which could be redeemed at any office of the issuing banker. These bills made it possible to transfer large sums of money without the complications of hauling large chests of gold and hiring armed guards to protect the gold from thieves.

Beginning around 1100, the need to transfer large sums of money to finance the Crusades stimulated the reemergence of banking in western Europe. In 1156, in Genoa, occurred the earliest known foreign exchange contract. Two brothers borrowed 115 Genoese pounds and agreed to reimburse the bank's agents in Constantinople the sum of 460 bezants one month after their arrival in that city. In the following century the use of such contracts grew rapidly, particularly since profits from time differences were seen as not infringing canon laws against usury. In 1162, Henry II levied a tax to support the crusades--the first of a series of taxes levied by Henry over the years with the same objective. The templars and hospitallers acted as Henry's bankers in the Holy Land. The Templars' wide flung, large land holdings across Europe also emerged in the 1100-1300 time frame as the beginning of Europe-wide banking, as their practice was to take in local currency, for which a demand note would be given that would be good at any of their castles across Europe, allowing movement of money without the usual risk of robbery while traveling.

By 1200 there was a large and growing volume of long-distance and international trade in a number of agricultural commodities and manufactured goods in western Europe, including corn, wool, finished cloth, wine, salt, wax and tallow, leather and leather goods, and weapons and armour. Individual trading concerns and combines often specialized in one or more of these, as did individual producers; because a large amount of capital was required to establish, e.g., a cloth manufacturing business, only the largest firms could diversify. As a result, businesses and clusters of businesses tended to market fairly narrow product lines. Big firms like the Medici bank could and did specialize; the Medici's manufacturing division had a number of manufacturing facilities producing many different types of cloth. Perhaps the best example of product policy comes from the Cistercian monastic order, where individual monasteries and granges tended to specialize in particular agricultural products or types of industrial production, usually with an eye to meeting particular local or regional market needs.

Ironically, the Papal bankers were the most successful of the Western world. When Pope John XXII (born Jacques d'Euse (1249-1334) was crowned in Lyon in 1316, he set up residency in Avignon. Civil war in Florence between the rival Guelph and Ghibelline factions resulted in victory for a group of Guelph merchant families in the city. They took over papal banking monopolies from rivals in nearby Siena and became tax collectors for the Pope throughout Europe. In 1306, Philip IV expelled

Jews from France. In 1311 he expelled Italian bankers and collected their outstanding credit. In 1327, Avignon had 43 branches of Italian banking houses. In 1347, Edward III of England defaulted on loans. Later there was the bankruptcy of the Peruzzi (1374) and Bardi (1353). The accompanying growth of Italian banking in France was the start of the Lombard moneychangers in Europe, who moved from city to city along the busy pilgrim routes important for trade. Key cities in this period were Cahors, the birthplace of Pope John XXII, and Figeac. Perhaps it was because of these origins that the term Lombard is synonymous with Cahorsin in medieval Europe, and means 'pawnbroker'. Banca Monte dei Paschi di Siena SPA (MPS) Italy, is the oldest surviving bank in the world.

After 1400, political forces turned against the methods of the Italian free enterprise bankers. In 1401, King Martin I of Aragon expelled them. In 1403, Henry IV of England prohibited them from taking profits in any way in his kingdom. In 1409, Flanders imprisoned and then expelled Genoese bankers. In 1410, all Italian merchants were expelled from Paris. In 1401, the Bank of Barcelona was founded. In 1407, the Bank of St George was founded in Genoa. This bank dominated business in the Mediterranean. In 1403 charging interest on loans was ruled legal in Florence despite the traditional Christian prohibition of usury. Italian banks such as the Lombards, who had agents in the main economic centres of Europe, had been making charges for loans. The lawyer and theologian Lorenzo di Antonio Ridolfi won a case which legalised interest payments by the Florentine government. In 1413, Giovanni di Bicci de'Medici appointed banker to the pope. In 1440, Gutenberg invents the modern printing press although Europe already knew of the use of paper money in China. The printing press design was subsequently modified, by Leonardo da Vinci among others, for use in minting coins nearly two centuries before printed banknotes were produced in the West.

By the 1390s silver was short all over Europe, except in Venice. The silver mines at Kutná Hora had begun to decline in the 1370s, and finally closed down after being sacked by King Sigismund in 1422. By 1450 almost all of the mints of northwest Europe had closed down for lack of silver. The last money-changer in the major French port of Dieppe went out of business in 1446. In 1455 the Turks overran the Serbian silver mines, and in 1460 captured the last Bosnian mine. The last Venetian silver grosso was minted in 1462. Several Venetian banks failed, and so did the Strozzi bank of Florence, the second largest in the city. Even the smallest of small change became scarce.

WESTERN BANKING HISTORY

Modern Western economic and financial history is usually traced back to the coffee houses of London. The London Royal Exchange was established in 1565. At that time moneychangers were already called bankers, though the term "bank" usually referred to their offices, and did not carry the meaning it does today.

There was also a hierarchical order among professionals; at the top were the bankers who did business with heads of state, next were the city exchanges, and at the bottom were the pawn shops or "Lombard"'s. Some European cities today have a Lombard street where the pawn shop was located.

After the siege of Antwerp trade moved to Amsterdam. In 1609 the Amsterdamsche Wisselbank (Amsterdam Exchange Bank) was founded which made Amsterdam the financial centre of the world until the Industrial Revolution.

Banking offices were usually located near centers of trade, and in the late 17th century, the largest centers for commerce were the ports of Amsterdam, London, and Hamburg. Individuals could participate in the lucrative East India trade by purchasing bills of credit from these banks, but the price they received for commodities was dependent on the ships returning (which often didn't happen on time) and on the cargo they carried (which often wasn't according to plan). The commodities market was very volatile for this reason, and also because of the many wars that led to cargo seizures and loss of ships.

Capitalism

Around the time of Adam Smith (1776) there was a massive growth in the banking industry. Within the new system of ownership and investment, the State's intervention in economic affairs was reduced and barriers to competition were removed.

Global Banking

In the 1970s, a number of smaller crashes tied to the policies put in place following the depression, resulted in deregulation and privatization of government-owned enterprises in the 1980s, indicating that governments of industrial countries around the world found private-sector solutions to problems of economic growth and development preferable to state-operated, semi-socialist programs. This spurred a trend that was already prevalent in the business sector, large companies becoming global and dealing with customers, suppliers, manufacturing, and information centres all over the world.

Global banking and capital market services proliferated during the 1980s and 1990s as a result of a great increase in demand from companies, governments, and financial institutions, but also because financial market conditions were buoyant and, on the whole, bullish. Interest rates in the United States declined from about 15% for two-year U.S. Treasury notes to about 5% during the 20-year period, and financial assets grew then at a rate approximately twice the rate of the world economy. Such growth rate would have been lower, in the last twenty years, were it not for the profound effects of the internationalization of financial markets especially U.S. Foreign investments, particularly from Japan, who not only provided the funds to corporations in the U.S., but also helped finance the federal government; thus, transforming the U.S. stock market by far into the largest in the world.

Nevertheless, in recent years, the dominance of U.S. financial markets has been disappearing and there has been an increasing interest in foreign stocks. The extraordinary growth of foreign financial markets results from both large increases in the pool of savings in foreign countries, such as Japan, and, especially, the deregulation of foreign financial markets, which has enabled them to expand their activities. Thus, American corporations and banks have started seeking investment opportunities abroad, prompting the development in the U.S. of mutual funds specializing in trading in foreign stock markets.

Such growing internationalization and opportunity in financial services has entirely changed the competitive landscape, as now many banks have demonstrated a preference for the "universal banking" model so prevalent in Europe. Universal banks are free to engage in all forms of financial services, make investments in client companies, and function as much as possible as a "one-stop" supplier of both retail and wholesale financial services. Many such possible alignments could be accomplished only by large acquisitions, and there were many of them. By the end of 2000, a year in which a record level of financial services transactions with a market value of $10.5 trillion occurred, the top ten banks commanded a market share of more than 80% and the top five, 55%. Of the top ten banks ranked by market share, seven were large universal-type banks (three American and four European), and the remaining three were large U.S. investment banks who between them accounted for a 33% market share.

This growth and opportunity also led to an unexpected outcome: entrance into the market of other financial intermediaries: nonbanks. Large corporate players were beginning to find their way into the financial service community, offering competition to established banks. The main services offered included insurances, pension, mutual, money market and hedge funds, loans and credits and securities. Indeed, by the end of 2001 the market capitalisation of the world's 15 largest financial services providers included four nonbanks.

In recent years, the process of financial innovation has advanced enormously increasing the importance and profitability of nonbank finance. Such profitability priorly restricted to the nonbanking industry, has prompted the Office of the Comptroller of the Currency (OCC)to encourage banks to explore other financial instruments, diversifying banks' business as well as improving banking economic health. Hence, as the distinct financial instruments are being explored and adopted by both the banking and nonbanking industries, the distinction between different financial institutions is gradually vanishing.

MAJOR EVENTS IN BANKING HISTORY

- Florentine banking-The Medicis and Pittis among others
- Knights Templar-earliest Euro wide /Mideast banking 1100-1300.

- Banknotes-Introduction of paper money
- 1602-First joint-stock company, the Dutch East India Company founded
- 1720-The South Sea Bubble and John Law's Mississippi Scheme, which caused a European financial crisis and forced many bankers out of business
- 1781-The Bank of North America was found by the Continental Congress
- 1800-Rothschild family founds Euro wide banking.
- 1803-The Louisiana Purchase was the largest land deal in history
- 1929-Stock market crash
- 1989-junk bond scandal and charges against Michael Milken resulted in new legislation for investment banks
- 2001-Enron bankruptcy, causing new legislation for annual reporting

Oldest Private Banks

- Monte dei Paschi di Siena 1472-present, the oldest surviving bank in the world. Founded in 1472 by the Magistrate of the city state of Siena, Italy.
- C. Hoare & Co founded 1672
- Barclays, which was founded by John Freame and Thomas Gould in 1690 and renamed to Barclays by Freame's son-in-law, James Barclay, in 1736
- Rothschild family 1700-present
- Hope & Co., founded in 1762

For French banking history, read the History of banks in France (in English or in French) on the FBF website.

Oldest National Banks

- Bank of Sweden-The rise of the national banks
- Bank of England-The evolution of modern central banking policies
- Bank of America-The invention of centralized check and payment processing technology
- Swiss banking
- United States Banking

- The Pennsylvania Land Bank, founded in 1723 and receiving the support of Benjamin Franklin who wrote "Modest Enquiry into the Nature and Necessity of a Paper Currency" in 1729.
- Imperial Bank of Persia (Iran)-History of banking in the Middle-East

HISTORY OF BANKING IN INDIA

Without a sound and effective banking system in India it cannot have a healthy economy. The banking system of India should not only be hassle free but it should be able to meet new challenges posed by the technology and any other external and internal factors.

For the past three decades India's banking system has several outstanding achievements to its credit. The most striking is its extensive reach. It is no longer confined to only metropolitans or cosmopolitans in India. In fact, Indian banking system has reached even to the remote corners of the country. This is one of the main reason of India's growth process.

The government's regular policy for Indian bank since 1969 has paid rich dividends with the nationalisation of 14 major private banks of India.

Not long ago, an account holder had to wait for hours at the bank counters for getting a draft or for withdrawing his own money. Today, he has a choice. Gone are days when the most efficient bank transferred money from one branch to other in two days. Now it is simple as instant messaging or dial a pizza. Money have become the order of the day.

The first bank in India, though conservative, was established in 1786. From 1786 till today, the journey of Indian Banking System can be segregated into three distinct phases. They are as mentioned below:

- Early phase from 1786 to 1969 of Indian Banks
- Nationalisation of Indian Banks and up to 1991 prior to Indian banking sector Reforms.
- New phase of Indian Banking System with the advent of Indian Financial & Banking Sector Reforms after 1991.

To make this write-up more explanatory, I prefix the scenario as Phase I, Phase II and Phase III.

Phase I

The General Bank of India was set up in the year 1786. Next came Bank of Hindustan and Bengal Bank. The East India Company established Bank of Bengal (1809), Bank of Bombay (1840) and Bank of Madras (1843) as independent units and called it Presidency Banks. These three banks were amalgamated in 1920 and Imperial Bank of India was established which started as private shareholders banks, mostly Europeans shareholders.

In 1865 Allahabad Bank was established and first time exclusively by Indians, Punjab National Bank Ltd. was set up in 1894 with headquarters at Lahore. Between 1906 and 1913, Bank of India, Central Bank of India, Bank of Baroda, Canara Bank, Indian Bank, and Bank of Mysore were set up. Reserve Bank of India came in 1935.

During the first phase the growth was very slow and banks also experienced periodic failures between 1913 and 1948. There were approximately 1100 banks, mostly small. To streamline the functioning and activities of commercial banks, the Government of India came up with The Banking Companies Act, 1949 which was later changed to Banking Regulation Act 1949 as per amending Act of 1965 (Act No. 23 of 1965). Reserve Bank of India was vested with extensive powers for the supervision of banking in india as the Central Banking Authority.

During those days public has lesser confidence in the banks. As an aftermath deposit mobilisation was slow. Abreast of it the savings bank facility provided by the Postal department was comparatively safer. Moreover, funds were largely given to traders.

Phase II

Government took major steps in this Indian Banking Sector Reform after independence. In 1955, it nationalised Imperial Bank of India with extensive banking facilities on a large scale specially in rural and semi-urban areas. It formed State Bank of india to act as the principal agent of RBI and to handle banking transactions of the Union and State Governments all over the country. Seven banks forming subsidiary of State Bank of India was nationalised in 1960 on 19th July, 1969, major process of nationalisation was carried out. It was the effort of the then Prime Minister of India, Mrs. Indira Gandhi. 14 major commercial banks in the country was nationalised.

Second phase of nationalisation Indian Banking Sector Reform was carried out in 1980 with seven more banks. This step brought 80% of the banking segment in India under Government ownership.

The following are the steps taken by the Government of India to Regulate Banking Institutions in the Country:

- 1949: Enactment of Banking Regulation Act.
- 1955: Nationalisation of State Bank of India.
- 1959: Nationalisation of SBI subsidiaries.
- 1961: Insurance cover extended to deposits.
- 1969: Nationalisation of 14 major banks.
- 1971: Creation of credit guarantee corporation.
- 1975: Creation of regional rural banks.
- 1980: Nationalisation of seven banks with deposits over 200 crore.

After the nationalisation of banks, the branches of the public sector bank India rose to approximately 800% in deposits and advances took a huge jump by 11,000%.

Banking in the sunshine of Government ownership gave the public implicit faith and immense confidence about the sustainability of these institutions.

Phase III

This phase has introduced many more products and facilities in the banking sector in its reforms measure. In 1991, under the chairmanship of M Narasimham, a committee was set up by his name which worked for the liberalisation of banking practices.

The country is flooded with foreign banks and their ATM stations. Efforts are being put to give a satisfactory service to customers. Phone banking and net banking is introduced. The entire system became more convenient and swift. Time is given more importance than money.

The financial system of India has shown a great deal of resilience. It is sheltered from any crisis triggered by any external macroeconomics shock as other East Asian Countries suffered. This is all due to a flexible exchange rate regime, the foreign reserves are high, the capital account is not yet fully convertible, and banks and their customers have limited foreign exchange exposure.

NATIONALISATION OF BANKS IN INDIA

The nationalisation of banks in India took place in 1969 by Mrs. Indira Gandhi the then prime minister. It nationalised 14 banks then. These banks were mostly owned by businessmen and even managed by them.

- Central Bank of India
- Bank of Maharashtra
- Dena Bank
- Punjab National Bank
- Syndicate Bank
- Canara Bank
- Indian Bank
- Indian Overseas Bank
- Bank of Baroda
- Union Bank
- Allahabad Bank
- United Bank of India
- UCO Bank
- Bank of India

Befor the steps of nationalisation of Indian banks, only State Bank of India (SBI) was nationalised. It took place in July 1955 under the SBI Act of 1955. Nationalisation of Seven State Banks of India (formed subsidiary) took place on 19th July, 1960.

The State Bank of India is India's largest commercial bank and is ranked one of the top five banks worldwide. It serves 90 million customers through a network of 9,000 branches and it offers--either directly or through subsidiaries--a wide range of banking services.

The second phase of nationalisation of Indian banks took place in the year 1980. Seven more banks were nationalised with deposits over 200 crores. Till this year, approximately 80% of the banking segment in India were under Government ownership.

After the nationalisation of banks in India, the branches of the public sector banks rose to approximately 800% in deposits and advances took a huge jump by 11,000%.

- 1955: Nationalisation of State Bank of India.
- 1959: Nationalisation of SBI subsidiaries.
- 1969: Nationalisation of 14 major banks.
- 1980: Nationalisation of seven banks with deposits over 200 crores.

SCHEDULED COMMERCIAL BANKS IN INDIA

The commercial banking structure in India consists of:

- Scheduled Commercial Banks in India
- Unscheduled Banks in India

Scheduled Banks in India constitute those banks which have been included in the Second Schedule of Reserve Bank of India(RBI) Act, 1934. RBI in turn includes only those banks in this schedule which satisfy the criteria laid down vide section 42 (6) (a) of the Act.

As on 30th June, 1999, there were 300 scheduled banks in India having a total network of 64,918 branches.The scheduled commercial banks in India comprise of State bank of India and its associates (8), nationalised banks (19), foreign banks (45), private sector banks (32), co-operative banks and regional rural banks.

"Scheduled banks in India" means the State Bank of India constituted under the State Bank of India Act, 1955 (23 of 1955), a subsidiary bank as defined in the State Bank of India (Subsidiary Banks) Act, 1959 (38 of 1959), a corresponding new bank constituted under section 3 of the Banking Companies (Acquisition and Transfer of Undertakings) Act, 1970 (5 of 1970), or under section 3 of the Banking Companies (Acquisition and Transfer of Undertakings) Act, 1980 (40 of 1980), or any other bank being a bank included in the Second Schedule to the Reserve Bank of India Act, 1934 (2 of 1934), but does not include a co-operative bank".

"Non-scheduled bank in India" means a banking company as defined in clause (c) of section 5 of the Banking Regulation Act, 1949 (10 of 1949), which is not a scheduled bank".

The following are the Scheduled Banks in India (Public Sector):

- State Bank of India
- State Bank of Bikaner and Jaipur
- State Bank of Hyderabad
- State Bank of Indore
- State Bank of Mysore
- State Bank of Patiala
- State Bank of Saurashtra
- State Bank of Travancore
- Andhra Bank
- Allahabad Bank
- Bank of Baroda
- Bank of India
- Bank of Maharashtra
- Canara Bank
- Central Bank of India
- Corporation Bank
- Dena Bank
- Indian Overseas Bank
- Indian Bank
- Oriental Bank of Commerce
- Punjab National Bank
- Punjab and Sind Bank
- Syndicate Bank
- Union Bank of India
- United Bank of India
- UCO Bank
- Vijaya Bank

The following are the Scheduled Banks in India (Private Sector):

- Vysya Bank Ltd
- Axis Bank Ltd
- Indusind Bank Ltd
- ICICI Banking Corporation Bank Ltd
- Global Trust Bank Ltd
- HDFC Bank Ltd
- Centurion Bank Ltd
- Bank of Punjab Ltd
- IDBI Bank Ltd

The following are the Scheduled Foreign Banks in India:

- American Express Bank Ltd.
- ANZ Gridlays Bank Plc.
- Bank of America NT & SA
- Bank of Tokyo Ltd.
- Banquc Nationale de Paris
- Barclays Bank Plc
- Citi Bank N.C.
- Deutsche Bank A.G.
- Hongkong and Shanghai Banking Corporation
- Standard Chartered Bank.
- The Chase Manhattan Bank Ltd.
- Dresdner Bank AG.

3

Essential Banking Law and Practice

INTRODUCTION

This paper is not intended to be a summary of banking law and practice: that would be impossible in a relatively short paper and a one and a half hour seminar. It is intended, however, to provide:

- o an overview of the some of the characteristics of banks and their legal relationship with their customers;
- o a summary of the regulatory framework within which they operate; and
- o an outline of some of the legal issues that arise for consideration by lawyers advising banks or their customers. A selection of useful texts and references for further reading and information is included in the Appendix.

What is Banking Law?

Banking law is not a discrete area of law like contract or torts. It conveniently describes, however, the collection of legal principles which impact on banking transactions and on the banker-customer relationship. In that sense, the activity of banking is the location at which a diverse range of legal principles intersect which we call banking law. Those legal principles are drawn from a range of sources, including common law, the Law Merchant, principles and rules incorporated into the contract between the bank and its retail customers.

Relevant legislation includes:

- o Banking Act 1959 (Cth)

- o Reserve Bank Act 1959 (Cth)
- o Australian Prudential Regulation Authority Act 1998 (Cth)
- o Australian Securities and Investments Commission Act 2001 (Cth), which contains in Division 2 the unconscionable conduct and consumer protection provisions in relation to financial services providers that are no longer in the Trade Practices Act
- o Corporations Act 2001 (Cth), in particular Pt 7
- o Privacy Act 1988 (Cth), in particular the credit information provisions in Part IIIA
- o Consumer Credit Code, usually referred to as the Uniform Consumer Credit Code
- o Cheques Act 1986 (Cth)
- o State Fair Trading Acts, e.g. Fair Trading Act 1999 (Vic) What is a bank?

It might be thought easier to start with a definition of 'bank' but this is also a fraught task. Weaver & Craigie's description of the search for a definition of a 'bank' in statute and case law, illustrates the difficulty of the task and the amount of judicial and legislative energy that has been given to it. Much of the difficulty has arisen from the circularity of the traditional definition-that a bank is a person or body authorized to carry on or recognized as carrying on the business of banking. What constitutes the business of banking is the vexed question. It is an important one, however, because depending on whether a person or body is classed as a bank it will have a range of additional rights and obligations.

Before setting out relevant Australian definitions, it is worth a short digression into history.

The modern term 'bank' comes from the 'banco' or merchant's bench in the marketplaces of medieval Italy: money dealing was conducted from a portable bench, which would be publicly broken in the event of failure of the merchant's business-the origins of the concept of bankruptcy. But banking as an activity is much older.

In ancient times the temple was likely to be the location of much of what we would recognise as banking business. In

Mesopotamia, money could be borrowed at interest from the temple; in Greece, sanctuaries and temples were often the store house or place of safe custody for bullion and valuables; and in Jerusalem money-changers located in the temple precinct would exchange currency and allow interest on deposits with them.

The code of laws devised by Hammurabi, King of Babylon, between 2084BC and 2081 BC included references to charging interest on loans and a right of privacy in lending transactions.

These early examples include some of the ingredients of what have come to be regarded as the key characteristics of banking: taking money on deposit and lending.

And the location within temples and their precincts would have provided another important ingredient-an air of security. Recognisable 'bankers' appeared again in the middle ages, financing trade and wars, including the crusades, although as Tyree notes, 'it was not until comparatively modern times that the deposit of funds by the wider community with a banker who was then expected to use the funds at his or her discretion for commercial lending was established.'

The historically close association of banking with trade means that the Law Merchant-a body of rules reflecting the custom of merchants which was once administered separately from the common law-is an additional historical source of what is now included in banking law.

MODERN AUSTRALIAN DEFINITIONS

Banking Act 1959

It can come as a surprise to find that the Banking Act 1959 (Cth) (Banking Act), does not contain a definition of 'bank'-that term was taken out of the Banking Act in 1999-although it does contain a definition of 'banking business' set out below.

This is not because banks have been abolished as a legal concept, but they have been re-named and other institutions brought under the new name. The financial services sector reforms of 1998 introduced the concept of an 'authorised deposit-taking institution' ('ADI').

Under s 5 of the Banking Act, an ADI is a body corporate authorized by the Australian Prudential Regulation Authority

(APRA) under s 9 of the Banking Act to carry on the business of banking.

Authorised ADIs now include banks, credit unions, building societies, specialist credit card institutions and others-a full list is available on APRA's website, www.apra.gov.au.

The use of the names 'bank', 'banker' and 'banking' by an authorised ADI is still, however, subject to control under s66 of the Banking Act and the consent of APRA is required to use them.

12 As a result, what we would readily identify as a bank is now, in legislative terms, an ADI which has the consent of APRA under s66 of the Banking Act 1959 to call itself a bank.

'Banking Business' under the Banking Act Under section 5(1) 'banking business' means:

(a) a business that consists of banking within the meaning of paragraph 51 (xiii) of the Constitution; or

(b) a business that is carried on by a corporation to which paragraph 51(xx)

  (i) both taking money on deposit (other than as part-payment for goods or services) and making advances of money; or

  (ii) other financial activities prescribed by the regulations for the purposes of this definition.

A noticeable omission from the definition of banking business was the involvement of banks in the Australian payments system under which payments are made or funds transferred by such mechanisms as the collection and payment of cheques, direct credits and debits, debit and credit card payments and high value payments.

This omission was partly rectified when two further activities were prescribed by the regulations to be 'banking business'.

By the 2001 amendments, the provision of a purchased payment facility (PPF) is banking business if APRA determines that:

o the purchaser may demand payment from the holder of stored value, in Australian currency of all or part of the balance held; and

- o the facility permits a relatively wide class of payments to be made by a relatively wide class of payers By the 2003 amendments, the acquiring and issuing of credit cards by participants in a designated credit card scheme (such as MasterCard and VISA) became prescribed activities and so fall within the definition of 'banking business'.

Cheques Act 1986

The definition of 'bank' was also deleted, in 1998, from the Cheques Act 1986 (Cth) (Cheques Act), which now refers to a 'financial institution'. 'Financial institution' in turn is defined in s 3 (1) to mean:

(a) the Reserve Bank;

(b) a body corporate that is an ADI (authorized deposit-taking institution) for the purposes of the Banking Act 1959; or

(c) (deleted)

(d) a person who carries on State banking within the meaning of paragraph 51(xiii) of the Constitution; or

(e) a person (other than a person referred to in paragraph (a), (b) or (d) who carries on the business of banking outside Australia.

Future Definitions?

One of the difficulties of a definition based on the functions of the institution-a check-list approach-is that the activities of and services offered by institutions most of us would recognise as banks is changing and the last decade in particular has been a period of accelerated change.

THE REGULATORY FRAMEWORK

Regulatory Agencies

There are three main regulatory agencies for the financial system in Australia and their responsibilities are:

- o Reserve Bank of Australia: monetary and banking policy and the stability of the Australian economy. The Reserve Bank includes within its structure the Payments System Board, which is responsible for payments system policy;

- o APRA: prudential regulation of a range of financial institutions including banks, credit unions, insurance companies and superannuation funds. The aim of prudential regulation is, essentially, to ensure sound practices and financial stability; and
- o Australian Securities and Investments Commission (ASIC): consumer protection and market integrity. It has responsibility for monitoring and reviewing financial industry codes of practice such as the Electronic Funds Transfer Code of Conduct. ASIC also has responsibility for enforcing company law and the licensing and conduct of corporations.

In addition the Australian Competition and Consumer Commission (ACCC) has an economy-wide role to protect competition. The responsibility for consumer protection in the financial services sector, however, lies with ASIC.

Banking and Financial Services Ombudsman

The Banking and Financial Services Ombudsman (BFSO) is not a regulator as such, nor is it a government agency: it is a dispute resolution scheme that is part of the regulatory framework.

The BFSO is approved by ASIC as an external dispute resolution scheme for financial services licensees under Part 7 of the Corporations Act 2001 (Cth) (Corporations Act). Membership of an approved scheme is a licence requirement.

An important part of the BFSO's role as an external dispute resolution scheme is identifying and addressing systemic issues-issues which affect a number of customers. The BFSO reports to ASIC on systemic issues identified in its dispute resolution work.

Consumer Protection in Financial Services: ASIC's Role

The role, powers and responsibilities of ASIC are set out in the Australian Securities and Investments Commission Act 2001 (Cth) (ASIC Act). They include the power to regulate unconscionable conduct and consumer protection in the financial services industry, contained in Part 2 Division 2. It is important to be aware that the consumer protection provisions contained in Part IVA and Part V of the Trade Practices Act 1974 (Cth)

(Trade Practices Act) no longer apply to financial services. This means that when considering bringing claims for misleading or deceptive conduct or unconscionable conduct, you will need to refer to and plead the relevant provisions in the ASIC Act. For example, the prohibition against misleading or deceptive conduct by a financial services provider is s12DA of the ASIC Act, not of the Trade Practices Act.

Regulation of Financial Services and Markets

Chapter 7 of the Corporations Act was a new chapter of the Corporations Act, replacing the previous chapters 7 and 8, and was introduced via what is commonly known as Financial Services Reform.

It contains the licensing, disclosure and other conduct requirements for the financial services industry, including banks, and is the source of the obligation, for example, to provide internal and external dispute resolution mechanisms to customers including the requirement that a licensed financial services provider be a member of an ASIC approved external dispute resolution scheme.

Regulation of Credit

The consumer credit provided by banks in Australia is regulated under the Consumer Credit Code, commonly referred to as the 'Uniform Consumer Credit Code'-hence the common acronym, 'UCCC' which is used in this paper.

The UCCC was introduced in 1996 to replace previous state-based credit legislation. It is 'template' legislation adopted in all states under a co-operative scheme, with the core statute being Queensland legislation. This means that when you buy a copy of the Consumer Credit Code, you buy the Queensland legislation, which has been adopted in Victoria via the Consumer Credit (Victoria) Act 1995.

The policy basis of the UCCC is 'truth in lending' and its objectives are to:

- o Provide meaningful disclosure to debtors, mortgagors and guarantors at relevant pre-contractual, contractual and post-contractual stages;
- o Ensure that the cost of credit is disclosed to prevent deception;

- o Enable comparison between products, and encourage competition; and
- o Achieve product flexibility by regulating substance not form.

The UCCC applies to credit:

- o provided to a natural person or a strata corporation;
- o wholly or predominantly (more than 50%) for personal, domestic or household purposes;
- o for which a charge is or may be made for providing the credit; and
- o where the credit provider is in the business of providing credit or credit provision is incidental to their business.

It covers credit contracts and by section 10, a hiring agreement where the hirer has a right or obligation to purchase the goods. It also, in a separate Part 10, covers consumer leases where the hirer does not have a right or obligation to purchase the goods.

So some of the questions to ask when determining whether the UCCC applies will go to:

- o the status of the debtor;
- o the purpose of the credit;
- o if there is a guarantor, what is the status of the guarantor (the guarantor also must be a natural person or a strata corporation);
- o the business of the person or body providing credit; and
- o whether there is a charge: charge includes interest, or other fee or charge.

Once those questions are answered, the exceptions set out in section 7 and in the Regulations will need to be considered.

They include in outline:

- o Short term credit-62 days or less unless the fees and charges exceed 5% of the amount of the loan, or the interest rate exceeds 24% p.a.;
- o Low value credit-$50 in most cases;
- o Credit provided with no prior agreement;
- o Where the only charge is an account charge not more than the prescribed maximum charge;

- o Bill facilities;
- o Where the credit provider is a pawnbroker trustee or employer-but the unjust transaction provisions will still apply and in the case of employer loans the UCCC will apply if the employer is a credit provider and the credit is on the same terms as to other customers There is also a monetary threshold for applications for changes to the credit contract on the grounds of hardship.

In Victoria, regulatory responsibility for the UCCC is with Consumer Affairs Victoria, and the Victorian Civil and Administrative Tribunal (VCAT) has exclusive jurisdiction or re-opening contracts under s 70 and for imposing civil penalties under s102 for breach of the 'key requirements', and in other cases, concurrent jurisdiction with other courts. The BFSO will also apply the UCCC, where relevant, to disputes that it considers.

THE BANKER-CUSTOMER RELATIONSHIP

What is the Basis of the Banker-customer Relationship?

The banker-customer relationship is essentially a contractual one. It is traditionally expressed as a 'debtor-creditor' relationship: the bank accepts deposits from its customers and becomes their debtor; the bank lends money to customers and becomes their creditor. It is more than that, however, and contains other contractual incidents implied by the courts.

In addition, the contract is overlaid by equity, tort to a lesser extent and statute including consumer protection legislation.

Although described in those terms, the banker-customer relationship is not a normal debtor-creditor relationship where the debtor is required to seek out his or her creditor and repay the debt when it is due. A bank is entitled to and should wait for a demand for repayment-a withdrawal slip or equivalent-and the timing of the demand may be prescribed by the express terms of the contract, such as with term deposits.

When considering the following incidents of the banker-customer contractual relationship, it is important to remember that these can be varied by express terms of the contract, which in turn are subject to limitations imposed by statute and rules of public policy. And as banking practice changes, the way in which they are expressed may also change. The normal incidents of the relationship The basic incidents of the banker-customer relationship have been identified as:

- o The bank undertakes to receive money and to collect bills for its customer's account;
- o The bank borrows the money and proceeds from the customer and undertakes to repay them:
- o on demand,
- o at the branch of the bank where the account is kept,
- o during ordinary working hours;
- o The bank promises to repay any part of the amount due against the unambiguous written order of the customer addressed to the branch of the bank where the account is kept;
- o Conversely the bank will not pay away any part of the amount due to the customer without such order or other compulsion recognized by law;
- o Any written order by the customer which requires the bank to pay a greater amount than the balance standing to the credit of the customer or an agreed overdraft limit may be declined in toto:
- o The bank will not cease to do business with the customer except on reasonable notice;
- o The bank undertakes to observe secrecy with respect to the customer's account, information acquired from the account, and other information acquired in the character of the customer's banker (subject to certain exceptions);
- o The custom and usage of bankers is implied into the contract (if known and accepted);
- o Both parties are bound by any statutory responsibilities or rights. What are the customer's duties?

Under common law, the customer has only two duties:

- o To use reasonable care in drawing cheques so as not to mislead the bank or facilitate forgery (the 'Macmillan duty'); and
- o To notify the bank of known forgeries or misuse of the account (the 'Greenwood duty').

Attempts have been made at various times to extend the duties owed at common law by a customer to such things as discovering forgeries by reading statements; taking care of a cheque book; and running an organized business.

These have largely failed.

The absence of a common law duty does not, of course, prevent an obligation being imposed under the express terms of the contract, although it is necessary to ensure that important obligations are sufficiently brought to the attention of the customer.

The non-excludable warranty provisions contained in the ASIC Act should also be kept in mind, as should the allocation of liability provisions of the Electronic Funds Transfers Code of Conduct.

And consumer protection provisions such as the prohibitions on misleading conduct and unconscionable conduct operate independently of the contract.

Does the Bank owe a Duty of Care?

The duty owed by a bank has been expressed as a contractual duty 'to exercise reasonable care in carrying out the bank's part' of the contract.

The standard is that of the reasonable competent banker acting in accordance with accepted current practice. Such a duty may, in limited circumstances, include a duty to question an otherwise valid mandate, e.g. a cheque validly drawn and signed by an authorised signatory.

Does the Bank owe a Fiduciary Duty?

The banker-customer relationship is not one of the accepted fiduciary relationships and the contractual duty of a banker to a customer is not a fiduciary duty, except in special circumstances.

In the usual course the bank is entitled to prefer its own interests to those of the customer, unlike a trustee or a professional adviser such as a lawyer, and does not have a duty to provide advice. This can come as a surprise to customers who may believe that a bank has a duty to advise them that a transaction or product is not in their interests, for example:

- o That a proposed business purchase is inadvisable because the business, to the knowledge of the bank, may not be sound;
- o That a proposed property purchase is inadvisable because, to the bank's knowledge from its valuation report, the value of the property is less than the purchase price; or
- o That there may be other loan products which are more advantageous or which are more suitable to the customer. A bank, however, does not usually have such duties and 'cases in which a bank lending to a customer comes to occupy a fiduciary position in which it must prefer the customer's interests to its own are rare'.

In cases where a bank has been found to have assumed a fiduciary duty, the common thread is that of some special feature in the facts: in simple terms that the banker has stepped, or been propelled by circumstances, out of his or her usual shoes and has engendered in the customer an expectation he or she will advise in the customer's interests.

The case of Commonwealth Bank of Australia v Smith is an example. In that case the borrowers were inexperienced and accustomed over a long period of time to rely on the bank manager's advice. The bank manager gave advice when sought about the viability of the business they proposed purchasing, describing it as 'a good buy'. His advice included discouraging other sources of advice. And the geographical context was a small town.

The facts will therefore be crucial.

Duty to Disclose?

Misleading or deceptive conduct by silence.

Claims of misleading conduct by silence are sometimes brought in the alternative to a claim of breach of fiduciary duty.

The claim is, usually, that the bank was under a duty to disclose certain information adverse to the customer's interests. But it can be unhelpful to frame the claim as arising from a duty to disclose.

As summarized by Black CJ in Demagogue Pty Limited v Ramensky:

> *'Silence is to be assessed as a circumstance like any other. To say this is certainly not to impose any general duty of disclosure; the question is simply whether, having regard to all the relevant circumstances, there has been conduct that is misleading or deceptive...to speak of "mere silence" or a duty of disclosure can divert attention from that primary question. Although "mere silence" is a convenient way of describing some fact situations, there is in truth no such thing as "mere silence" because the significance of silence always falls to be considered in the context in which it occurs. That context may or may not include facts giving rise to a reasonable expectation, in the circumstances of the case, that if particular matters exist, they will be disclosed.'*

In the context of guarantees, however, it may be appropriate to speak of a duty to disclose, based on the judgment of Gibbs CJ in Commercial Bank of Amadio.

Unlike the other members of the majority in the High Court, Gibbs CJ based his decision that the guarantee should be set aside not on unconscionable conduct but on undue concealment of unusual features of the transaction which the guarantors would not naturally expect to exist.

Must the Silence be Deliberate?

One question that arises in a claim of misleading conduct by silence is whether the omission to speak must be deliberate or advertent: which in turn will have evidential importance for those seeking to prove it.

Conduct may be misleading or deceptive at law, even though it was not intentionally so. Intention is regarded as an unnecessary ingredient.

There is a suggestion in Miller's Annotated Trade Practices Act, 2004, at 1.52.50 that intention is relevant where it is claimed that silence or omission, rather than positive conduct, constitutes a breach of the statutory obligation. Where the silence in issue is a failure to provide information then, Miller suggests, the plaintiff must show that the defendant deliberately withheld that information. This is based on section 4(2) of the Trade Practices Act which states that a 'reference to engaging in conduct shall be read as a reference to do or refusing to do an act'. In turn a reference to refusing to do an act is stated to include a reference to refraining (other than inadvertently) from doing an act.

Miller's suggestion is supported by Rhone-Poulenc Agrochimie SA v UIM Chemical Services Pty Ltd (1986) 68 ALR 77. Section 4(2) of the Trade Practices Act is mirrored in s12BA(2) of the ASIC Act.

Other Sources of Liability

Apart from statutory causes of action, a bank may have liability under a number of heads. A discussion of the duty of confidentiality is contained below. A useful analysis both of the sources of liability for a bank as lender and the entry-points in the relationship when they can arise can be found in the text by Professor James O'Donovan, 'Lender Liability'.

Apart from banking law texts, BFSO Bulletins are another source of information about the ways in which a bank can be found liable to its customer. They cover issues such as:

- o A bank's obligations as mortgagee exercising a power of sale;
- o A bank's obligations in the collection of debts or when a customer is in financial difficulty;
- o A bank's obligations in making assessments of credit before lending; and
- o Issues that can arise when a customer has a decision-making disability.

Breach of Confidentiality

This is usually expressed as the duty in Tournier's case.

The duty arises out of contract and is founded on the historical expectations of banks that they will keep their customers' personal and financial information secret. It is qualified-Bankes LJ in Tournier articulated three qualifications:

- o Where disclosure is under compulsion of law;
- o Where the interests of the bank require disclosure; and
- o Where the disclosure is made by the express or implied consent of the customer.

The Code of Banking Practice, in clause 22, contains an express acknowledgment of the common law duty, together with obligations under the Privacy Act 1988 (Cth). Clause 22 sets out four exceptions:

- o Where disclosure is compelled by law;
- o Where there is a duty to the public to disclose;
- o Where 'our' interests require disclosure; or
- o Where disclosure is made with 'your' express or implied consent.

The duty covers the state of the customer's account-how much they owe and what their other account balances are; the individual transactions on the accounts, the securities held by the bank and other information gained by the bank in the capacity as banker.

A claim for breach of the duty might arise where information is given to a person with no authority in relation to the account such as a spouse or relative; where information is given to a person the bank mistakenly believes to be the account holder or where information is insecurely held and as a result is inadvertently made available to third parties.

The Special Wives' Equity

What is called the 'special wives' equity' is an equitable basis for setting aside a guarantee given by a wife to secure borrowings of her husband. Although it can appear to be closely related, it has a different rationale to equitable principles relating to unconscionable conduct which are based on notions of a person under a special disability or disadvantage being exploited by a stronger party.

The High Court in Garcia v National Australia Bank Ltd stated that the rationale for the equity is:

> *'not to be found in notions based on the subservience or inferior economic position of women. Nor is it based on their vulnerability to exploitation because of their emotional involvement.'*

It is based instead on the trust and confidence presumed to exist between a married couple.

Garcia v National Australia Bank Ltd affirmed the 'rule', derived primarily from the judgment of Dixon J in Yerkey v Jones, that applies where a husband obtains the execution of a guarantee by his wife. The special wives' equity applies to make a guarantee/mortgage unenforceable if given by a wife and:

- o She did not in fact understand the purport and effect of the transaction;
- o She was a 'volunteer' that is, she gained no real benefit-with 'benefit' being given a narrow construction; and
- o The bank took no steps to explain the transaction and she did not receive independent legal advice.

The rule in Yerkey v Jones is separate from undue influence so it is not necessary to show that the wife's will was overborne by the influence of her husband. The rule in Yerkey v Jones is also not subsumed by Amadio.

Liability for unconscionable conduct under Amadio contemplates that the creditor has notice of unconscionability factors: the rule in Yerkey v Jones does not require the lender to be on notice of any special disadvantage or disability.

A lender will not avoid the operation of the special wives' equity by recommending that a wife obtain independent advice. It must either explain the purport and effect of the guarantee to her or ensure that an independent adviser has explained it. The equity does not depend on the husband acting for the creditor in obtaining the wife's agreement to the transaction: the High Court declined to follow Barclay's Bank v O'Brien

The important findings of fact in the Garcia case were that Mrs Garcia did misunderstand the application of the guarantee and did not understand that her obligations under it were secured by the mortgage over her home.

It is also important that a narrow view of benefit was taken by the High Court-it found on the facts that Mrs Garcia obtained no real benefit from the transaction even though she was a director and shareholder in the debtor company. This was because of the court's view that the company was under the complete control of her husband.

And although bank officers explained the general effect of the documentation to Mrs Garcia, they didn't explain that the guarantees were secured by and linked to the mortgage of the jointly owned property

A further discussion of issues to do with guarantees is set out below in the section on the Code of Banking Practice.

DISPUTE RESOLUTION AND THE CODE OF BANKING PRACTICE

The Role and Significance of the Code of Banking Practice

The 2004 revised Code of Banking Practice (the revised Code) is a document with which all lawyers who advise clients in relation to their financial or property-related affairs or disputes should be familiar. Although it is described as a voluntary code, once adopted by a bank it becomes contractually enforceable. Unlike most consumer protection legislation it applies to small business and investment customers as well as individuals. It gives customers of adopting banks an important set of rights in relation to matters including:

- o Disclosure;
- o Conduct;
- o Provision of documents;
- o Contractual enforceability of statutory obligations;
- o Debt collection;
- o Dispute resolution.

It contains obligations towards guarantors which go beyond the common law and provide for detailed information about the debtor's financial position to be given by banks to potential guarantors. It contains a key commitment to act fairly and reasonably in a consistent and ethical manner. It sets out a compulsory dispute resolution framework that should not be ignored by lawyers whose clients are in dispute with a bank.

The revised Code is the successor to the 1993 Code of Banking Practice (the 1993 Code). The revised Code took three years to come to fruition. Mr Richard Viney was appointed in May 2000. Following submissions from and consultation with interested parties, he published an Issues Paper in May 2001. There was further consultation and his Final Report with 61 recommendations was published in October 2001. The drafting process itself involved further consultation into 2002. A version of the revised Code was then launched in August 2002 for implementation in August 2003. The publication and implementation of the revised Code was not straightforward. Prior to implementation, amendments were made to the 'launch publication' and even after implementation, some modifications were made by the ABA, mainly in relation to the guarantee provisions. As a consequence, apart from the 2002 'launch publication (which should be disregarded), there are in fact two revised Codes, one published and implemented in 2003, which some banks adopted, and a second modified version, published in 2004, which has been adopted by a greater number of bank members of the ABA.

Lawyers will therefore need to make sure that they know which version of the Code of Banking Practice they are looking at and whether the bank about whom or to whom they are providing advice has adopted the 1993, the 2003 or the modified 2004 Code.

And they should note that the Code of Banking Practice has come up for review again this year. Issues arising from particular provisions of the revised Code A detailed discussion of the main provisions of the revised Code (2003 version) is contained in BFSO Bulletin 39, published in September 2003, and it is not proposed to set out such a discussion here. There are, however, some provisions which raise relatively complex issues.

Acting Fairly and Reasonably

Clause 2.2 of the revised Code is a promise in the following terms:

> *'We will act fairly and reasonably towards you in a consistent and ethical manner. In doing so we will consider your conduct, our conduct and the contract between us.'*

The inclusion of fairness and ethical behaviour as a contractual obligation in the agreement between a bank and its customer may be a startling concept to black letter lawyers, raising both eyebrows and questions such as, "What does that mean?", or even, "Where would such an obligation end?". Those used to a traditional banking culture may also ask, "Why does that need to be put in writing?".

The inclusion of fairness, however, sits reasonably comfortably with a bank's existing obligations in equity and under statute, including its obligations under the Corporations Act as a financial services licensee.

Acting ethically, arguably, is no more than is required by an obligation to act fairly and honestly-although it may require a more considered choice between two legally available courses of action. It does not necessarily involve a duty to advise-a banker has not, traditionally, owed fiduciary duties to their customers.

But if, as social commentators such as Hugh Mackay suggest, there are increasing pressures on the staff of corporate institutions in Australia to cut moral corners and put the bottom line first, a clause such as 2.2 may nevertheless have work to do.

It will be interesting to see whether the courts, when they come to decide cases raising interpretation and application of the Code of Banking Practice, identify conduct as being in breach of clause 2.2 that would not otherwise be in breach of statutory prohibitions such as those against misleading, deceptive or unconscionable conduct.

Financial Hardship

The revised Code has introduced an obligation to try to help customers overcome their financial difficulties and, where appropriate, provide information about the hardship variation provisions of the Consumer Credit Code (UCCC).

Clause 25.2 sets out the promise of an adopting bank:

> *'With your agreement, we will try to help you overcome your financial difficulties with any credit facility you have with us. We could, for example, work with you to develop a repayment plan. If at the time, the hardship variation provisions of the Uniform Consumer Credit Code could apply to your circumstances, we will inform you about them.'*

These are positive contractual obligations and a dispute about a breach of them could be brought to the relevant external scheme or even to a court or tribunal if the loss involved warranted the cost. It is important to understand that despite the reference to the UCCC, the first part of clause 25.2 applies not only to individual customers fitting the definition of a consumer but also to small business and investment customers. It is a promise to try to help customers overcome their financial difficulties not a promise to succeed, which raises interesting questions of how to establish that there has been a breach. It may, for example, have application where a customer is in default but makes an offer to repay the debt via a repayment plan or other arrangement. Responsible collection activity will not always, in any event, involve demand followed up in the shortest possible time by legal action, including bankruptcy or liquidation proceedings and will usually involve consideration of a reasonable, realistic proposal. This obligation, however, may provide a useful additional negotiating tool for lawyers acting for bank customers in difficulty with the repayment of a loan or other facility and should be kept in mind by lawyers acting on behalf of a bank to ensure that prior to taking legal action the bank has complied with its obligations.

Given also that the obligation in 25.2 is overlaid by the key commitment in clause 2.2 to act fairly and reasonably in a consistent and ethical manner, it might be argued that a bank is required to give genuine consideration to a repayment proposal, give legitimate reasons for any rejection of the proposal, consider alternatives, communicate in a fair and reasonable manner and not start or conclude enforcement action before communicating a response to any reasonable repayment proposal.

ADVISING GUARANTORS

Lawyers advising potential guarantors, whether in the context of providing a certificate of independent advice or in the context of small business advice, need to be aware of what a potential guarantor is entitled to expect from a bank under the revised Code, including what information must be provided. They will also need to make the appropriate decision about what to do with any information provided.

Given the extended and explicit warnings required to be included in the guarantee document, prominent notice stating, for example, that the potential guarantor can refuse to enter into the guarantee. While this goes without saying in law, the blunt terms of the notice may well prompt the question "Should I do so?"

Problems with Guarantees

The provisions of the revised Code significantly extend a bank's obligation to disclose information to potential guarantors, essentially limited at common law to an obligation to disclose information only if the transaction has unusual features.

An adopting bank is required, before taking a guarantee, to provide meaningful financial information to the potential guarantor, which should assist them to assess the level of risk involved in providing the particular guarantee. The provisions of clause 28 also have the important effect of extending to small businesses some of the protections offered by the guarantee provisions of the UCCC.

What has traditionally been the difficulty for guarantors, in making the decision to give a guarantee, is not so much understanding what will happen if the debtor doesn't pay but is assessing the chance that the debtor will not or will be unable to repay. The BFSO Bulletin 22, Report on Relationship Debt, published in September 1999, observed in relation to family and spouse guarantee cases that:

While a guarantor may be made aware of the consequences if the borrower defaults, the expectation appears to be that the possibility of the borrower defaulting is a remote one. This may be influenced in particular cases by statements by the debtor or the lender or both that "your house is not at risk". It may result from a natural unwillingness on the part of the guarantor to believe that the worst will happen. The expectation was they would be helping the person to whom they were related, not giving their house to the bank.

The necessary information might conceivably include:

- Whether the guarantee is being asked for as 'top up' security because of concerns by the lender about increased risk of default;
- Whether the debtor has a history of overdrawings, excesses, arrears or significant defaults;
- The nature and the duration of the facility being secured by the guarantee and any related security arrangements.

In the absence of information from the bank about account history and past defaults or irregularities the debtor themselves will be the guarantor's only source of information about the state of the debtor's affairs. There are obvious problems with this-a debtor in financial difficulty or otherwise unable to qualify for the facility sought, will have an interest in encouraging the guarantor to proceed with the guarantee by minimising negative information about the debtor's affairs. The instinct of the debtor, even a well-meaning one, may be to reassure the potential guarantor that the guarantee is only a formality. The related problem of obtaining information from the bank is that, because of the banker's duty of confidentiality, to do so requires the debtor's consent.

How does the revised Code deal with the issue of the debtor's consent? It does not seek to override the banker's duty of confidentiality to the debtor-that consent is required is implicit. Rather it prohibits the taking of the guarantee unless the required information is provided. It therefore has a simple practical effect-if the debtor doesn't consent for whatever reason the bank cannot take the guarantee.

Overview of Clause 28

The revised Code seeks to address the information imbalance between the bank and many guarantors by requiring the bank:

- o to provide warning notices similar to those required by the UCCC but with the additional statement that 'you can refuse to enter into the guarantee'; and
- o to provide information and copies of documents intended to give the potential guarantor or their financial adviser a picture of the financial situation of the debtor and the means to assess the financial risk of giving the guarantee.

The Code also seeks to control the circumstances in which the guarantee is signed and the timing of signing. For most guarantors not involved in the business directly there will be a required one day gap between provision of information and being asked to sign the document, unless the guarantor has had same day independent legal advice after receiving the information.

The bank promises not to give the guarantee to the debtor for signing by the guarantor. Clause 28 also provides some important post guarantee protections including:

- o a limited right of withdrawal [cl 28.11];
- o important provisions about future credit provision to the debtor [cl 28.12 and 28.13] and
- o provisions about enforcement of judgments against guarantors.

And, under cl 28.2 the guarantor's liability under the guarantee must be limited either to a specific amount plus other liabilities, such as interest and recovery costs, described in the guarantee or the value of a specified security at the time of recovery.

The Modifications to the Guarantee Provisions

As noted above, changes were made to clause 28 in the one year period between launch and implementation, and again after the revised Code was implemented in 2003. Copies labelled as 'Launch Publication August 2002' should not therefore be used or relied on. The discussion below is about modifications made after the publication of the August 2003 version.

The main modifications were:

- o to limit the obligation to disclose excesses or overdrawings to those of $100 or more;
- o to change the obligation to provide copies of related security documents to an obligation to provide a descriptive list of related security documents and copies on request;
- o to include an opt out provision for director guarantors in relation to the information and one day gap requirements.

In both the 2003 and 2004 versions, a number of the provisions of clause 28 do not apply to guarantors of commercial asset financing facilities and sole director guarantors.

The Code of Banking Practice-Dispute Resolution Framework

The dispute resolution framework described in clauses 35-37 of the Code of Banking Practice is an important part of the structure of the revised Code. It mirrors the dispute resolution requirements mandated by the 2001 amendments to the Corporations Act, in sections 912A.

Lawyers therefore need to be aware that even if a bank or other financial services provider has not adopted the revised Code, it will still have similar dispute resolution obligations to those set out in the revised Code. The revised Code provides for a two step process:

- o Access to a free internal dispute resolution process that meets the Australian Standard AS4269-1995; and
- o Subject to jurisdictional limits, progress of an unresolved dispute to an ASIC approved external dispute resolution scheme.

The ASIC approval policy, contained in Policy Statement 139, requires an approved scheme to be:

- o accessible;
- o independent;
- o fair;
- o accountable;
- o efficient; and
- o effective.

Currently, there are seven ASIC approved external schemes in the financial services sector:

- o Banking & Financial Services Ombudsman Ltd (BFSO, formerly the Australian Banking Industry Ombudsman Ltd)-disputes about banks, their associated entities and other financial services providers
- o Credit Ombudsman Service Limited (COSL, formerly the Mortgage Industry Ombudsman Service, MIOS),-disputes about mortgage originators and finance brokers and others that are members of the scheme.
- o Credit Union Dispute Resolution Centre (CUDRC)-disputes about those Australian credit unions that are members of that scheme. CUDRC is managed under agreement by the BFSO.
- o Financial Industry Complaints Service (FICS)-disputes about financial services providers including life insurers, funds managers, investment advisers and planners, stockbrokers and some superannuation providers.
- o Financial Co-operative Dispute Resolution Scheme (FCDRS)-disputes from consumers about those

Australian credit unions and building societies that are members of the scheme.

- o Insurance Brokers Disputes Limited (IBD)-disputes about general or life insurance brokers. IBD is managed by agreement by the BFSO
- o Insurance Ombudsman Service Ltd (IOS, formerly Insurance Enquiries and Complaints Ltd)-disputes about general insurance companies.

The majority of the schemes, together with the Superannuation Complaints Tribunal, which has a separate statutory basis, operate a shared 'front end' with a single telephone number, 1300 78 08 08 under the name 'Financial Ombudsman Service' and share other resources. As at August 2007, the BFSO, IOS and FICS are in the process of converging.

What the schemes have in common is that there will usually be an initial facilitated negotiation period followed by investigation and decision (binding on the industry member only) if the dispute is otherwise unresolved.

The Work of the BFSO

The legal issues arising in the banker-customer disputes that the BFSO deals with may include:

- o Breach of contract, including the contractual duty to provide services with care and skill;
- o Misleading or deceptive conduct;
- o Unconscionable conduct;
- o Breach of the provisions of the UCCC;
- o Breach of the Code of Banking Practice;
- o Inappropriate allocation of liability for an unauthorised electronic funds transfer under the EFT Code; and
- o Breach of the Privacy Act, including the National Privacy Principles, or the bankers' duty of confidentiality.

The subject matter of disputes can include:

- o Unauthorised withdrawals from bank accounts by a third party or by error of the bank;
- o Whether the bank undertook a reasonable assessment of a customer's ability to repay a loan or other facility before making the decision to lend;

- o Representations made to customers about a product or service;
- o The price obtained for a property on sale by the bank as mortgagee;
- o Other action taken in enforcement of a debt;
- o Delays in settlement;
- o Errors in the calculation of repayments required on a loan;
- o Non-disclosure of material information in the taking of a guarantee.

Banks will commonly be members of the BFSO scheme and may also belong to one or more other schemes depending on the range of their business. Non-bank members of the BFSO, which now outnumber bank members, include payment system providers, brokers, building societies, debt collection agencies and credit reference bodies.

Advising Clients using an External Dispute Resolution Scheme

What does this mean for a lawyer whose client is in dispute with a member of an external dispute resolution scheme such as the BFSO or who is acting for a member in a dispute with a customer?

Victorian lawyers have a professional conduct obligation to inform clients about 'reasonably available alternatives to fully contested adjudication' where appropriate.

Advisers need to be aware of and ready to engage in the internal dispute resolution processes promised by an adopting bank or required under the Corporations Act of financial services licensee. Lawyers need to familiarise themselves with the available external schemes to ensure that they are able to advise their clients about any appropriate scheme in jurisdiction terms and to know when a court or tribunal will be the more appropriate forum. They need to understand the processes involved, the rules or terms of reference, and understand what will be the most cost-effective way of assisting their client. And they need to understand the non-adversarial, inquisitorial nature of the investigation processes used by most schemes.

In some ways an external dispute resolution scheme is a foreign concept to many lawyers used to the adversarial system or to traditional forms of mediation. It involves some ingredients such as shuttle mediation and a form of arbitration which will be familiar to lawyers engaged in dispute resolution. The processes are conducted under the without prejudice privilege unless there is a resolution by agreement or decision accepted by both parties. But there are some differences to traditional forms of dispute resolution. The ASIC approved schemes:

- o are free for customers to use;
- o may involve some investigation, including asking both parties for information and documents;
- o although there are procedures, have relatively informal processes and the claim does not have to put in the form of pleadings;
- o the decision is binding only on the industry member and not on the customer;
- o hearings in person are rarely conducted-a decision will usually be made on the papers.

The processes are designed to be accessible to lay people without legal representation and to operate Australia-wide. Some schemes discourage legal representation; others such as the BFSO do not discourage it but make it clear that legal costs will not usually be recoverable as part of any compensation awarded. This means that it may not be cost-effective for the lawyer to be the point of contact with the scheme throughout the dispute but they may nevertheless be of assistance in helping their clients write the initial letter setting out the dispute and identifying the relevant documents to attach to the letter. Lawyers may also be of assistance to their clients in evaluating any offer made or formulating any counter offer.

CONCLUSION

Banking law is a wide-ranging and constantly changing area of the law. It focuses on an activity which has been at the heart of a strong economy since ancient times and which intersects with the lives of most individuals-anyone with a bank account. It is a challenging, interesting and important body of knowledge for lawyers.

4

Banking Companies (Acquisition and Transfer of Undertakings) Act, 1970

THE BANKING COMPANIES (ACQUISITION AND TRANSFER OF UNDERTAKINGS) ACT,1970

ACT NO. 5 OF 1970

[31st March, 1970.] B

An Act to provide for the acquisition and transfer of the undertakings of certain banking companies, having regard to their size, resources, coverage and organisation, in order to control the heights of the economy and to meet progressively, and serve better, the needs of development of the economy in conformity with national policy and objectives and for matters connected therewith or incidental thereto.

SHORT TITLE AND COMMENCEMENT

(1) This Act may be called the Banking Companies (Acquisition and Transfer of Undertakings) Act,

(2) The provisions of this Act (except section 21, which shall come into force on the appointed day) shall be deemed to have come into force on the 19th day of July, 1969.

DEFINITIONS

In this Act, unless the context otherwise requires,--

(a) "appointed day" means the 14th day of February, 1970, being the day on which the Banking Companies (Acquisition and Transfer of Undertakings) Ordinance, 1970 (3 of 1970), was promulgated;

(b) "banking company" does not include a foreign company within the meaning of section 591 of the Companies Act, 1956 (1 of 1956);

(c) "commencement of this Act" means the 19th day of July, 1969;

(d) "corresponding new bank", in relation to an existing bank, means the body corporate specified against such bank in column 2 of the First Schedule;

(e) "Custodian" means the person who becomes, or is appointed, a Custodian under section 7;

(f) "existing bank" means a banking company specified in column 1 of the First Schedule, being a company the deposits of which, as 78 shown in the return as on the last Friday of June, 1969, furnished to the Reserve Bank under section 27 of the Banking Regulation Act, 1949 (10 of 1949), were not less than rupees fifty crores; 1*[(fa) "prescribed" means prescribed by regulations made under this Act;]

(g) "Schedule" means a Schedule to this Act;

(h) words and expressions used herein and not defined but defined in the Banking Regulation Act, 1949 (10 of 1949), have the meanings respectively assigned to them in that Act.

(i) words and expressions used herein and not defined either in this Act or in the Banking regulation Act. 1949 (10 of 1949) in the Companies Act, 1956 (1 of 1956) shall have the meanings respectively assigned to them in the Companies Act, 1956.

Establishment of corresponding new banks and business thereof.

3. Establishment of corresponding new banks and business thereof.

(1) On the commencement of this Act, there shall be constituted such corresponding new banks as are specified in the First Schedule.

(2) The paid-up capital of every corresponding new bank constituted under sub-section (1) shall, until any provision is made in this behalf in any scheme made under section 9, be

equal to the paid-up capital of the existing bank in relation to which it is the corresponding new bank.

2*[(2A) Notwithstanding anything contained in subs-section (2), the paid-up capital of every corresponding new bank constituted under sub-section (1) may from time to time be increased by--(a) such amounts as the Board of Directors of the corresponding new bank may, after consultation with the Reserve Bank and with the previous sanction of the Central Government, transfer from the reserve fund established by such bank to such capital: (b) such amounts as the Central Government may, in consultation with the Reserve Bank, contribute to such paid-up capital; Provided that the paid-up capital of any such bank shall in no case be in excess of 3*[4*[rupees one thousand five hundred crores].

(3) The entire capital of each corresponding new bank shall stand vested in, and allotted to, the Central Government.

(4) Every corresponding new bank shall be a body corporate with perpetual succession and a common seal with power, subject to the provisions of this Act, to acquire, hold and dispose of property, and to contract, and may sue and be sued in its name.

(5) Every corresponding new bank shall carry on and transact the business of banking as defined in clause (b) of section 5 of the Banking Regulation Act, 1949 (10 of 1949), and may engage in 5*[one or more of the other forms of business] specified in sub-section (1) of section 6 of that Act.

(6) Every corresponding new bank shall establish a reserve fund to which shall be transferred the share premiums and the balance, if any, standing to the credit of the reserve fund of the existing bank in relation to which it is the corresponding new bank, and such further sums, if any, as may be transferred in accordance with the provisions of section 17 of the Banking Regulation Act, 1949 (10 of 1949).

6*[(7) (i) The corresponding new bank shall, if so required by the Reserve Bank, act as agent of the Reserve Bank at all places in India where it has a branch, for--(a) paying, receiving, collecting and remitting money, bullion and securities on behalf of any Government in India; and (b) undertaking and transacting any other business which the Reserve Bank may from time to time entrust to it. (ii) The terms and conditions on which any such agency business shall be carried on by the corresponding new bank on behalf of the Reserve Bank shall be such as may be agreed upon. (iii) If no agreement can be reached on any matter referred to in clause (ii), or if a dispute arises between the corresponding new bank and the Reserve Bank as to the interpretation of any agreement between them, the matter shall be referred to the Central Government and the decision of the Central Government thereon shall be final. (iv) The corresponding new bank may transact any business or perform any functions entrusted to it under clause (i), by itself or through any agent approved by the Reserve Bank.]

Undertaking of existing banks to vest in corresponding new banks. 4. Undertaking of existing banks to vest in corresponding new banks. On the commencement of this Act, the undertaking of every existing bank shall be transferred to, and shall vest in, the corresponding new bank.--1 Subs. & ins. by Act 1 of 1984, s. 65 (w.e.f. 15-2-1984). 2 Ins. by Act 81 of 1985, s. 7 (w.e.f. 30-12-1985). 3 Subs. by Act 66 of 1988, s. 30 (w.e.f. 30-12-1988). 4 Subs. by Act 36 of 1992, s. 2 (w.e.f. 30-12-1988).

General effect of vesting.

5. General effect of vesting. (1) The undertaking of each existing bank shall be deemed to include all assets, rights, powers, authorities and privileges and all property, movable and immovable, cash balances, reserve funds, investments and all other rights and interests in, or arising out of, such property as were immediately before the commencement of this Act in the ownership, possession, power or control of the existing bank in relation to the undertaking, whether within or without India, and all books of accounts, registers, records and all other documents of whatever nature relating thereto and shall also be deemed to include all borrowings, liabilities and obligations of whatever kind then subsisting of the existing bank in relation to the undertaking.

(2) If, according to the laws of any country outside India, the provisions of this Act by themselves are not effective to transfer or vest any asset or liability situated in that country which forms part of the undertaking of an existing bank to, or

in, the corresponding new bank, the affairs of the existing bank in relation to such asset or liability shall, on and from the commencement of this Act, stand entrusted to the chief executive officer for the time being of the corresponding new bank, and the chief executive officer may exercise all powers and do all such acts and things as may be exercised or done by the existing bank for the purpose of effectively transferring such assets and discharging such liabilities.

(3) The chief executive officer of the corresponding new bank shall, in exercise of the powers conferred on him by sub-section (2), take all such steps as may be required by the laws of any such country outside India for the purpose of effecting such transfer or vesting, and may either himself or through any person authorised by him in this behalf realise any asset and discharge any liability of the existing bank.

(4) Unless otherwise expressly provided by this Act, all contracts, deeds, bonds, agreements, powers of attorney, grants of legal representation and other instruments of whatever nature subsisting or having effect immediately before the commencement of this Act and to which the existing bank is a party or which are in favour of the existing bank shall be of as full force and effect against or in favour of the corresponding new bank, and may be enforced or acted upon as fully and effectually as if in the place of the existing bank the corresponding new bank had been a party thereto or as if they had been issued in favour of the corresponding new bank.

(5) If, on the appointed day, any suit, appeal or other proceeding of whatever nature in relation to any business of the undertaking which has been transferred under section 4, is pending by or against the existing bank, the same shall not abate, be discontinued or be, in any way, prejudicially affected by reason of the transfer of the undertaking of the existing bank or of anything contained in this Act but the suit, appeal or other 80 proceeding may be continued, prosecuted and enforced by or against the corresponding new bank.

(6) Nothing in this Act shall be construed as applying to the assets, rights, powers, authorities and privileges and property, movable and immovable, cash balances and investments in any country outside India (and other rights and interests in, or arising out of, such property) and borrowings,

liabilities and obligations of whatever kind subsisting at the commencement of this Act, of any existing bank operating in that country if, under the laws in force in that country, it is not permissible for a banking company, owned or controlled by Government, to carry on the business of banking there.

Payment of Compensation

(1) Every existing bank shall be given by the Central Government such compensation in respect of the transfer, under section 4, to the corresponding new bank of the undertaking of the existing bank as is specified against each such bank in the Second Schedule.

(2) The amount of compensation referred to in sub-section (1) shall be given to every existing bank, at its option,--(a) in case (to be paid by cheque drawn on the Reserve Bank) in three equal annual instalments, the amount of each instalment carrying interest at the rate of four per cent. per annum from the commencement of this Act, or (b) in saleable or otherwise transferable promissory notes or stock certificates of the Central Government issued and repayable at par, and maturing at the end of--(i) ten years from the commencement of this Act and carrying interest from such commencement at the rate of four and a half per cent. per annum, or (ii) thirty years from the commencement of this Act and carrying interest from such commencement at the rate of five and a half per cent. per annum, or (c) partly in cash (to be paid by cheque drawn on the Reserve Bank) and partly in such number of securities specified in sub-clause (i) or sub-clause (ii), or both, of clause (b), as may be required by the existing bank, or 81 (d) partly in such number of securities specified in sub-clause (i) of clause (b) and partly in such number of securities specified in sub-clause (ii) of that clause, as may be required by the existing bank.

(3) The first of the three equal annual instalments referred to in clause (a) of sub-section (2) shall be paid, and the securities referred to in clause (b) of that sub-section shall be issued, within sixty days from the date of receipt by the Central Government of the option referred to in that sub-section, or where no such option has been exercised, from the latest date before which such option ought to have been exercised.

(4) The option referred to in sub-section (2) shall be exercised by every existing bank before the expiry of a period of three months from the appointed day (or within such further time, not exceeding three months, as the Central Government may, on the application of the existing bank, allow) and the option so exercised shall be final and shall not be altered or rescinded after it has been exercised.

(5) Any existing bank which omits or fails to exercise the option referred to in sub-section (2), within the time specified in sub-section (4), shall be deemed to have opted for payment in securities specified in sub-clause (i) of clause (b) of sub-section (2).

(6) Notwithstanding anything contained in this section, any existing bank may, before the expiry of three months from the appointed day (or within such further time, not exceeding three months, as the Central Government may, on the application of the existing bank, allow) make an application in writing to the Central Government for an interim payment of an amount equal to seventy-five per cent. of the amount of the paid-up capital of such bank, as on the commencement of this Act, indicating therein whether the payment is desired in cash or in securities specified in sub-section (2), or in both.

(7) The Central Government shall, within sixty days from the receipt of the application referred to in sub-section (6), make the interim payment to the existing bank in accordance with the option indicated in such application.

(8) The interim payment made to an existing bank under sub-section (7) shall be set off against the total amount of compensation payable to such existing bank under this Act and the balance of the compensation remaining outstanding after such payment shall be given to the existing bank in accordance with the option exercised, or deemed to have been exercised, under sub-section (4) or sub-section

(5), as the case may be: Provided that where any part of the interim payment is obtained by an existing bank in cash, the payment so obtained shall be set off, in the first instance, against the first instalment of the cash payment referred 82 in sub-section (2), and in case the payment so obtained exceeds the amount of the first instalment, the excess amount shall be adjusted against the second instalment and the balance of such excess amount, if any, against the third instalment of the cash payment.

(9) Any payment purported to have been made to an existing bank under sub-section (3) of section 15 of the Banking Companies (Acquisition and Transfer of Undertakings) Act, 1969 (22 of 1969), shall be deducted by the Central Government from the amount of the interim payment made to such existing bank under sub-section (7), or where no such interim payment has been made, from the total amount of the compensation due to such existing bank, and the amount so deducted shall be paid by the Central Government to the corresponding new bank. CHAP MANAGEMENT OF CORRESPONDING NEW BANKS CHAPTER IV MANAGEMENT OF CORRESPONDING NEW BANKS

HEAD OFFICE AND MANAGEMENT

(1) The head office of each corresponding new bank shall be at such place as the Central Government may, by notification in the Official Gazette, specify in this behalf, and, until any such place is so specified, shall be at such place at which the head office of the existing bank, in relation to which it is the corresponding new bank, is on the commencement of this Act, located.

(2) The general superintendence, direction and management of the affairs and business of a corresponding new bank shall vest in a Board of Directors which shall be entitled to exercise all such powers and do all such acts and things as the corresponding new bank is authorised to exercise and do.

(3) (a) As soon as may be after the appointed day, the Central Government shall, in consultation with the Reserve Bank, constitute the first Board of Directors of a corresponding new bank, consisting of not more than seven persons, to be appointed by the Central Government, and every director so appointed shall hold office until the Board of Directors of such corresponding new bank is constituted in accordance with the scheme made under section 9: Provided that the Central Government may, if it is of opinion that it is necessary in the interests of the corresponding new bank so to do, remove a person from the membership of the first Board of Directors and

appoint any other person in his place. (b) Every member of the first Board of Directors (not being an officer of the Central Government or of the Reserve Bank) shall receive such remuneration as is equal to the remuneration which a member of the Board of Directors of the existing bank was entitled to receive immediately before the commencement of this Act. 83

(4) Until the first Board of Directors is appointed by the Central Government under sub-section (3), the general superintendence, direction and management of the affairs and business of a corresponding new bank shall vest in a Custodian, who shall be the chief executive officer of that bank and may exercise all powers and do all acts and things as may be exercised or done by that bank.

(5) The Chairman of an existing bank holding office as such immediately before the commencement of this Act, shall be the Custodian of the corresponding new bank and shall receive the same emoluments as he was receiving immediately before such commencement: Provided that the Central Government may, if the Chairman of an existing bank declines to become, or to continue to function as, a Custodian of the corresponding new bank, or, if it is of opinion that it is necessary in the interests of the corresponding new bank so to do, appoint any other person as the Custodian of a corresponding new bank and the Custodian so appointed shall receive such emoluments as the Central Government may specify in this behalf.

(6) The Custodian shall hold office during the pleasure of the Central Government.

Corresponding new banks to be guided by the directions of the CentralGovernment. 8. Corresponding new banks to be guided by the directions of the Central Government. Every corresponding new bank shall, in the discharge of its functions, be guided by such directions in regard to matters of policy involving public interest as the Central Government may, after consultation with the Governor of the Reserve Bank, give.

POWER OF CENTRAL GOVERNMENT TO MAKE SCHEME

(1) The Central Government may, after consultation with the Reserve Bank, make a scheme for carrying out the provisions of this Act.

(2) In particular, and without prejudice to the generality of the foregoing power, the said scheme may provide for all or any of the following matters, namely:--(a) the capital structure of the corresponding new bank1***. (b) the constitution of the Board of Directors, by whatever name called, of the corresponding new bank and all such matters in connection therewith or incidental thereto as the Central Government may consider to be necessary or expedient; (c) the reconstitution of any corresponding new bank into two or more corporations, the amalgamation of any corresponding new bank with any other corresponding new bank or with another banking institution, the transfer of the whole or any part of the------- ---1 Omitted by Act 37 of 1994, s. 6 (w.e.f. 3-4-1995). 84 undertaking of a 1*[corresponding new bank to any other corresponding new bank or banking institution] or the transfer of the whole or any part of the undertaking of any other banking institution to a corresponding new bank; (d) such incidental, consequential and supplemental matters as may be necessary to carry out the provisions of this Act.

(3) Every Board of Directors of a corresponding new bank, constituted under any scheme made under sub-section (1), shall include--(a) representatives of the employees, and of depositors, of such bank, and (b) such other persons as may represent the interests of each of the following categories, namely, farmers, workers and artisans, to be elected or nominated in such manner as may be specified in the scheme.

(4) The Central Government may, after consultation with the Reserve Bank, make a scheme to amend or vary any scheme made under sub-section (1).

3*[(5) On and from the date of coming into operation of a scheme made under this section with respect to any of the matters referred to in clause (c) of sub-section (2) or any matters incidental, consequential and supplemental thereto,--(a) the scheme shall be binding on the corresponding new bank or corporations or banking institutions, and also on the members, if any, the depositors, and other creditors and employees of each of them and on any other persons having any right or liability in relation to any of them including the trustees or other persons, managing or in any other manner connected with, any provident fund or other fund maintained by any of them; (b) the properties and assets of the corresponding new bank, or as the case may be, of the banking institution shall, by virtue of and to the extent provided in the scheme, stand transferred to, and vested in, and the liabilities of the corresponding new bank, or, as the case may be, of the banking institution shall, by virtue of, and to the extent provided in the scheme, stand transferred to, and become the liabilities of, the corporation or corporations brought into existence by reconstitution of the banking institution or the corresponding new bank, as the case may be. 4[Explanation I].--In this section, "banking institution" means a banking company and includes the State Bank of India or a subsidiary bank.] 5*['Explanation II.--For the purposes of this section, the expression "corresponding new bank" shall include a corresponding new bank within the meaning of the Banking Companies (Acquisition and Transfer of Undertakings) Act, 1980 (40 of 1980).]

6*[(6)] Every scheme made by the Central Government under this Act shall be laid, as soon as may be after it is made, before each House of Parliament while it is in session for a total period of thirty days 7*[which may be comprised in one session or in two or more successive sessions, and if, before the expiry of the session immediately following the session or the successive sessions aforesaid], both Houses agree in making any modification in the scheme or both Houses agree that the scheme should not be made, the scheme shall thereafter have effect only in such modified form or be of no effect, as the case may be; so, however, that any such modification or annulment shall be without prejudice to the validity of anything previously done under that scheme. CHAP MISCELLANEOUS CHAPTER V MISCELLANEOUS

CLOSURE OF ACCOUNTS AND DISPOSAL OF PROFITS

(1) Every corresponding new bank shall cause its books to be closed and balanced on the 31st day of December 8*[or such other date in each year as the Central Government may, by notification in the Official Gazette, specify] and shall appoint, with the previous approval of the Reserve Bank, auditors for the audit of its accounts: 9*[Provided that with a view to facilitating the transition from one period of accounting to

another period of accounting under this sub-section, the Central Government may, by order published in the Official Gazette, make such provisions as it considers necessary or expedient for the closing and balancing of, or for other matters relating to, the books in respect of the concerned years.]

(2) Every auditor of a corresponding new bank shall be a person who is qualified to act as an auditor of a company under section 226 of the Companies Act, 1956, (1 of 1956.) and shall receive such remuneration as the Reserve Bank may fix in consultation with the Central Government.

(3) Every auditor shall be supplied with a copy of the annual balance-sheet and profit and loss account and a list of all books kept by the corresponding new bank, and it shall be the duty of the auditor to examine the--1 Re-numbered, ins. & subs. by Act 1 of 1984, s. 66 (w.e.f. 15-2-1984). 2 Subs., numbered and ins. by Act 66 of 1988, s. 31 (w.e.f. 30-12-88). 3 Subs. & ins. by s. 32, ibid. (w.e.f. 30-12-1988). 85 balance-sheet and profit and loss account with the accounts and vouchers relating thereto, and in the performance of his duties, the auditor--(a) shall have, at all reasonable times, access to the books, accounts and other documents of the corresponding new bank, (b) may, at the expense of the corresponding new bank, employ accountants or other persons to assist him in investigating such accounts, and (c) may, in relation to such accounts, examine the Custodian or any officer or employee of the corresponding new bank.

(4) Every auditor of a corresponding new bank shall make a report to the Central Government upon the annual balance-sheet and accounts and in every such report shall state--(a) whether, in his opinion, the balance-sheet is a full and fair balance-sheet containing all the necessary particulars and is properly drawn up so as to exhibit a true and fair view of the affairs of the corresponding new bank, and in case he had called for any explanation or information, whether it has been given and whether it is satisfactory; (b) whether or not the transactions of the corresponding new bank, which have come to his notice, have been within the powers of that (c) whether or not the returns received from the offices and branches of the corresponding new bank have been found adequate for the purpose of his audit; (d) whether the profit and loss account

shows a true balance of profit or loss for the period covered by such account; and (e) any other matter which he considers should be brought to the notice of the Central Government. 1*["Explanation I.--For the purposes of this Act--(a) the balance-sheet shall not be treated as not disclosing a true and fair view of the affairs of the corresponding new bank, and (b) the profit and loss account shall not be treated as not showing a true balance of profit or loss for the period covered by such account, merely by reason of the fact that the balance-sheet or, as the case may be, the profit and loss account does not disclose any matters which are by the provisions of the Banking Regulation Act, 1949, read with the relevant provisions of this Act or any other Act, not required to be disclosed. Explanation II.--For the purposes of this Act the accounts of the corresponding new bank shall not be deemed as having not been properly drawn up on the ground merely that they do not disclose certain matters if--(i) those matters are such as the corresponding new bank is, by virtue of any provision contained in the Banking Regulation Act, 1949, read with the relevant provisions of this Act, or any other Act, not required to disclose; and (ii) the provisions referred to in clause (i) are specified in the balance-sheet and profit and loss account of the corresponding new bank or in the auditor's report."]

(5) The report of the auditor shall be verified, signed and transmitted to the Central Government.

(6) The auditor shall also forward a copy of the audit report to the corresponding new bank and to the Reserve Bank.

(7) After making provision for bad and doubtful debts, depreciation in assets, contributions to staff and superannuation funds and all other matters for which provision is necessary under any law, or which are usually provided for by banking companies, a corresponding new bank shall transfer the balance of profits to the Central Government. 1*["(7A) Every corresponding new bank shall furnish to the Central Government the annual balance-sheet, the profit and loss account, and the auditor's report and a report by its Board of directors on the working and activities of the bank during the period covered by the accounts."]

(8) The Central Government shall cause every auditor's report and report on the working and activities of each

corresponding new bank to be laid 1*["as soon as may be after they are received before each House of Parliament 2*xxx)---- --1 Ins. & subs. by Act 1 of 1984. s. 67 (w.e.f. 15-2-1984). 2 Omitted by Act 81 of 1985, s. 9 (w.e.f. 1-5-1986). 86

1*["(9) Without prejudice to the foregoing provisions, the Central Government may, at any time, appoint such number of auditors as it thinks fit to examine and report on the accounts of a corresponding new bank and the auditors so appointed shall have all the rights, privileges and authority in relation to the audit of the accounts of the corresponding new bank which an auditor appointed by the corresponding new bank has under this section."]

Corresponding new bank deemed to be an Indian company. 11. Corresponding new bank deemed to be an Indian company. For the purposes of the Income-tax Act, 1961, (43 of 1961.) every corresponding new bank shall be deemed to be an Indian company and a company in which the public are substantially interested.

Removal of Chairman from office.

12. Removal of Chairman from office. (1) Every person holding office, immediately before the commencement of this Act, as Chairman of an existing bank shall, if he becomes Custodian of the corresponding new bank, be deemed, on such commencement, to have vacated office as such Chairman.

(2) Save as otherwise provided in sub-section (1), every officer or other employee of an existing bank shall become, on the commencement of this Act, an officer or other employee, as the case may be, of the corresponding new bank and shall hold his office or service in that bank on the same terms and conditions and with the same rights to pension, gratuity and other matters as would have been admissible to him if the undertaking of the existing bank had not been transferred to and vested in the corresponding new bank and continue to do so unless and until his employment in the corresponding new bank is terminated or until his remuneration, terms or conditions are duly altered by the corresponding new bank.

(3) For the persons who immediately before the commencement of this Act were the trustees for any pension,

provident, gratuity or other like fund constituted for the officers or other employees of an existing bank, there shall be substituted as trustees such persons as the Central Government may, by general or special order, specify.

(4) Notwithstanding anything contained in the Industrial Disputes Act, 1947 (14 of 1947), or in any other law for the time being in force, the transfer of the services of any officer or other employee from an existing bank to a corresponding new bank shall not entitle such officer or other employee to any compensation under this Act or any other law for the time being in force and no such claim shall be entertained by any court, tribunal or other authority.

12A. Bonus

3*["12A. Bonus. (1) No officer or other employee [other than an employee within the meaning of clause (13) of section 2 of the Payment of Bonus Act, 1965 (21 of 1965)] of a corresponding new bank shall be entitled to be paid any bonus.]

(2) No employee of a corresponding new bank, being an employee within the meaning of clause (13) of section 2 of the Payment of Bonus Act, 1965, shall be entitled to be paid any bonus except in accordance with the provisions of that Act.

(3) The provisions of this section shall have effect notwithstanding any judgment, decree or order of any court, tribunal or other authority and notwithstanding anything contained in any other provision of this Act or in the Industrial Disputes Act, 1947 (14 of 1947), or any other law for the time being in force or any practice, usage or custom or any contract, agreement, settlement, award or other instrument.]

OBLIGATIONS AS TO FIDELITY AND SECRECY

(1) Every corresponding new bank shall observe, except as otherwise required by law, the practices and usages customary among bankers, and, in particular, it shall not divulge any information relating to or to the affairs of its constituents except in circumstances in which it is, in accordance with law or practices and usages customary among bankers, necessary or appropriate for the corresponding new bank to divulge such information.

(2) Every director, member of a local board or a committee, or auditor, adviser, officer or other employee of a corresponding new bank shall, before entering upon his duties, make a declaration of fidelity and secrecy in the form set out in the Third Schedule.--

------1 Ins. by Act 1 of 1984, s. 67 (w.e.f. 15-2-1984). 2 Ins. by Act 37 of 1994, s. 9 (w.e.f. 15-7-1994). 3 Ins. by Act 64 of 1984, s. 4. 87

(3) Every Custodian of a corresponding new bank shall, as soon as possible, make a declaration of fidelity and secrecy in the form set out in the Third Schedule.

Custodian to be public servant. 14. Custodian to be public servant. Every Custodian of a corresponding new bank shall be deemed to be a public servant for the purposes of Chapter IX of the Indian Penal Code (45 of 1860).

Certain defects not to invalidate acts or proceedings

(1) All acts done by the Custodian, acting in good faith, shall, notwithstanding any defect in his appointment or in the procedure, be valid.

(2) No act or proceeding of any Board of Directors or a local board or committee of a corresponding new bank shall be invalid merely on the ground of the existence of any vacancy in, or defect in the constitution of, such board or committee, as the case may be.

(3) All acts done by a person acting in good faith as a director or member of a local board or committee of a corresponding new bank shall be valid, notwithstanding that it may afterwards be discovered that his appointment was invalid by reason of any defect or disqualification or had terminated by virtue of any provision contained in any law for the time being in force: Provided that nothing in this section shall be deemed to give validity to any act by a director or member of a local board or committee of a corresponding new bank after his appointment has been shown to the corresponding new bank to be invalid or to have terminated.

Indemnity

(1) Every Custodian of a corresponding new bank and every officer of the Central Government or of the Reserve Bank and

every officer or other employee of a corresponding new bank, shall be indemnified by such bank against all losses and expenses incurred by him in or in relation to the discharge of his duties except such as have been caused by his own wilful act or default.

(2) A director or member of a local board or committee of a corresponding new bank shall not be responsible for any loss or expense caused to such bank by the insufficiency or deficiency of the value of, or title to, any property or security acquired or taken on behalf of the corresponding new bank, or by the insolvency or wrongful act of any customer or debtor, or by anything done in or in relation to the execution of the duties of his office, unless such loss, expense, insufficiency or deficiency was due to any wilful act or default on the part of such director or member.

16A. Arrangement with corresponding new bank on appointment of directors toprevail. 1*[16A. Arrangement with corresponding new bank on appointment of directors to prevail. (1) Where any arrangement entered into by a corresponding new bank with a company provides for the appointment by the corresponding new bank of one or more directors of such company, such provision and any appointment of directors made in pursuance thereof shall be valid and effective notwithstanding anything to the contrary contained in the Companies Act, 1956 (1 of 1956), or in any other law for the time being in force or in the memorandum, articles of association or any other instrument relating to the Company, and any provision regarding share qualification, age limit, number of directorships, removal from office of directors and such like conditions contained in any such law or instrument aforesaid, shall not apply to any director appointed by the corresponding new bank in pursuance of the arrangement as aforesaid.

(2) Any director appointed as aforesaid shall--(a) hold office during the pleasure of the corresponding new bank and may be removed or substituted by any person by order in writing of the corresponding new bank; (b) not incur any obligation or liability by reason only of his being a director or for anything done or omitted to be done in good faith in the discharge of his duties as a director or anything in relation thereto; (c) not be liable to retirement by rotation and shall not be taken into

account for computing the number of directors liable to such retirement.]

References to existing banks on and from the commencement of this Act. 17. References to existing banks on and from the commencement of this Act. Any reference to any existing bank in any law, other than this Act, or in any contract or other instrument shall, in so far as it relates to the undertaking which has been transferred by section 4, be construed as a reference to the corresponding new bank.

Dissolution. 18. Dissolution. No provision of law relating to winding up of corporations shall apply to a corresponding new bank and no corresponding new bank shall-----------------
--1 Ins. by Act 1 of 1984, s. 68 (w.e.f. 15-2-1984). 88 be placed in liquidation save by order of the Central Government and in such manner as it may direct.

Power to Make Regulations

(1) The Board of Directors of a corresponding new bank may, after consultation with the Reserve Bank and with the previous sanction of the Central Government, 1*[by notification in the Official Gazette,] make regulations, not inconsistent with the provisions of this Act or any scheme made thereunder, to provide for all matters for which provision is expedient for the purpose of giving effect to the provisions of this Act.

(2) In particular, and without prejudice to the generality of the foregoing power, the regulations may provide for all or any of the following matters, namely:--(a) the powers, functions and duties of local boards and restrictions, conditions or limitations, if any, subject to which they may be exercised or performed, the formation and constitution of local committees and committees of local board (including the number of members of any such committee), the powers, functions and duties of such committees, the holding of meetings of local committees and committees of local boards and the conduct of business thereat; (b) the manner in which the business of the local boards shall be transacted and the procedure in connection therewith; 2*[(ba) the nature of shares of the corresponding new bank, the manner in which and the conditions subject to which shnres may be held and transferred and generally all

matters relating to the rights and duties of shareholders; (bb) the maintenance of register, and the particulars to be entered in the register in addition to those specified in sub section (2F) of section 3, the safeguards to be observed in the maintenance of register on computer floppieg or diskettes, inspection and closure of the register and all other matters connected there with: (bc) the manner in which general meetings shall be convered, the procedure to be followed thereat and the manner in which voting rights may be exercised; (bd) the holding of meetings of shareholders and the business to be transacted thereat; (be) the manner in which notices may be served on behalf of the corresponding new bank upon shareholders or other persons; (bf) the manner in which the directors nominated under clause (h) of sub-section (3) of section 9 shall retire;] (c) the delegation of powers and functions of the board of directors of a corresponding new bank to the general manager, director, officer or other employee of that bank; (d) the conditions or limitations subject to which the corresponding new bank may appoint advisers, officers or other employees and fix their remuneration and other terms and conditions of service; (e) the duties and conduct of advisers, officers or other employees of the corresponding new bank; (f) the establishment and maintenance of superannuation, pension, provident or other funds for the benefit of officers or other employees of the corresponding new bank or of the dependants of such officers or other employees and the granting of superannuation allowances, annuities and pensions payable out of such funds; (g) the conduct and defence of legal proceedings by or against the corresponding new bank and the manner of signing pleadings; (h) the provision of a seal for the corresponding new bank and the manner and effect of its use; (i) the form and manner in which contracts binding on the corresponding new bank may be executed;--1 Ins. by Act 4 of 1986, s. 2 and Sch. (w.e.f. 15-5-1986). 2 ins. by Act 37 of 1994, s. 9 (w.e.f. 15-7-1994). 89 (j) the conditions and the requirements subject to which loans or advances may be made or bills may be discounted or purchased by the corresponding new bank; (k) the persons or authorities who shall administer any pension, provident or other fund constituted for the benefit of officers or other employees of the corresponding new bank or their dependants; (l) the preparation and submission of statements of programmes of activities and financial statements of the corresponding new bank and the period for which and the time within which such statements and estimates are to be prepared and submitted; and (m) generally for the efficient conduct of the affairs of the corresponding new bank.

(3) Until any regulation is made under sub-section (1), the articles of association of the existing bank and every regulation, rule, bye-law or order made by the existing bank shall, if in force at the commencement of this Act, be deemed to be the regulations made under sub-section (1) and shall have effect accordingly and any reference therein to any authority of the existing bank shall be deemed to be a reference to the corresponding a thority of the corresponding new bank and until any such corresponding authority is constituted under this Act, shall be deemed to refer to the Custodian.

1*[or(4) Every regulation shall, as soon as may be after it is made under this Act by the Board of directors of a corresponding new bank, be forwarded to the Central Government and that Government shall cause a copy of the same to be laid before each House of Parliament, while it is in session, for a total period of thirty days which may be comprised in one session or in two or more successive sessions, and if, before the expiry of the session immediately following the session or the successive sessions aforesaid, both Houses agree in making any modification in the regulation or both Houses agree that the regulation should not be made, the regulation shall thereafter have effect only in such modified form or be of no effect, as the case may be; so, however, that any such modification or annulment shall be without prejudice to the validity of anything previously done under that regulation.]

Amendment of Certain Enactments

(1) In the Banking Regulation Act, 1949 (10 of 1949),--

(a) in section 34A, in sub-section (3), for the words "and any subsidiary bank", the words, figures and brackets "a corresponding new bank constituted under section 3 of the Banking Companies (Acquisition and Transfer of Undertakings)

Act, 1970 (5 of 1970) and any subsidiary bank" shall be substituted;

(b) in section 36AD, in sub-section (3), for the words "and any subsidiary bank", the words, figures and brackets "a corresponding new bank constituted under section 3 of the Banking Companies (Acquisition and Transfer of Undertakings) Act, 1970 (5 of 1970), and any subsidiary bank" shall be substituted; (c) in section 51, for the words "or any other banking institution notified by the Central Government in this behalf", the words, figures and brackets "or any corresponding new bank constituted under section 3 of the Banking Companies (Acquisition and Transfer of Undertakings) Act, 1970 (5 of 1970), or any other banking institution notified by the Central Government in this behalf" shall be substituted; (d) in the Fifth Schedule, in Part I of paragraph 1, in clause (e), the Explanations shall be deemed never to have been inserted.--1 Ins. by Act 1 of 1984, s. 69 (w.e.f. 15-2-1984). 90

(2) In the Industrial Disputes Act, 1947 (14 of 1947), in section 2, in clause (bb), for the words "and any subsidiary bank", the words, figures and brackets "a corresponding new bank constituted under section 3 of the Banking Companies (Acquisition and Transfer of Undertakings) Act, 1970 (5 of 1970), and any subsidiary bank" shall be substituted.

(3) In the Banking Companies (Legal Practitioners, Clients, Accounts) Act, 1949 (46 of 1949), in section 2, in clause (a), for the words "and any subsidiary bank", the words, figures and brackets "a corresponding new bank constituted under section 3 of the Banking Companies (Acquisition and Transfer of Undertakings) Act, 1970 (5 of 1970), and any subsidiary bank" shall be substituted.

(4) In the Deposit Insurance Corporation Act, 1961 (47 of 1961).--(a) in section 2,--(i) after clause (e), the following clause shall be inserted, namely:--'(ee) "corresponding new bank" means a corresponding new bank constituted under section 3 of the Banking Companies (Acquisition and Transfer of Undertakings) Act, 1970 (5 of 1970)'; (ii) in clause (g),--(a) for the words or a banking company", the words "a corresponding new bank or a banking company", and (b) for the words "with a banking

company", the words "with a corresponding new bank or with a banking company", shall be substituted; (iii) in clause (i), after the words "banking company", the words "or a corresponding new bank" shall be inserted;

(b) section 13 shall be re-numbered as sub-section (1) thereof and after sub-section (1) as so re-numbered, the following sub-section shall be inserted, namely:--

"(2) The provisions of clauses (a), (b), (c), (d) and (h) of sub-section (1) shall apply to a corresponding new bank as they apply to a banking company.".

(5) In the State Agricultural Credit Corporations Act, 1968 (60 of 1968),--(a) in section 2, after clause (i), the following clause shall be inserted, namely:--'(ii) "corresponding new bank" means a corresponding new bank constituted under section 3 of the Banking Companies (Acquisition and Transfer of Undertakings) Act, 1970 (5 of 1970)'; (b) after the words "subsidiary banks" or "subsidiary bank", as the case may be, occurring in clause (d) of sub-section (3) of 91 section 5, in clause (b) of section 9 and in the proviso to section 18, the words "corresponding new banks" or "corresponding new bank", as the case may be, shall be inserted.

Repeal and Savings

(1) The Banking Companies (Acquisition and Transfer of Undertakings) Ordinance, 1970 (3 of 1970), is hereby repealed.

(2) Notwithstanding such repeal and notwithstanding any judgment, decree or order of any court or tribunal,--(a) any action taken, or purported to have been taken, or anything done, or purported to have been done, between the 19th day of July, 1969, and the 10th day of February, 1970, by any corresponding new bank purported to have been constituted under the Banking Companies (Acquisition and Transfer of Undertakings) Ordinance, 1969 (8 of 1969), or the Banking Companies (Acquisition and Transfer of Undertakings) Act, 1969 (22 of 1969), or by any person purporting to act on behalf of such bank and any right, obligation or liability acquired or incurred, between the said dates, by or on behalf of such corresponding new bank shall be deemed to have been taken, done, acquired or incurred under the provisions of this Act by

or on behalf of the corresponding new bank constituted thereunder; (b) any action taken, or purported to have been taken, or anything done, or purported to have been done, between the 10th day of February, 1970, and the appointed day, by an existing Bank or by any person acting on behalf of such bank, and any right, obligation or liability acquired or incurred, between the said dates, by or on behalf of such existing bank shall be deemed to have been taken, done, acquired or incurred under the provisions of this Act by or on behalf of the corresponding new bank constituted thereunder; (c) anything done or any action taken, including any order made, notification issued or directions given under the Banking Companies (Acquisition and Transfer of Undertakings) Ordinance, 1970 (3 of 1970), shall be deemed to have been done, taken, made, issued or given, as the case may be, under the corresponding provisions of this Act.

(3) Any suit, appeal or other proceeding of whatever nature instituted on or after the 19th day of July, 1969, by or against a corresponding new bank purported to have been constituted by the Banking Companies (Acquisition and Transfer of Undertakings) Ordinance, 1969 (8 of 1969), or the Banking Companies (Acquisition and Transfer of Undertakings) Act, 1969 (22 of 1969), shall not abate, be discontinued, or be, in any way, prejudicially affected by reason of the expiry of the said Ordinance or the invalidation of the said Act, as the case may be, but such suit, appeal or other proceeding may be 92 continued, prosecuted and enforced by or against the corresponding new bank as if such suit, appeal or other proceeding had been instituted by or against the corresponding new bank constituted under this Act. SCHE See sections 2, 3 and 4 THE FIRST SCHEDULE (See sections 2, 3 and 4)--Existing bank Corresponding new bank---Column 1 Column 2--The Central Bank of India Limited.. Central Bank of India. The Bank of India Limited.... Bank of India. The Punjab National Bank Limited.. Punjab National Bank. The Bank of Baroda Limited... Bank of Baorda. The United Commercial Bank Limited.. 1*[Uco Bank] Canara Bank

Limited.... Canara Bank. United Bank of India Limited... United Bank of India. Dena Bank Limited.... Dena Bank. Syndicate Bank Limited.... Syndicate Bank. The Union Bank of India Limited.. Union Bank of India. Allahabad Bank Limited.... Allahabad Bank. The Indian Bank Limited.... Indian Bank. The Bank of Maharashtra Limited.. Bank of Maharashtra. The Indian Overseas Bank Limited.. Indian Overseas Bank.------- ---SCHE See section 6 THE SECOND SCHEDULE (See section 6)-------------------- ---Name of existing bank Amount of compensation-- ------------------(in lakhs of rupees) The Central Bank of India Limited.. 1750 The Bank of India Limited.. 1470 The Punjab National Bank Limited.. 1020 The Bank of Baroda Limited.. 840 The United Commercial Bank Limited.. 830 Canara Bank Limited.. 360 United Bank of India Limited.. 420 Dena Bank Limited.. 360 Syndicate Bank Limited.. 360 The Union Bank of India Limited.. 310 Allahabad Bank Limited.. 310 The Indian Bank Limited.. 230 The Bank of Maharashtra Limited.. 230 The Indian Overseas Bank Limited.. 250------------------------- -------------------------------------1 Subs. by Act 81 of 1985, s. 10 (w.e.f. 30-12-1985). 93 SCHE DECLARATION OF FIDELITY AND SECRECY THE THIRD SCHEDULE

(See sub-sections (2) and (3) of section 13] DECLARATION OF FIDELITY AND SECRECY I,---------, do hereby declare that I will faithfully, truly and to the best of my skill and ability execute and perform the duties required of me as Custodian, Director, member of Local Board, member of Local Committee, auditor, adviser, officer or other employee (as the case may be) of the * and which properly relate to the office or position in the said* held by me. I further declare that I will not communicate or allow to be communicated to any person not legally entitled thereto any information relating to the affairs of the * or to the affairs of any person having any dealing with the*;nor will I allow any such person to inspect or have access to any books or documents belonging to or in the possession of the* and relating to the business of the* or to the business of any person having any dealing with the* * Name of corresponding new bank to be filled in.

THE DEPARTMENTAL INQUIRIES (ENFORCEMENT OF ATTENDANCE OF WITNESSES AND PRODUCTION OF DOCUMENTS) ACT, 1972

No. 18 of 1972

An Act to provide for the enforcement of attendance of witnesses and production of documents in certain departmental inquiries and for matters connected therewith or incidental thereof.

Be it enacted by Parliament in the Twenty-third Year of the Republic of India as follows:-

Short Title and Extent

1. (1) This Act may be called the Departmental Inquiries (Enforcement of Attendance of Witnesses and Production of Documents) Act, 1972.

(2) It extends to the whole of India except the State of Jammu and Kashmir.

Departmental Inquiries to which the Act shall Apply

2. The provisions of this Act shall apply to every departmental inquiry made in relation to-

(a) persons appointed to public services or posts in connection with the affairs of the Union;

(b) persons who, having been appointment to any public service or post in connection with the affairs of the Union, are in service or pay of-

(i) any local authority in any Union Territory,

(ii) any corporation established by or under a Central Act and owned or controlled by the Central Governmen,

(iii) any Government company within the meaning of section 617 of the Companies Act, 1956, (1 of 1956) in which not less than fifty-one percent of the paid-up share capital is held by the Central Government or any company which is a subsidiary of such Government company,

(iv) any society registered under the Societies Registration Act, 1860, (21 of 1960) which is subject to the control of the Central Government.

3. For the purposes of this Act,-

(a) "departmental inquiry" means an inquiry held under and in accordance with-

(i) any law made by Parliament or any rule made thereunder, or

(ii) any rule made under the proviso to articles 309, or continued under article 313 of the Constitution of India, into any allegation of lack of integrity against any person to whom this Act applies;

(b)"inquiring authority" means an officer or authority appointed by the Central Government or by any officer or authority subordinate to that Government to hold a departmental inquiry and includes any officer or authority who is empowered by or under any law or rule for the time being in force to hold such inquiry;

(c) 'lack of integrity includes bribery or corruption.

Power of Central Government to authorise the exercise of powers specified in Section 5

4. (1) where the Central Government is of opinion that for the purposes of any departmental inquiry it is necessary to summon as witnesses, or call for any document from any class or category of persons, it may, by notification in the Official Gazette, authorise the inquiring authority to exercise the power specified in section 5 in relation to any person within such class or category and thereupon the inquiring authority may exercise such power at any stage of the departmental inquiry.

(2) The power conferred on the Central Government by sub-section (1) may also be exercised by such authority, not being an authority inferior to the appointing authority in relation to the person against whom the departmental inquiry is being held, as the Central Government may, by notification in the Official Gazette, specify in this behalf.

Power of authorised inquiring authority to enforce attendance of witnesses and production of documents

5. (1) Every inquiring authority authorised under section 4,(hereafter referred to as the "authorised inquiring authority") shall have the same powers as are vested in a civil court under the Code of Civil Procedure, 1908, (5 of 1908) while trying a suit, in respect of the following matters, namely:-

(a) the summoning and enforcing the attendance of any witness and examining him on oath;

(b) requiring the discovery and production of any document or other material which is producible as evidence;

(c) the requisitioning of any public record from any court or office;

(2) Notwithstanding anything contained in sub-section (1), the authorised inquiring authority shall not compel the Reserve Bank of India, the State bank of India, any subsidiary bank as defined in clause (k) of section 2 of the State Bank of India (Subsidiary Banks) Act 1959, (38 of 1959) or any corresponding new bank constituted under section 3 of the Banking Companies (Acquisition and Transfer of Undertakings) Act, 1970, (5 of 1970).-

(a) to produce any books of account or other documents which the Reserve Bank of India, the State Bank of India, the subsidiary bank or the corresponding new bank claims to be of a confidential nature, or

(b) to make any such books or documents a part of the record of the proceedings of the departmental inquiry, or

(c) to give inspection of any such books or documents if produced, to any party before it or to any other person.

(3) Every process issued by an authorised inquiring authority for the attendance of any witness or for the production of any document shall be served and executed through the District Judge within the local limits of whose jurisdiction the witness or other person, on whom the process is to be served or executed, voluntarily resides or carries on business or personally works for gain, and for the purpose of taking any action for the disobedience of any such process, every such process shall be deemed to be a process issued by the District Judge.

(4) Every authorised inquiring authority making any departmental inquiry under this Act shall be deemed to be a civil court for the purposes of sections 480 and 482 of the Code of Criminal Procedure, 1898, (5 of 1898).

Territorial limits in which powers specified in section 5 may by exercised.

6. For the purpose of exercising the powers specified in section 5, the territorial jurisdiction of every authorised inquiring authority shall extend to the limits of the territory to which this Act extends.

Power to make rules

7. (1) The Central Government may, by notification in the Official Gazette, make rules for the purpose of giving effect to the provisions of this Act.

(2) Every rule made by the Central Government under this section shall be laid, as soon as may be after it, is made, before each House of Parliament while it is in session for a total period of thirty days which may be comprised in one session or in two or more successive sessions, and if, before the expiry of the session immediately following the session or the successive sessions aforesaid, both Houses agree in making any modification in the rule or both Houses agree that the rule should not be made, the rule shall thereafter have effect only in such modified form or be of no effect, as the case may be; so however., that the modification or annulment shall be without prejudice to the validity of anything previously done under that rule.

5

The Banking Regulation Act, 1949

(Act No. 10 of 1949)

[10th March, 1949]

PRELIMINARY

Sections

1. Short title, extent and commencement

2. Application of other laws not barred

3 Act to apply to co-operative societies in certain cases.

4. Power to suspend operation of Act

5. Interpretation

5A. Act to override memorandum, articles, etc.

BUSINESS OF BANIKNG COMPANIES

6. Forms of business in which banking companies may engage

7. Use of words "bank", "banker", "banking" or "banking company"

8. Prohibition of trading

9. Disposal of non-banking assets

10. Prohibition of employment of managing agents and restrictions on certain forms of employment

10A. Board of directors to include persons with professional or other experience

10B Ranking company to be managed by whole-time chairman

27. Monthly returns and power to call for other returns and information

28. Power to publish information

29. Accounts and balance-sheet

30. Audit

31. Submission of returns

32. Copies of balance-sheets and accounts to be sent to registrar

33. Display of audited balance-sheet by companies incorporated outside India

34. Accounting provisions of this Act not retrospective

34A. Production of documents of confidential nature

35. Inspection

35A Power of the Reserve Bank to give directions

35B. Amendments of provisions relating to appointments of managing directors, etc., to be subject to previous approval of the Reserve Bank

36. Further powers and functions of Reserve Banks

36A. Certain provisions of the Act not to apply to certain banking companies

CONTROL OVER MANAGEMENT

36AA Power of Reserve Bank to remove managerial and other persons from office

36AB Power of Reserve Bank to appoint additional directors

36AC Part IIA to override other laws

PROHIBITION OF CERTAIN ACTIVITIES IN RELATION TO BANKING COMPANIES

36AD. Punishments for certain activities in relation to banking companies

ACQUISITION OF THE UNDERTAKINGS OF BANKING COMPANIES IN CERTAIN CASES

36AE. Power of Central Government to acquire undertakings of banking companies in certain cases

36AF Power of the Central Government to make scheme

SUSPENSION OF BUSINESS AND WINDING UP OF BANKING COMPANIES

SPECIAL PROVISIONS FOR SPEEDY DISPOSAL OF WINDING UP PROCEEDINGS

PROVISIONS RELATING TO CERTAIN OPERATIONS OF BANKING COMPANIES

SCHEDULES

THE FIRST SCHEDULE

THE SECOND SCHEDULE [Repealed]

THE THIRD SCHEDULE

THE FOURTH SCHEDULE

THE FIFTH SCHEDULE

Amending Act (24 of 2004)

PREAMBLE

An Act to consolidate and amend the law relating to banking 1[***].

WHEREAS it is expedient to consolidate and amend the law relating to banking 2[* **].

It is hereby enacted as follows.-

THE BANKING REGULATION ACT, 19491

(Act No. 10 of 1949)

[10th March, 1949]

PRELIMINARY

1. Short title, extent and commencement.-(1) This Act may be called the Banking 2[Regulation] Act, 1949.

3[(2) It extends to the whole of India 4[* * *].]

(3) It shall come into force on such date5as the Central Government may, by notification in the Official Gazette, appoint in this behalf.

2. Application of other laws not barred.-The provisions of this Act shall be in addition to, and not, save as hereunder expressly provided, in derogation of the 6[Companies Act, 1956 (1 of 1956)], and any other law for the time being in force.

7[3. Act to apply to co-operative societies in certain cases.-Nothing in this Act shall apply to.-

(a) a primary agricultural credit society;

(b) a co-operative land mortgage bank; and

(c) any other co-operative society, except in the manner and to the extent specified in Part V.]

4. Power to suspend operation of Act.-(1) The Central Government, if on a representation made by the Reserve Bank in this behalf it is satisfied that it is expedient so to do, may by notification in the Official Gazette suspend for such period, not exceeding sixty days, as may be specified in the notification, the operation of all or any of the provisions of this Act, either generally or in relation to any specified banking company.

(2) In a case of special emergency, the Governor of the Reserve Bank, or in his absence a Deputy Governor of the Reserve Bank nominated by him in this behalf may, by order in writing, exercise the powers of the Central Government under sub-section (1) so however that the period of suspension shall not exceed thirty days, and where the Governor or the Deputy Governor, as the case may be, does so, he shall report the matter to the Central Government forthwith, and the order shall, as soon as may be, be published in the Gazette of India.

(3) The Central Government may, by notification in the Official Gazette, extend from time to time the period of any suspension ordered under sub-section (1) or subsection (2) for such period, not exceeding sixty days at any one time, as it thinks fit so however that the total period does not exceed one year.

(4) A copy of any notification issued under sub-section (3) shall be laid on the table of 8[Parliament] as soon as may be after it is issued.

5. Interpretation.-9[In this Act], unless there is anything repugnant in the subject or context,-

10[(a) "approved securities" means--

(i) securities in which a trustee may invest money under clause (a), clause (b), clause (bb), clause (c) or clause (d) of section 20 of the Indian Trusts Act, 1882 (2 of 1882);

(ii) such of the securities authorised by the Central Government under clause (f) of section 20 of the Indian Trusts Act, 1882 (2 of 1882), as may be prescribed;]

(b) "banking" means the accepting, for the purpose of lending or investment, of deposits of money from the public, repayable on demand or otherwise, and withdrawal by cheque, draft, order or otherwise;

(c) "banking company" means any company which transacts the business of banking 11[in India];

Explanation.-Any company which is engaged in the manufacture of goods or carries on any trade and which accepts deposits of money from the public merely for the purpose of financing its business as such manufacturer or trader shall not be deemed to transact the business of banking within the meaning of this clause;

12[(ca) "banking policy" means any policy which is specified from time to time by the Reserve Bank in the interest of the banking system or in the interest of monetary stability or sound economic growth, having due regard to the interests of the depositors, the volume of deposits and other resources of the bank and the need for equitable allocation and the efficient use of these deposits and resources;]

13[(cc) "branch" or "branch office", in relation to a banking company, means any branch or branch office, whether called a pay office or sub-pay office or by any other name, at which deposits are received, cheques cashed or moneys lent, and for the purposes of section 35 includes any place of business where any other form of business referred to in sub-section (1) of section 6 is transacted;]

14[(d) "company" means any company as defined in section 3 of the Companies Act, 1956 (1 of 1956); and includes a foreign company within the meaning of section 591 of that Act;)

15[(da) "corresponding new bank" means a corresponding new bank constituted under section 3 of the Banking Companies (Acquisition and Transfer of Undertakings) Act, 1970 (5 of 1970); or under section 3 of the Banking Companies (Acquisition and Transfer of Undertakings) Act, 1980 (40 of 1980);]

16[* * * * *]

(f) "demand liabilities" means liabilities which must be met on demand, and "time liabilities" means liabilities which are not demand liabilities;

17[(ff) "Deposit Insurance Corporation" means the Deposit Insurance Corporation established under section 3 of the Deposit Insurance Corporation Act, 1961 (47 of 1961);]

18[(ffa) "Development Bank" means the Industrial Development Bank of India established under section 3 of the Industrial Development Bank of India Act, 1964 (18 of 1964);

(ffb) "Exim Bank" means the Export-Import Bank of India established under section 3 of the Export-Import India Act, 1981 (28 of 1981);]

19[(ffc) "Reconstruction Bank" means the Industrial Reconstruction Bank of India established under section 3 of the Industrial Reconstruction Bank of India Act, 1984 (62 of 1984);]

20[(ffd) "National Housing Bank" means the National Housing Bank established under section 3 of the National Housing Bank Act, 1987;]

(g) "gold" includes gold in the form of coin, whether legal tender or not, or in the form of bullion or ingot, whether refined or not;

21[(gg) "managing agent" includes.-

(i) Secretaries and Treasurers;

(ii) Where the managing agent is a company, and director of such company, and any member thereof who holds substantial interest in such company;

(iii) Where the managing agent is a firm, any partner of such firm;]

22[(h) "managing director", in relation to a banking company, means a director who, by virtue of an agreement with the banking company or of a resolution passed by the banking company in general meeting or by its Board of directors or, by virtue of its memorandum or articles of association, is entrusted with the management of the whole, or substantially the whole of the affairs of the company, and includes a director occupying the position of a managing director, by whatever name called:]

23[Provided that the managing director shall exercise his powers subject to the superintendence, control and direction of the Board of Directors;]

24[(ha) "National Bank" means the National Bank for Agriculture and Rural Development established under section 3 of the National Bank for Agriculture and Rural Development Act, 1981;]

25[* * * * *]

(j) "prescribed" means prescribed by rules made under this Act;

24[(ja) "regional rural bank" means a regional rural bank established under section 3 of the Regional Rural Banks Act, 1976 (21 of 1976);]

25[* * * * *]

26[(1) "Reserve Bank" means the Reserve Bank of India constituted under section 3 of the Reserve Bank of India Act, 1934 (2 of 1934);]

25[* * * * *]

(n) "secured loan or advance" means a loan or advance made on the security of assets the market value of which is not at any time less than the amount of such loan or advance; and "unsecured loan or advance" means a loan or advance not so secured;

27[(ni) "Small Industries Bank" means the Small Industries Development Bank of India established under section 3 of the Small Industries Development Bank of India, 1989;]

28[(na) "small-scale industrial concern" means an industrial concern in which the investment in plant and machinery is not in excess of seven and a half lakhs of rupees or such higher amount, not exceeding twenty lakhs of rupees, as the Central Government may, by notification in the Official Gazette, specify in this behalf, having regard to the trends in industrial development and other relevant factors;]

29[(nb) "Sponsor Bank" has the meaning assigned to it in the Regional Rural Banks Act, 1976 (21 of 1976);

(nc) "State Bank of India" means the State Bank of India constituted under section 3 of the State Bank of India Act, 1955 (23 of 1955);]

30[(nd)] "subsidiary bank" has the meaning assigned to it in the State Bank of India (Subsidiary Banks) Act, 1959;

31[(ne)] " substantial interest".-

(i) in relation to a company, means the holding of a beneficial interest by an individual or his spouse or minor child, whether singly or taken together, in the shares thereof, the amount paid up on which exceeds five lakhs of rupees or ten percent of the paid-up capital of the company, whichever is less;

(ii) in relation to a firm, means the beneficial interest held therein by an individual or his spouse o r minor child, whether singly or taken together, which represents more than ten per cent of the total capital subscribed by all the partners of the said firm;]]

32[(o) all other words and expressions used herein but not defined and defined in the Companies Act, 1956 (1 of 1956), shall have the meanings respectively assigned to them in that Act.]

33[* * * * *]

34[5A. Act to override memorandum, articles, etc.-Save as otherwise expressly provided in this Act.-(a) the provisions of this Act shall have effect notwithstanding anything to the contrary contained in the memorandum or articles of a banking company, or in any agreement executed by it, or in any resolution passed by the banking company in general meeting or by its Board of Directors, whether the same be registered, executed or passed, as the case may be, before or after the commencement of the Banking Companies (Amendment) Act, 1959 (33 of 1959); and

(b) any provision contained in the memorandum, articles, agreement or resolution aforesaid shall, to the extent to which it is repugnant to the provisions of this Act, become or be void, as the case may be.]

BUSINESS OF BANKING COMPANIES

6. Forms of business in which banking companies may engage.-(1) In addition to the business of banking, a banking company may engage in any one or more of the following forms of business, namely:-

(a) the borrowing, raising, or taking up of money; the lending or advancing of money either upon or without security; the drawing, making, accepting, discounting, buying, selling, collecting and dealing in bills of exchange, hoondees, promissory notes, coupons, drafts, bills of lading, railway receipts, warrants, debentures, certificates, scrips and other instruments and securities whether transferable or negotiable or not; the granting and issuing of letters of credit, traveller's cheques and circular notes; the buying, selling and dealing in bullion and specie; the buying and selling of foreign exchange including foreign bank notes; the acquiring, holding, issuing on commission, underwriting and dealing in stock, funds, shares, debentures, debenture stock, bonds, obligations, securities and investments of all kinds; the purchasing and selling of bonds, scrips or other forms of securities on behalf of constituents or others, the negotiating of loans and advances; the receiving of all kinds of bonds, scrips or valuables on deposit or for safe custody or otherwise; the providing of safe deposit vaults; the collecting and transmitting of money and securities;

(b) acting as agents for any Government or local authority or any other person or persons; the carrying on of agency business of any description including the clearing and forwarding of goods, giving of receipts and discharges and otherwise acting as an attorney on behalf of customers, but excluding the business of a 1[managing agent or secretary and treasurer] of a company;

(c) contracting for public and private loans and negotiating and issuing the same;

(d) the effecting, insuring, guaranteeing, underwriting, participating in managing and carrying out of any issue, public or private, of State, municipal or other loans or of shares, stock, debentures, or debenture stock of any company, corporation or association and the lending of money for the purpose of any such issue;

(e) carrying on and transacting every kind of guarantee and indemnity business;

(f) managing, selling and realising any property which may come into the possession of the company in satisfaction or part satisfaction of any of its claims;

(g) acquiring and holding and generally dealing with any property or any right, title or interest in any such property which may form the security or part of the security for any loans or advances or which may be connected with any such security;

(h) undertaking and executing trusts;

(i) undertaking the administration of estates as executor, trustee or otherwise;

(j) establishing and supporting or aiding in the establishment and support of associations, institutions, funds, trusts and conveniences calculated to benefit employees or ex-employees of the company or the dependents or connections of such persons; granting pensions and allowances and making payments towards insurance; subscribing to or guaranteeing moneys for charitable or benevolent objects or for any exhibition or for any public, general or useful object;

(k) the acquisition, construction, maintenance and alteration of any building or works necessary or convenient for the purposes of the company;

(l) selling, improving, managing, developing, exchanging, leasing, mortgaging, disposing of or turning into account or otherwise dealing with all or any part of the property and rights of the company;

(m) acquiring and undertaking the whole or any part of the business of any person or company, when such business is of a nature enumerated or described in this sub-section;

(n) doing all such other things as are incidental or conducive to the promotion or advancement of the business of the company;

(o) any other form of business which the Central Government may, by notification in the Official Gazette, specify as a form of business in which it is lawful for a banking company to engage.

(2) No banking company shall engage in any form of business other than those referred to in sub-section (1).

2[7. Use of words "bank", "banker", "banking" or "banking company".-(1) No company other than a banking company shall use as part of its name 3[or in connection with its business] any of the words "bank", "banker" or "banking" and no company shall carry on the business of banking in India unless it uses as part of its name at least one of such words.

(2) No firm, individual or group of individuals shall, for the purpose of carrying on any business, use as part of its or his name any of the words "bank", "banking" or "banking company".

(3) Nothing in this section shall apply to.-

(a) a subsidiary of a banking company formed for one or more of the purposes mentioned in sub-section (1) of section 19, whose name indicates that it is a subsidiary of that banking company;

(b) any association of banks formed for the protection of their mutual interests and registered under section 25 of the Companies Act, 1956 (1 of 1956).]

8. Prohibition of trading.-Notwithstanding anything contained in section 6 or in any contract, no banking company shall directly or indirectly deal in the buying or selling or bartering of goods, except in connection with the realisation of security given to or held by it, or engage in any trade, or buy, sell or barter goods for others otherwise than in connection with bills of exchange received for collection or nego-tiation or with such of its business as is referred lo in clause (i) of sub-section (1) of section 6:

4[Provided that this section shall not apply to any such business as is specified in pursuance of clause (o) of sub-section (1) of section 6.

Explanation.-For the purposes of this section, "goods" means every kind of movable property, other than actionable claims, stocks, shares, money, bullion and specie, and all instruments referred to in clause (a) of sub-section (1) of section 6.

9. Disposal of non-banking assets.-Notwithstanding anything contained in section 6, no banking company shall hold any immovable property howsoever acquired, except such as is required for its own use, for any period exceeding seven years from the acquisition thereof or from the commencement of this Act, whichever is later or any extension of such period as in this section provided, and such properly shall be disposed of within such period or extended period, as the case may be:

Provided that the banking company may, within the period of seven years as aforesaid deal or trade in any such property for the purpose of facilitating the disposal thereof:

Provided further that the Reserve Bank may in any particular case extend the aforesaid period of seven years by such period not exceeding five years where it is satisfied that such extension would be in the interests of the depositors of the banking company.

5[10. Prohibition of employment of managing agents and restrictions on certain forms of employment.-(1) No banking company-

(a) shall employ or be managed by a managing agent; or

(b) shall employ or continue the employment of any person-

(i) who is, or at any time has been, adjudicated insolvent, or has suspended payment or has compounded with his creditors, or who is, or has been, convicted by a criminal court of an offence involving moral turpitude; or

(ii) whose remuneration or part of whose remuneration takes the form of commission or of a share in the profits of the company:

6[Provided that nothing contained in this sub-clause shall apply to the payment by a banking company of-

(a) any bonus in pursuance of a settlement or award arrived at or made under any law relating to industrial disputes or in accordance with any scheme framed by such banking company or in accordance with the usual practice prevailing in banking business;

(b) any commission to any broker (including guarantee broker), cashier-contractor, clearing and forwarding agent, auctioneer or any other person, employed by the banking company under a contract otherwise than as a regular member of the staff of the company; or]

(iii) whose remuneration is, in the opinion of the Reserve Bank, excessive; or

(c) shall be managed by any person-

7[(i) who is a director of any other company not being-

(a) a subsidiary of the banking company, or

(b) a company registered under section 25 of the Companies Act, 1956 (1 of 1956):

Provided that the prohibition in this sub-clause shall not apply in respect of any such director for a temporary period not exceeding three months or such further period not exceeding nine months as the Reserve Bank may allow; or]

(ii) who is engaged in any other business or vocation; or

(iii) 8[whose term of office as a person managing the company is] for period exceeding five years at any one time:

9[Provided that the term of office of any such person may be renewed or extended by further periods not exceeding five

years on each occasion subject to the condition that such renewal/ extension shall not be sanctioned earlier than two years from the date on which it is to come into force:

Provided also that where the term of office of such person is for an indefinite period, such term, unless it otherwise comes to an end earlier, shall come to an end immediately on the expiry of five years from the date of his appointment or on the expiry of three months from the date of commencement of section 8 of the Banking Laws (Miscellaneous Provisions) Act, 1963 (55 of 1963), whichever is later:]

Provided further that nothing in this clause shall apply to a director, other than the managing director, of a banking company by reason only of his being such director.

Explanation.-For the purpose of sub-clause (iii) of clause (b), the expression "remuneration", in relation to person employed or continued in employment, shall include salary, fees and perquisites but shall not include any allowances or other amounts paid to him for the purpose of reimbursing him in respect of the expense actually incurted by him in the performance of his duties.

(2) In forming its opinion under sub-clause (iii) of clause (b) of sub-section (1), the Reserve Bank may have regard among other matters to the following:-

(i) the financial condition and history of the banking company, its size and area of operation, its resources, the volume of its business, and the trend of its earning capacity;

(ii) the number of its branches or offices;

(iii) the qualifications, age and experience of the person concerned;

(iv) the remuneration paid to other persons employed by the banking company or to any person occupying a similar position in any other banking company similarly situated; and

(v) the interests of its depositors.

10[11[***].]

(6) Any decision or order of the Reserve Bank made under

contained in any other law for the time being in force, every banking company,

(a) in existence on the commencement of section 3 of the Banking Laws (Amendment) Act, 1968 (58 of 1968), or

(b) which comes into existence thereafter, shall comply with the requirements of this section:

Provided that nothing contained in this sub-section shall apply to a banking company referred to in clause (a) for a period of three months from such commencement.

(2) Not less than fifty-one per cent, of the total number of members of the Board of directors of a banking company shall consist of persons, who-

(a) shall have special knowledge or practical experience in respect of one or more of the following matters, namely:-

(i) accountancy,

(ii) agriculture and rural economy,

(iii) banking,

(iv) co-operation,

(v) economics,

(vi) finance,

(vii) law,

(viii) small-scale industry,

(ix) any other matter the special knowledge of, and practical experience in, which would, in the opinion of the Reserve Bank, be useful to the banking company: Provided that out of the aforesaid number of directors, not less than two shall be persons having special knowledge or practical experience in respect of agriculture and rural economy, co-operation or small-scale industry; and

(b) shall not-

(1) have substantial interest in, or be connected with, whether as employee, manager or managing agent,-

(i) any company, not being a company registered under section 25 of the Companies Act, 1956 (1 of 1956), or

(ii) any firm, which carries on any trade, commerce or industry and which, in either case, is not a small-scale industrial concern, or

(2) be proprietors of any trading, commercial or industrial concern, not being a small-scale industrial concern.

13[(2A) Notwithstanding anything to the contrary contained in the Companies Act, 1956 (1 of 1956), or in any other law for the time being in force,-

(i) no director of a banking company, other than its chairman or whole-time director, by whatever name called, shall hold office continuously for a period exceeding eight years;

(ii) a chairman or other whole-time director of a banking company who has been removed from office as such chairman, or whole-time director, as the case may be, under the provisions of this Act shall also cease to be a director of the banking company and shall also not be eligible to be appointed as a director of such banking company, whether by election or co-option or otherwise, for a period of four years from the date of his ceasing to be the-chairman or whole-time director as the case may be.]

(3) If, in respect of any banking company the requirements, as laid down in subsection (2), are not fulfilled at any time, the Board of directors of such banking company shall re-constitute such Board so as to ensure that the said requirements are fulfilled.

(4) If, for the purpose of re-constituting the Board under sub-section (3), it is necessary to retire any director or directors, the Board may, by lots drawn in such manner as may be prescribed, decide which director or directors shall cease to hold office and such decision shall be binding on every director of the Board.

(5) Where the Reserve Bank is of opinion that the composition of the Board of directors of a banking company is such that it does not fulfil the requirements of subsection (2), it may, after giving to such banking company a reasonable opportunity of being heard, by an order in writing, direct the banking company to so re-constitute its Board of directors as to ensure that the said requirements are fulfilled and, if within two months from the date of receipt of that order, the banking company does not comply with the directions made by the Reserve Bank, that Bank may, after determining, by lots drawn in such manner as may be prescribed, the person who ought

to be removed from the membership of the Board of directors, remove such person from the office of the director of banking company and with a view to complying with the provision of sub-section (2) appoint a suitable person as a member of the Board of directors in the place of the person so removed whereupon the person so appointed shall be deemed to have been duly elected by the banking company as its director.

(6) Every appointment, removal or reconstitution duly made, and every election duly held, under this section shall be final and shall not be called into question in any court.

(7) Every director elected or, as the case may be, appointed under this section shall hold office until the date up to which his predecessor would have held office, if the election had not been held, or, as the case may be, the appointment had not been made.

(8) No act or proceeding of the Board of directors of a banking company shall be invalid by reason only of any defect in the composition thereof or on the ground that it is subsequently discovered that any of its members did not fulfil the requirements of this section.

10B. Banking company to be managed by whole time chairman.-14[(1) Notwithstanding anything contained in any law for the time being in force or in any contract to the contrary, every banking company in existence on the commencement of the Banking Regulation (Amendment) Act, 1994 (20 of 1944), or which comes into existence thereafter shall have one of its directors, who may be appointed on a whole-time or a part-time basis, as chairman of its board of directors, and where he is appointed on a whole-time basis, as chairman of its board of directors, he shall be entrusted with the management of the whole of the affairs of the banking company: Provided that the chairman shall exercise his powers subject to the superintendence, control and direction of the board of directors.

(1A) Where a chairman is appointed on a part-time basis,-

(i) such appointment shall be with the previous approval of the Reserve Bank and be subject to such conditions as the Reserve Bank may specify while giving such approval;

(ii) the management of the whole of the affairs of such banking company shall be entrusted to a managing director who shall exercise his powers subject to the superintendence, control and direction of the board of directors.]

(2) 15[Every chairman of the board of directors who is appointed on a whole-time basis and every managing director] of a banking company shall be in the whole-time employment of such company and shall hold office for such period, not exceeding five years, as the board of directors may fix, but shall, subject to the provisions of this section, be eligible for re-election of reappointment:

Provided that nothing in this sub-section shall be construed as prohibiting a chairman from being a director of a subsidiary of the banking company or a director of a company registered under section 25 of the Companies Act, 1956 (1 of 1956).

(3) Every person holding office on the commencement of section 3 of the Banking Laws (Amendment) Act, 1968 (58 of 1968), as managing director of a banking company shall-(a) if there is a chairman of its board of directors, vacate office on such commencement, or (b) if there is no chairman of its board of directors, vacate office on the date on which the chairman of its board of directors is elected or appointed in accordance with the provisions of this section.

(4) 16[Every chairman who is appointed on a whole-time basis and every managing director of a banking company appointed under sub-section (1A)] shall be person who has special knowledge and practical experience of-(a) the working of a banking company, or of the State Bank of India or any subsidiary bank or a financial institution, or (b) financial, economic or business administration:

Provided that a person shall be disqualified for being a 16[chairman who is appointed on a whole time basis or a managing director], if be-

(a) is a director of any company other than a company referred to in the proviso to sub-section (2), or

(b) is a partner of any firm which carries on any trade, business or industry, or

(c) has substantial interest in any other company or firm, or

(d) is a director, manager, managing agent, partner or proprietor of any trading, commercial or industrial concern, or

(e) is engaged in any other business or vocation.

(5) 16[A chairman of the board of directors appointed on a whole-time basis or a managing director] of a banking company may, by writing, under his hand addressed to the company, resign his office, 17[* * *].

18[(5A) 16[A chairman of the board of directors appointed on a whole-time basis or a managing director] whose term of office has come to an end, either by reason of his resignation or by reason of expiry of the period of his office, shall, subject to the approval of the Reserve Bank, continue in office until his successor assumes office.

(6) Without prejudice to the provisions of section 36AA where the Reserve Bank is of opinion that any person who, is, or has been elected to be, the 16[chairman of the board of directors who is appointed on a whole-time basis or the managing director] of a banking company is not a fit and proper person to hold such office, it may, after giving to such person and to the banking company a reasonable opportunity of being heard by order in writing, require the banking company to elect or appoint any other person as the 16[chairman of the board of directors who is appointed on a whole-time basis or the managing director] and if, within a period of two months from the date of receipt of such order, the banking company fails to elect or appoint a suitable person as the 16[chairman of the board of directors who is appointed on a whole-time basis or the managing director], the Reserve Bank may, by order, remove the first-mentioned person from the office of the 19[chairman of the board of directors who is appointed on a whole-time basis or the managing director] of the banking company and appoint a suitable person in his place whereupon the person so appointed shall be deemed to have been duly elected or appointed, as the case may be, as the 19[chairman of the board of directors who is appointed on a whole-time basis or the managing director] of such banking company and any person elected or 19[appointed as chairman on a whole-time basis or managing director] under this sub-section shall hold office for the residue of the period of office of the person in whose place he has been so elected or appointed.

(7) The banking company and any person against whom an order of removal is made under sub-section (6) may, within

thirty days from the date of communication to it or to him of the order, prefer an appeal to the Central Government and the decision of the Central Government thereon, and subject thereto, the order made by the Reserve Bank under sub-section (6), shall be final and shall not be called into question in any court.

(8) Notwithstanding anything contained in this section, the Reserve Bank may, if in its opinion it is necessary in the public interest so to do, permit 19[the chairman of the board of directors who is appointed on a whole-time basis or the managing director] to undertake such part-time honorary work as is not likely to interfere with his duties as 19[such chairman or managing director].

(9) Notwithstanding anything contained in this section, where a person 19[appointed on a whole-time basis, as chairman of the board of directors or the managing director] dies or resigns or is by infirmity or otherwise rendered incapable of carrying out his duties or is absent on leave or otherwise in circumstances not involving the vacation of his office, the banking company may, with the approval of the Reserve Bank, make suitable arrangements for carrying out the 19[duties of chairman or managing director] for a total period not exceeding four months.

20[10BB. Power of Reserve Bank to appoint [Chairman of the Board of directors appointed on a whole-time basis or a managing director] of a banking company.-(1) Where the office, of the 21[chairman of the board of directors appointed on a whole-time basis or a managing director] of a banking company is vacant, the Reserve Bank may, if it is of opinion that the continuation of such vacancy is likely to adversely affect the interests of the banking company, appoint a person eligible under sub-section (4) of section 10B to be so appointed, to be the 21[chairman of the board of directors appointed on a whole-time basis or a managing director] of the banking company and where the person so appointed is not a director of such banking company, he shall, so long as he holds the office of the 21[chairman of the board of directors appointed on a whole-time basis or a managing director], be deemed to be director of the banking company.

(2) The 22[chairman of the board of directors appointed on a whole-lime basis or a managing director] so appointed by the

Reserve Bank shall be in the whole-time employment of the banking company and shall hold office for such period not exceeding three years, as the Reserve Bank may specify, but shall, subject to other provisions of this Act, be eligible for reappointment.

(3) The 22[chairman of the board of directors appointed on a whole-time basis or a managing director] so appointed by the Reserve Bank shall draw from the banking company such pay and allowances as the Reserve Bank may determine and may be removed from office only by the Reserve Bank.

(4) Save as otherwise provided in this section, the provisions of section 10B shall, as far as may be, apply to the 22[chairman of the board of directors appointed on a whole-time basis or a managing director] appointed by the Reserve Bank under subsection (1) as they apply to a 22[chairman of the board of directors appointed on a whole-time basis or a managing director] appointed by the banking company.]

23[10C. Chairman and certain directors not to be required to hold qualification shares.-24[Chairman of the board of directors who is appointed on a whole-lime basis or a managing director] of a banking company (by whomsoever appointed) and a director of a banking company (appointed by the Reserve Bank under section 10A) shall not be required to hold qualification shares in the banking company.]

10D. Provisions of sections 10A and 10B to override all other laws, contracts, etc.-Any appointment or removal of a 25[director, chairman of the board of directors who is appointed on a whole-time basis or a managing director] in pursuance of section IOA or section 10B 26[or section 10BB] shall have effect and any such person shall not be entitled to claim any compensation for the loss or termination of office, notwithstanding anything contained in any law or in any contract, memorandum or articles of association.]

11. Requirement as to minimum paid-up capital and reserves.-(1) Notwithstanding anything contained in 27[section 149 of the Companies Act, 1956 (1 of 1956)], no banking company in existence on the commencement of this Act, shall, after the expiry of three years from such commencement or of such further period not exceeding one year as the Reserve Bank,

having regard to the interests of the depositors of the company, may think fit in any particular case to allow, carry on business 28[in India], and no other banking company shall after the commencement of this Act, commence or carry on business 28[in India] 29[unless it complies with such of the requirements of this section as are applicable to it].

30[(2) In the case of a banking company incorporated outside India-(a) the aggregate value of its paid-up capital and reserves shall not be less than fifteen lakhs of rupees and if it has a place or places of business in the city of Bombay or Calcutta or both, twenty lakhs of rupees; and (b) 31[the banking company shall deposit and keep deposited with the Reserve Bank either in cash or in the form of unencumbered approved securities, or partly in cash and partly in the form of such securities-(i) an amount which shall not be less than the minimum required by clause (a); and (ii) as soon as may be after the expiration of each 32[* * *] year, an amount calculated at twenty per cent of its profit for that year in respect of all business transacted through its branches in India, as disclosed in the profit and loss account prepared with reference to that year under section 29:]

Provided that any such banking company may at any time replace-

(i) any securities so deposited by cash or by any other unencumbered approved securities or partly by cash and partly by other such securities, so however, that the total amount deposited is not affected;

(ii) any cash so deposited by unencumbered approved securities of an equal value.]

33[(2A) Notwithstanding anything contained in sub-section (2), the Central Government may, on the recommendation of the Reserve Bank, and having regard to the adequacy of the amounts already deposited and kept deposited by a banking company under sub-section (2), in relation to its deposit liabilities in India, declare by order in writing that the provisions of sub-clause (ii) of clause (b) of sub-section (2) shall not apply to such banking company for such period as may be specified in the order.]

(3) In the case of any banking company to which the provisions of sub-section (2) do not apply, the aggregate value of its paid-up capital and reserves shall not be less than-

(i) if it has places of business in more than one State, five lakhs of rupees, and if any such place or places of business is or are situated in the city of Bombay or Calcutta or both, ten lakhs of rupees;

(ii) if it has all its places of business in one State none of which is situated in the city of Bombay or Calcutta, one lakh of rupees in respect of its principal place of business, plus ten thousand rupees in respect of each of its other places of business situated in the same district in which it has its principal place of business, plus twenty-five thousand rupees in respect of each place of business situated elsewhere in the State otherwise than in the same district:

Provided that no banking company to which this clause applies shall be required to have paid-up capital and reserves exceeding an aggregate value of five lakhs of rupees:

Provided further that no banking company to which this clause applies and which has only one place of business, shall be required to have paid-up capital and reserves exceeding an aggregate value of fifty thousand rupees:

34[Provided further that in the case of every banking company to which this clause applies and which commences banking business for the first time after the commencement of the Banking Companies (Amendment) Act, 1962 (36 of 1962), the value of its paid-up capital shall not be less than five lakhs of rupees;]

(iii) if it has all its places of business in one State, one or more of which is or are situated in the city of Bombay or Calcutta, five lakhs of rupees, plus twenty-five thousand rupees in respect of each place of business situated outside the city of Bombay or Calcutta, as the case may be:

Provided that no banking company to which this clause applies shall be required to have paid-up capital and reserves exceeding an aggregate value of ten lakhs of rupees.

Explanation.-For the purposes of this sub-section, a place of business situated 35[in a State] other than that in which the principal place of business of the banking company is situated shall, if it is not more than twenty-five miles distant from such principal place of business, be deemed to be situated within the same State as such principal place of business.

(4) Any amount deposited and kept deposited with the Reserve Bank under 36[* * *] sub-section (2) by any banking company incorporated 37[outside India] shall, in the event of the company ceasing for any reason to carry on banking business 38[in India], be an asset of the company on which the claims of all the creditors of the company 38[in India] shall be a first charge.

39[(5) For the purposes of this section,-

(a) "place of business" means any office, sub-office, sub-pay office and any place of business at which deposits are received, cheques cashed, or moneys lent;

(b) "value" means the real or exchangeable value, and not the nominal value which may be shown in the books of the banking company concerned.]

(6) If any dispute arises in computing the aggregate value of the paid-up capital and reserves of any banking company, a determination thereof by the Reserve Bank shall be final for the purposes of this section.

40[12. Regulation of paid-up capital, subscribed capital and authorised capital and voting rights of shareholders.-(1) No banking company shall carry on business in India, unless it satisfies the following conditions, namely:-

(i) that the subscribed capital of the company is not less than one-half of the authorised capital, and the paid-up capital is not less than one-half of the subscribed capital and that, if the capital is increased, it complies with the conditions prescribed in this clause within such period not exceeding two years as the Reserve Bank may allow;

(ii) that the capital of the company consists of ordinary shares only or of ordinary shares or equity shares and such preferential shares as may have been issued prior to the 1st day of July, 1944:

Provided that nothing contained in this sub-section shall apply to any banking company incorporated before the 15th day of January, 1937.

[(2) No person holding shares in a banking company shall, in respect of any shares held by him, exercise voting rights 41[on poll] 42[in excess of 43(ten per cent)] of the total voting rights of all the shareholders of the banking company.]

(3) Notwithstanding anything contained in any law for the time being in force or in any contract or instrument no suit or other proceeding shall be maintained against any person registered as the holder of a share in a banking company on the ground that the title to the said share vests in a person other than the registered holder:

Provided that nothing contained in this sub-section shall bar a suit or other proceeding-

(a) by a transferee of the share on the ground that he has obtained from the registered holder a transfer of the share in accordance with any law relating to such transfer; or

(b) on behalf of a minor or a lunatic on the ground that the registered holder holds the share on behalf of the minor or lunatic.

(4) Every chairman, managing director or chief executive officer by whatever name called of a banking company shall furnish to the Reserve Bank through that banking company returns containing full particulars of the extent and value of his holding of shares, whether directly or indirectly, in the banking company and of any change in the extent of such holding or any variation in the rights attaching thereto and such other information relating to those shares as the Reserve Bank may, by order, require and in such form and at such time as may be specified in the order.]

44[12A. Election of new directors.-(1) The Reserve Bank may, by order, require any banking company to call a general meeting of the shareholders of the company within such time, not less than two months from the date of the order, as may be specified in the order or within such further time as the Reserve Bank may allow in this behalf, to elect in accordance with the voting rights permissible under this Act fresh directors, and the banking company shall be bound to comply with the order.

(2) Every director elected under sub-section (1) shall hold office until the date up to which his predecessor would have held office, if the election had not been held.

(3) Any election duly held under this section shall not be called in question in any court.]

13. Restriction on commission, brokerage, discount, etc. on sale of shares.-Notwithstanding anything to the contrary contained in 45[sections 76 and 79 of the Companies Act, 1956 (1 of 1956)], no banking company shall pay out directly or indirectly by way of commission, brokerage, discount or remuneration in any form in respect of any shares issued by it, any amount exceeding in the aggregate two and one-half per cent of the paid-up value of the said shares.

14. Prohibition of charge on unpaid capital.-No banking company shall create any charge upon any unpaid capital of the company, and any such charge shall be invalid.

46[14A. Prohibition of floating charge on assets.-(1) Notwithstanding anything contained in section 6, no banking company shall create a floating charge on the undertaking or any property of the company or any part thereof, unless the creation of such floating charge is certified in writing by the Reserve Bank as not being detrimental to the interests of the depositors of such company.

(2) Any such charge created without obtaining the certificate of the Reserve Bank shall be invalid.

(3) Any banking company aggrieved by the refusal of a certificate under subsection (1) may, within ninety days from the date on which such refusal is communicated to it, appeal to the Central Government.

(4)The decision of the Central Government where an appeal has been preferred to it under sub-section (3) or of the Reserve Bank where no such appeal has been preferred shall be final.]

15. Restrictions as to payment of dividend.-47[(1)] No banking company shall pay any dividend on its shares until all its capitalised expenses (including preliminary expenses, organisation expenses, share-selling commission, brokerage, amounts of losses incurred and any other item of expenditure not represented by tangible assets) have been completely written off.

48[(2)] Notwithstanding anything to the contrary contained in sub-section (1) or in the Companies Act, 1956(1 of 1956), a banking company may pay dividends on its shares without writing off-

(i) the depreciation, if any, in the value of its investments in approved securities in any case where such depreciation has not actually been capitalised or otherwise accounted for as a loss;

(ii) the depreciation, if any, in the value of its investments in shares, debentures or bonds (other than approved securities) in any case where adequate provision for such depreciation has been made to the satisfaction of the auditor of the banking company;

(iii) the bad debts, if any, in any case where adequate provision for such debts has been made to the satisfaction of the auditor of the banking company.]

49[(16. Prohibition of common directors.-50[(1) No banking company incorporated in India shall have as a director in its Board of directors any person who is a director of any other banking company.

(1A) No banking company referred to in sub-section (1) shall have in its Board of directors, more than three directors who are directors of companies which among themselves are entitled to exercise voting rights in excess of twenty per cent of the total voting rights of all the shareholders to that banking company.]

(2) If immediately before the commencement of the Banking Companies (Amendment) Act, 1956 (95 of 1956), any person holding office as a director of a banking company is also a director of companies which among themselves are entitled to exercise voting rights in excess of twenty percent of the total voting rights of all the shareholders of the banking company, he shall, within such period from such commencement as the Reserve Bank may specify in this behalf-

(a) either resign his office as a director of the banking company; or

(b) choose such number of companies as among themselves are not entitled to exercise voting rights in excess of twenty per cent, of the total voting rights of all the shareholders of the banking company as companies in which he wishes to continue to hold the office of a director and resign his office as a director in the other companies.]

51[(3) Nothing in sub-section (1) shall apply to, or in relation to, any director appointed by the Reserve Bank.]

52[17. Reserve Fund.-(1) Every banking company incorporated in India shall create a reserve fund and 53[* * *] shall, out of the balance of profit of each year as disclosed in the profit and loss account prepared under section 29 and before any dividend is declared, transfer to the reserve fund a sum equivalent to not less than twenty per cent of such profit.

54[(1A) Notwithstanding anything contained in sub-section (1), the Central Government may, on the recommendation of the Reserve Bank and having regard to the adequacy of the paid-up capital and reserves of a banking company in relation to its deposit liabilities, declare by order in writing that the provisions of sub-section (1) shall not apply to the banking company for such period as may be specified in the order:

Provided that no such order shall be made unless, at the time it is made, the amount in the reserve fund under sub-section (1), together with the amount in the share premium account is not less than the paid-up capital of the banking company.]

(2) Where a banking company appropriates any sum or sums from the reserve fund or the share premium account, it shall, within twenty-one days from the date of such appropriation, report the fact to the Reserve Bank, explaining the circumstances relating to such appropriation:

Provided that the Reserve Bank may, in any particular case, extend the said period of twenty-one days by such period as it thinks fit or condone any delay in the making of such report.

55[18. Cash reserve.-(1) Every banking company, not being a scheduled bank, shall maintain in India by way of cash reserve with itself or by way of balance in a current account with the Reserve Bank, or by way of net balance in current accounts or in one or more of the aforesaid ways, a sum equivalent to at least three per cent of the total of its demand and time liabilities in India as on the last Friday of the second preceding fortnight and shall submit to the Reserve Bank before the twentieth day of every month a return showing the amount so held on alternate Fridays during a month with particulars of its demand and time liabilities in India on such Fridays or if any such Friday is a public holiday under the Negotiable Instruments Act, 1881 (26 of 1881), at the close of business on the preceding working day.

Explanation.-In this section, and in section 24,-

(a) "liabilities in India" shall not include-

(i) the paid-up capital or the reserves or any credit balance in the profit and loss account of the banking company;

(ii) any advance taken from the Reserve Bank or from the Development Bank or from the Exim Bank 56[or from the Reconstruction Bank] 57[or from the National Housing Bank] or from the National Bank 58[or from the Small Industries Bank] by the banking company;

(iii) in the case of a Regional Rural Bank, also any loan taken by such bank from its Sponsor Bank;

(b) "fortnight" shall mean the period from Saturday to the second following Friday, both days inclusive;

(c) "net balance in current accounts" shall, in relation to a banking company, mean the excess, if any, of the aggregate of the credit balances in current account maintained by that banking company with State Bank of India or a subsidiary bank or a corresponding new bank over the aggregate of the credit balances in current account held by the said banks with such banking company;

(d) for the purposes of computation of liabilities, the aggregate of the liabilities of a banking company to the State Bank of India, a subsidiary bank, a corresponding new bank, a regional rural bank, another banking company, a co-operative bank or any other financial institution notified by the Central Government in this behalf, shall be reduced by the aggregate of the liabilities of all such banks and institutions to the banking company;

(e) the expression "co-operative bank" shall have the meaning assigned to it in clause (cci) of section 56.

(2) The Reserve Bank may, for the purposes of this section and section 24, specify from time to time, with reference to any transaction or class of transactions, that such transaction or transactions shall be regarded as liability in India of a banking

company and, if any question arises as to whether any transaction or class of transactions shall be regarded for the purposes of this section and section 24 as liability in India of a banking company, the decision of the Reserve Bank thereon shall be final.]

19. Restriction on nature of subsidiary companies.-59[(1) A banking company shall not form any subsidiary company except a subsidiary company formed for one or more of the following purposes, namely:-

(a) the undertaking of any business which, under clauses (a) to (o) of subsection (3) of section 6, is permissible for a banking company to undertake, or

(b) with the previous permission in writing of the Reserve Bank, the carrying on of the business of banking exclusively outside India, or

(c) the undertaking of such other business, which the Reserve Bank may, with the prior approval of the Central Government, consider to be conducive to the spread of banking in India or to be other wise useful or necessary in the public interest.

Explanation.-For the purposes of section 8, a banking company shall not be deemed, by reason of its forming or having a subsidiary company, to be engaged indirectly in the business carried on by such subsidiary company.]

(2) Save as provided in sub-section (1), no banking company shall hold shares in any company, whether as pledgee, mortgagee or absolute owner, of an amount exceeding thirty per cent of the paid-up share capital of that company or thirty per cent of its own paid-up share capital and reserves, whichever is less:

Provided that any banking company which is on the date of the commencement of this Act holding any shares in contravention of the provisions of this sub-section shall not be liable to any penalty therefor if it reports the matter without delay to the Reserve Bank and if it brings its holding of shares into conformity with the said provisions within such period, not exceeding two years, as the Reserve Bank may think fit to allow.

(3) Save as provided in sub-section (1) and notwithstanding anything contained in sub-section (2), a banking company shall

not, after the expiry of one year from the date of the commencement of this Act, hold shares, whether as pledgee, mortagagee or absolute owner, in any company in the management of which any managing director or manager of the banking company is in any manner concerned or interested.

60[20. Restrictions on loans and advances.-(1) Notwithstanding anything to the contrary contained in section 77 of the Companies Act, 1956 (1 of 1956), no banking company shall,-

(a) grant any loans or advances on the security of its own shares, or-

(b) enter into any commitment for granting any loan or advance to or on behalf of-

(i) any of its directors,

(ii) any firm in which any of its directors is interested as partner, manager, employee or guarantor, or

(iii) any company [not being a subsidiary of the banking company or a company registered under section 25 of the Companies Act, 1956 (1 of 1956), or a Government company] of which 61[or the subsidiary or the holding company of which] any of the directors of the banking company is a director, managing agent, manager, employee or guarantor or in which he holds substantial interest, or

(iv) any individual in respect of whom any of its directors is a partner or guarantor.

(2) Where any loan or advance granted by a banking company is such that a commitment for granting it could not have been made if clause (b) of sub-section (1) had been in force on the date on which the loan or advance was made, or is granted by a banking company after the commencement of section 5 of the Banking Laws (Amendment) Act, 1968 (58 of 1968), but in pursuance of a commitment entered into before such commencement, steps shall be taken to recover the amounts due to the banking company on account of the loan, or advance together with interest, if any, due thereon within the period stipulated at the time of the grant of the loan or advance, or where no such period has been stipulated, before the expiry of one year from the commencement of the said section 5:

Provided that the Reserve Bank may, in any case, on an application in writing made to it by the banking company in this behalf, extend the period for the recovery of the loan or advance until such date, not being a date beyond the period of three years from the commencement of the said section 5, and subject to such terms and conditions, as the Reserve Bank may deem fit:

Provided further that this sub-section shall not apply if and when the director concerned vacates the office of the director of the banking company, whether by death, retirement, resignation or otherwise.

(3) No loan or advance, referred to in sub-section (2), or any part thereof shall be remitted without the previous approval of the Reserve Bank, and any remission without such approval shall be void and of no effect.

(4) Where any loan or advance referred to in sub-section (2), payable by any person, has not been repaid to the banking company within the period specified in that subsection, then, such person shall, if he is a director of such banking company on the date of the expiry of the said period, be deemed to have vacated his office as such on the said date.

Explanation.-In this section-

(a) "loans or advance" shall not include any transaction which the Reserve Bank may, having regard to the nature of the transaction, the period within which, and the manner and circumstances in which, any amount due on account of the transaction is likely to be realised, the interest of the depositors and other relevant considerations, specify by general or special order as not being a loan or advance for the purpose of this section;

(b) "director" include a member of any board or committee in India constituted by a banking company for the purpose of managing, or for the purpose of advising it in regard to the management of, all or any of its affairs.

(5) If any question arises whether any transaction is a loan or advance for the purposes of this section, it shall be referred to the Reserve Bank, whose decision thereon shall be final.]

C2[20A. Restrictions on power to remit debts.- (1) Notwithstanding anything to the contrary contained in section 293 of the Companies Act, 1956 (1 of 1956), a banking company shall not, except with the prior approval of the Reserve Bank, remit in whole or in part any debt due to it by-

(a) any of its directors, or

(b) any firm or company in which any of its directors is interested as director, partner, managing agent or guarantor, or

(c) any individual if any of its directors is his partner or guarantor.

(2) Any remission made in contravention of the provisions of sub-section (1) shall be void and of no effect.]

21. Power of Reserve Bank to control advances by banking companies.-(1) Where the Reserve Bank is satisfied that it is necessary or expedient in the public interest 63[or in the interests of depositors] 64[or banking policy] so to do, it may determine the policy in relation to advances to be followed by banking companies generally or by any banking company in particular, and when the policy has been so determined, all banking companies or the banking company concerned, as the case may be, shall be bound to follow the policy as so determined.

(2) Without prejudice to the generality of the power vested in the Reserve Bank under sub-section (1) the Reserve Bank may give directions to banking companies, either generally or to any banking company or group of banking companies in particular, 65[as to-

(a) the purposes for which advances may or may not be made,

(b) the margins to be maintained in respect of secured advances,

(c) the maximum amount of advances or other financial accommodation which, having regard to the paid-up capital, reserves and deposits of a banking company and other relevant considerations, may be made by that banking company to any one company, firm, association of persons or individual,

(d) the maximum amount up to which, having regard to the considerations referred to in clause (c), guarantees may be given by a banking company on behalf of any one company, firm, association of persons or individual, and

(e) the rate of interest and other terms and conditions on which advances or other financial accommodation may be made or guarantees may be given.]

66[(3) Every banking company shall be bound to comply with any directions given to it under this section.]

67[21A. Rates of interest charged by banking companies not to be subject to scrutiny by courts.-Notwithstanding anything contained in the Usurious Loans Act, 1918 (10 of 1918), or any other law relating to indebtedness in force in any State, a transaction between a banking company and its debtor shall not be re-opened by any court on the ground that the rate of interest charged by the banking company in respect of such transaction is excessive.]

22. Licensing of banking companies.-68[(1) Save as hereinafter provided, no company shall carry on banking business in India unless it holds a licence issued in that behalf by the Reserve Bank and any such licence may be issued subject of such conditions as the Reserve Bank may think fit to impose.]

(2) Every banking company in existence on the commencement of this Act, before the expiry of six months from such commencement, and every other company before commencing banking business 69[in India], shall apply in writing to the Reserve Bank for a licence under this section:

Provided that in the case of a banking company in existence on the commencement of this Act, nothing in sub-section (1) shall be deemed to prohibit the company from carrying on banking business until it is granted a licence in pursuance of 70is section] or is by notice in writing informed by the Reserve Bank that a licence cannot be granted to it:

Provided further that the Reserve Bank shall not give a notice as aforesaid to a banking company in existence on the commencement of this Act before the expiry of the three years referred to in sub-section (1) of section 11 or of such further period as the Reserve Bank may under that sub-section think fit to allow.

(3) Before granting any licence under this section, the Reserve Banking may require to be satisfied by an inspection

of the books of the company or otherwise that 71[***] the following conditions are fulfilled, namely:-

72[(a) that the company is or will be in a position to pay its present or future depositors in full as their claims accrue;

(b) that the affairs of the company are not being, or are not likely to be, conducted in a manner deterimental to the interests of its present or future depositors;]

73[(c) that the general character of the proposed management of the company will not be prejudicial to the public interest or the interest of its depositors;

(d) that the company has adequate capital structure and earning prospects;

(e) that the public interest will be served by the grant of a licence to the company to carry on banking business in India;

(f) that having regard to the banking facilities available in the proposed principal area of operations of the company, the potential scope for expansion of banks already in existence in the area and other relevant factors the grant of the licence would not be prejudicial to the operation and consolidation of the banking system consistent with monetary stability and economic growth;

(g) any other condition, the fulfilment of which would, in the opinion of the Reserve Bank, be necessary to ensure that the carrying on of banking business in India by the company will not be prejudicial to the public interest or the interests of the depositors.]

74[(3A) Before granting any licence under this section to a company incorporated outside India, the Reserve Bank may require to be satisfied by an inspection of the books of the company or otherwise that the conditions specified in sub-section (3) are fulfilled and that the carrying on of banking business by such company in India will be in the public interest and that the Government or law of the country in which it is incorporated does not discriminate in any way against banking companies registered in India and that the company complies with all the provisions of this Act applicable to banking companies incorporated outside India.]

75[(4) The Reserve Bank may cancel a licence granted to a banking company under this section-

(i) if the company ceases to carry on banking business in India; or

(ii) if the company at any time fails to comply with any of the conditions imposed upon it under sub-section (1); or

(iii) if at any time, any of the conditions referred to in sub-section (3) 74[and sub-section (3A)] is not fulfilled:

Provided that before cancelling a licence under clause (ii) or clause (iii) of this sub-section on the ground that the banking company has failed to comply with or has failed to fulfil any of the conditions referred to therein, the Reserve Bank, unless it is of opinion that the delay will be prejudicial to the interests of the company's depositors or the public, shall grant to the company on such terms as it may specify, an opportunity of taking the necessary steps for complying with or fulfilling such condition.

(5) Any banking company aggrieved by the decision of the Reserve Bank cancelling a licence under this section may, within thirty days from the date on which such decision is communicated to it, appeal to the Central Government.

(6) The decision of the Central Government where an appeal has been preferred to it under sub-section (5) or of the Reserve Bank where no such appeal has been preferred shall be final.]

76[23. Restrictions on opening of new, and transfer of existing, places of business.-(1) Without obtaining the prior permission of the Reserve Bank-

(a) no banking company shall open a new place of business in India or change otherwise than within the same city, town or village, the location of an existing place of business situated in India; and

(b) no banking company incorporated in India shall open a new place of business outside India or change, otherwise than within the same city, town or village in any country or area outside India, the location of an existing place of business situated in that country or area:

Provided that nothing in this sub-section shall apply to the opening for a period not exceeding one month of a temporary place of business within a city, town or village or the environs thereof within which the banking company already has a place of business, for the purpose of affording banking facilities to the public on the occasion of an exhibition, a conference or a mela or any other like occasion.

(2) Before granting any permission under this section, the Reserve Bank may require to be satisfied by an inspection under section 35 or otherwise as to the financial condition and history of the company, the general character of its management, the adequacy of its capital structure and earning prospects and that public interest will be served by the opening or, as the case may be, change of location, of the place of business.

(3) The Reserve Bank may grant permission under sub-section (1) subject to such conditions as it may think fit to impose either generally or with reference to any particular case.

(4) Where, in the opinion of the Reserve Bank, a banking company has, at any time, failed to comply with any of the conditions imposed on it under this section, the Reserve Bank may, by order in writing and after affording reasonable opportunity to the banking company for showing cause against the action proposed to be taken against it, revoke any permission granted under this section.

77[(4A) Any regional rural bank requiring the permission of the Reserve Bank under this section shall forward its application to the Reserve Bank through the National Bank which shall give its comments on the merits of the application and send it to the Reserve Bank:

Provided that the regional rural bank shall also send an advance copy of the application directly to the Reserve Bank.]

(5) For the purpose of this section "place of business" includes any sub-office, pay office, subpay office and any place of business at which deposits are received, cheques cashed or moneys lent.]

24. Maintenance of a percentage of assets.-(1) After the expiry of two years from the commencement of this Act, every banking company shall maintain 78[in India] in cash, gold or unencumbered approved securities, valued at a price not exceeding the current market price, an amount which shall not

at the close of business on any day be less than 20 percent of the total of its 79[demand and time liabilities] 80[in India].

81[Explanation-For the purposes of this section, "unencumbered approved securities" of a banking company shall include its approved securities lodged with another institution for an advance or any other credit arrangement to the extent to which such securities have not been drawn against or availed of.]

82[(2) In computing the amount for the purposes of sub-section (1), the deposit required under sub-section (2) of section 11 to be made with the Reserve Bank by a banking company incorporated outside India and any balances maintained in India by a banking company in current account with the Reserve Bank or the State Bank of India or with any other bank which may be notified in this behalf by the Central Government, including in the case of a scheduled bank the balance required under section 42 of the Reserve Bank of India Act, 1934 (2 of 1934) to be so maintained, shall be deemed to be cash maintained in India.]

83[(2A)(a) Notwithstanding anything contained in sub-section (1) or in sub-section (2), after the expiry of two years from the commencement of the Banking Companies (Amendment) Act, 1962 (36 of 1962),-

(i) a scheduled bank, in addition to the average daily balance which it is, or may be, required to maintain under section 42 of the Reserve Bank of India Act, 1934 (2 of 1934), and

(ii) every other banking company, in addition to the cash reserve which it is required to maintain under section 18,

84[shall maintain in India,-

(A) in cash, or

(B) in gold valued at a price not exceeding the current market price or in unencumbered approved securities valued at a price determined in accordance with such one or more of, or combination of, the following methods of valuation, namely, valuation with reference to cost price, market price, book value or face value, as may be specified by the Reserve Bank from time to time, an amount which shall not, at the close of business on any day, be less than twenty-five per cent or such other percentage not exceeding forty per cent, as the Reserve Bank may, from time to time, by notification in the Official Gazette, specify, of the total of its demand and time liabilities in India, as on the last Friday of the second preceding fortnight;]

85[(b) in computing the amount for the purposes of clause (a),-

(i) the deposit required under sub-section (2) of section 11 to be made with the Reserve Bank by a banking company incorporated outside India;

(ii) any cash or balances maintained in India by a banking company other than a scheduled bank with itself or with the Reserve Bank or by way of net balance in current account in excess of the aggregate of the cash or balance or net balance required to be maintained under section 18;

(iii) any balances maintained by a scheduled bank with the Reserve Bank in excess of the balance required to be maintained by it under section 42 of the Reserve Bank of India Act, 1934 (2 of 1934);

(iv) the net balance in current accounts maintained in India by a scheduled bank;

(v) any balances maintained by a Regional Rural Bank in call or fixed deposit with its Sponsor Bank, shall be deemed to be cash maintained in India].

86[Explanation.-For the purpose of clause (a) of this sub-section, the market price of an approved security shall be the price as on the date of the issue of the notification or as on any earlier or later date as may be notified from time to time by the Reserve Bank in respect of any class or classes of securities.]

87[(2B) The Reserve Bank may, by notification in the Official Gazette, vary the percentage referred to in sub-section (2A) in respect of a Regional Rural Bank 88[***].]

89[(3) For the purpose of ensuring compliance with the provisions of this section, every banking company shall, not later than twenty days after the end of the month to which it relates, furnish to the Reserve Bank in the prescribed form and manner a monthly return showing particulars of its assets maintained in accordance with this section, and its demand and time liabilities in India at the close of business on each alternate Friday during the month, or if any such Friday is a public holiday, at the close of business on the preceding working day:

Provided that every Regional Rural Bank shall also furnish a copy of the said return to the National Bank.]

(4)(a) If on any alternate Friday or, if such Friday is a public holiday, on the preceding working day, the amount maintained by a banking company at the close of business on that day falls below the minimum prescribed by or under clause (a) of sub-section (2A) such banking company shall be liable to pay to the Reserve Bank in respect of that day's default, penal interest for that day at the rate of three per cent per annum above the bank rate on the amount by which the amount actually maintained falls short of the prescribed minimum on that day; and

(b) If the default occurs again on the next succeeding alternate Friday, or, if such Friday is a public holiday, on the preceding working day, and continues on succeeding alternate Fridays or preceding working days, as the case may be, the rate of penal interest shall be increased to a rate of five per cent per annum above the bank rate on each such shortfall in respect of that alternate Friday and each succeeding alternate Friday or preceding working day, if such Friday is a public holiday, in which the default continues.

(5)(a) Without prejudice to the provisions of sub-section (3), the Reserve Bank may require a banking company to furnish to it a return in the form and manner specified by it showing particulars of its assets maintained in accordance with this section and its demand and time liabilities in India, as at the close of business on each day of a month; and

(b) Without prejudice to the provisions of sub-section (4), on the failure of a banking company to maintain as on any day, the amount so required to be maintained by or under clause (a) of sub-section (2A) the Reserve Bank may, in respect of such default, require the banking company to pay penal interest for that day as provided in clause (a) of sub-section (4) and if the default continues on the next succeeding working day, the penal interest may be increased as provided in clause (b) of sub-section (4) for the concerned days.

(6)(a) The penalty payable under sub-section (4) and sub-section (5) shall be paid within a period of fourteen days from the date on which a notice issued by the Reserve Bank demanding payment of the same is served on the banking company and in the event of failure of the banking company to pay the same within such period, the penalty may be levied by a direction of the principal civil court having jurisdiction in the area where an office of the defaulting banking company is situated, such direction to be made only upon an application made by the Reserve Bank in this behalf to the court; and

(b) When the court makes a direction under clause (a), it shall issue a certificate specifying the sum payable by the banking company and every such certificate shall be enforceable in the same manner as if it were a decree made by the court in a suit.

(7) When under the provisions of clause (b) of sub-section (4), penal interest at the increased rate of five per cent, above the bank rate has become payable by a banking company, if thereafter the amount required to be maintained on the next succeeding alternate Friday, or if such Friday is a public holiday, the next preceding working day, is still below the prescribed minimum, every director, manager or secretary of the banking company, who is knowingly and wilfully a party to the default, shall be punishable with fine which may extend to five hundred rupees and with a further fine which may extend to five hundred rupees for each subsequent alternate Friday or the preceding working day, as the case may be, on which the default continues.

(8) Notwithstanding anything contained in this section, if the Reserve Bank is satisfied, on an application in writing by the defaulting banking company, that the banking company had sufficient cause for its failure to comply with the provisions of clause (a) of sub-section (2A), the Reserve Bank may not demand the payment of the penal interest.

Explanation.-In this section, the expression "public holiday" means a day which is a public holiday under the Negotiable Instruments Act, 1881 (26 of 1881)].

25. Assets in India.-90[(1) The assets in India of every banking company at the close of business on the last Friday of every quarter or, if that Friday is a public holiday under the

Negotiable Instruments Act, 1881 (26 of 1881), at the close of the business on the preceding working day, shall not be less than seventy-five percent of its demand and time liabilities in India.

(2) Every banking company shall, within one month from the end of every quarter, submit to the Reserve Bank a return in the prescribed form and manner of the assets and liabilities referred to in sub-section (1) as at the close of business on the last Friday of the previous quarter, or, if that Friday is a public holiday under the Negotiable Instruments Act, 1881 (26 of 1881) at the close of business on the preceding working day:]

91[Provided that every regional rural bank shall also furnish a copy of the said return to the National Bank.]

For the purposes of this section,-

92[(a) "assets in India" shall be deemed to include export bills drawn in, and import bills drawn on and payable in India and expressed in such currencies as the Reserve Bank may from time to time approve in this behalf and also such securities as the Reserve Bank may approve in this behalf notwithstanding that all or any of the said bills or securities are held outside India;]

93[(b) "liabilities in India" shall not include the paid-up capital or the reserves or any crredit balance in the profit and loss account of the banking company;]

94[(c)] "quarter" means the period of three months ending on the last day of March, June, September or December.

26. Return of unclaimed deposits.-Every banking company shall, within thirty days after the close of each calendar year, submit a return in the prescribed form and manner to the Reserve Bank as at the end of such calendar year of all accounts 95[in India] which have not been operated upon for ten years 96[* * *]:

Provided that in the case of money deposited for a fixed period the said term of ten years shall be reckoned from the date of the expiry of such fixed period:

97[Provided further that every regional rural bank shall also furnish a copy of the said return to the National Bank.]

27. Monthly returns and power to call for other returns and information.-(I) Every banking company shall, before me close of the month succeeding that to which it relates, submit to the Reserve Bank a return in the prescribed form and manner showing its assets and liabilities [in India] as at the close of business on the last Friday of every month or if that Friday is a public holiday under the Negotiable Instruments Act, 1881 (26 of 1881), at the close of business on the preceding working day.

98[(2) The Reserve Bank may at any time direct a banking company to furnish it within such time as may be specified by the Reserve Bank, with such statements and information relating to the business or affairs of the banking company (including any business or affairs with which such banking company is concerned) as the Reserve Bank may consider necessary or expedient to obtain for the purposes of this Act, and without prejudice to the generality of the foregoing power may call for information every half-year regarding 99[the investments of a banking company and the classification of its advances in respect of industry, commerce and agriculture].]

97[(3). Every regional rural bank shall submit a copy of the return which it submits to the Reserve Bank under sub-section (1) also to the National Bank and the powers exercisable by the Reserve Bank under sub-section (2) may also be exercised by the National Bank in relation to regional rural banks.]

100[28. Power to publish information.-The Reserve Bank or the National Bank, or both, if they consider it in the public interest so to do, may publish any information obtained by them under this Act in such consolidated form as they think fit.]

29. Accounts and balance-sheet.-(1) At the expiration of each calendar year 101[or at the expiration of a period of twelve months ending with such date102 as the Central Government may, by notification in the Official Gazette, specify in this behalf,] every banking company incorporated 95[in India], in respect of all business transacted by it, and every banking company incorporated 103[outside India], in respect of all business transacted through its branches 104[in India], shall prepare with reference to 105[that year or period, as the case

may be,] a balance-sheet and profit and loss account as on the last working day of 106[that year or the period, as the case may be] in the Forms set out in the Third Schedule or as near thereto as circumstances admit:

107[Provided that with a view to facilitating the transition from one period, of accounting to another period of-accounting under this sub-section, the Central Government may, by order published in the Official Gazette, make such provisions as it considers necessary or expedient for the preparation of, or for other matters relating to, the balance sheet or profit and loss account in respect of the concerned year or period, as the case may be.]

(2) The balance-sheet and profit and loss account shall be signed-

(a) in the case of a banking company incorporated 104[in India], by the manager or the principal officer of the company and where there are more than three directors of the company, by at least three of those directors, or where there are not more than three directors, by all the directors, and

(b) in the case of a banking company incorporated 103[outside India] by the manager or agent of the principal office of the company 104[in India].

(3) Notwithstanding that the balance-sheet of a banking company is under subsection (I) required to be prepared in a form other than the form 108[set out in Part I-of Schedule VI to the Companies Act, 1956 (1 of 1956)], the requirements of that relating to the balance-sheet and profit and loss account of a company shall, in so far as they are not inconsistent with this Act, apply to the balance-sheet or profit and loss account, as the case may be, of a banking company.

109[(3A) Notwithstanding anything to the contrary contained in sub-section (3) of section 210 of the Companies Act, 1956 (1 of 1956), the period to which the profit and loss account relates shall, in the case of a banking company, be the period ending with the last working day of the year immediately preceding the year in which the annual general meeting is held.]

110[Explanation.-In sub-section (3A), "year" means the year or, as the case may be, the period referred to in sub-section (1).]

(4) The Central Government, after giving not less than three months' notice of its mention so to do by a notification in the Official Gazette, may from time to time by a like notification amend the Form set out in the Third Schedule.

30. Audit.-111[(1) The balance-sheet and profit and loss account prepared in accordance with section 29 shall be audited by a person duly qualified under any law for the time being in force to be an auditor of companies.]

112[(1A) Notwithstanding anything contained in any law for the time being in force or in any contract to the contrary, every banking shall, before appointing re-appointing or removing any auditor or auditors, obtain the previous approval of the Reserve Bank.

(1B) Without prejudice to anything contained in the Companies Act, 1956 (1 of 1956), or any other law for the time being in force, where the Reserve Bank is of opinion that it is necessary in the public interest or in the interest of the banking company or its depositors so to do, 113[it may at any time by order direct that a special audit of the banking company's accounts, for any such transaction or class of transactions or for such period or periods as may be specified in the order, shall be conducted and may by the same or a different order either appoint a person duly qualified under any law for the time being in force to be an auditor of companies or direct the auditor of the banking company himself to conduct such special audit] and the auditor shall comply with such directions and make a report of such audit to the Reserve Bank and forward a copy thereof to the company.

(1C) The expenses of, or incidental to 113[the special audit] specified in the order made by the Reserve Bank shall be borne by the banking company.]

(2) The auditor shall have the powers of, exercise the functions vested in, and discharge the duties and be subject to the liabilities and penalties imposed on, auditors of companies by 114[section 227 of the Companies Act, 1956 (1 of 1956), 115[,and auditors, if any, appointed by the law establishing, constituting or forming the banking company concerned.]

(3) In addition to the matters which under the aforesaid Act the auditor is required to state in his report, he shall, in

the case of a banking company incorporated 116[in India], state in his report,-

(a) whether or not the information and explanation required by him have been found to be satisfactory;

(b) whether or not the transactions of the company which have come to his notice have been within the powers of the company;

(c) whether or not the returns received from branch offices of the company have been found adequate for the purposes of his audit;

(d) whether the profit and loss account shows a true balance 117[of profit or loss] for the period covered by such account;

(e) any other matter which he considers should be brought to the notice of the shareholders of the company.

31. Submission of returns.-The accounts and balance-sheet referred to in section 29 together with the auditor's report shall be published in the prescribed manner and three copies thereof shall be furnished as returns to the Reserve Bank within three months from the end of the period to which they refer:

Provided that the Reserve Bank may in any case extend the said period of three months for the furnishing of such returns by a further period not exceeding three months:

118[Provided further that a regional rural bank shall furnish such returns also to the National Bank.]

32. Copies of balance-sheets and accounts to be sent to registrar.-119[(1) Where a banking company in any year furnishes its accounts and balance-sheet in accordance with the provisions of section 31, it shall at the same time send to the registrar three copies of such accounts and balance-sheet and of the auditor's report, and where such copies are so sent, it shall not be necessary to file with the registrar, in the case of a public company, copies of the accounts and balance-sheet and of the auditor's report, and, in the case of a private company, copies of the balance-sheet and of the auditor's report as required by sub-section (1) of section 220 of the Companies Act, 1956 (1 of 1956); and the copies so sent shall be chargeable with the same fee and shall be dealt with in all respects as if they were filed in accordance with that section.]

(2) When in pursuance of sub-section (2) of section 27 the Reserve Bank requires any additional statement or information in connection with the balance-sheet and accounts furnished under section 31, the banking company shall, when supplying such statement or information, send a copy thereof to the registrar.

33. Display of audited balance-sheet by companies incorporated outside India.-Every banking company incorporated 120[outside India] shall, not later than the first Monday in August of any year in which it carries on business, display in a conspicuous place in its principal office and in every branch office 121[in India] a copy of its last audited balance-sheet and profit and loss account prepared under section 29, and shall keep the copy so displayed until replaced by a copy of the subsequent balance-sheet and profit and loss account so prepared, and every such banking company shall display in like manner copies of its complete audited balance-sheet and profit and loss account relating to its banking business as soon as they are available, and shall keep the copies so displayed until copies of such subsequent accounts are available.

34. Accounting provisions of this Act not retrospective.- Nothing in this Act shall apply to the preparation of accounts by a banking company and the audit and submission thereof in respect of any accounting year which has expired prior to the commencement of this Act, and notwithstanding the other provisions of this Act, such accounts shall be prepared, audited and submitted in accordance with the law in force immediately before the commencement of this Act.

122[34A. Production of documents of confidential nature.- (1) Notwithstanding anything contained in section 11 of the Industrial Disputes Act, 1947 (14 of 1947), or any other law for the time being in force, no banking company shall, in any proceeding under the said Act or in any appeal or other proceeding arising therefrom or connected therewith, be compelled by any authority before which such proceeding is pending to produce, or give inspection of, any of its books of account or other document or furnish or disclose any statement or information, when the banking company claims that such document, statement or information is of a confidential nature and that the production or inspection of such document or the furnishing or disclosure of such statement or information would involve disclosure of information relating to-

(a) any reserves not shown as such in its published balance-sheet; or

(b) any particulars not shown therein in respect of provisions made for bad and doubtful debts and other usual or necessary provisions.

(2) If, in any such proceeding in relation to any banking company other than the Reserve Bank of India, any question arises as to whether any amount out of the reserves or provisions referred to in sub-section (1) should be taken into account by the authority before which such proceeding is pending, the authority may, if it so thinks fit, refer the question to the Reserve Bank and the Reserve Bank shall, after

taking into account principles of sound banking and all relevant circumstances concerning the banking company, furnish to the authority a certificate stating that the authority shall not take into account any amount as such reserves and provisions of the banking company or may take them into account only to the extent of the amount specified by it in the certificate, and the certificate of the Reserve Bank on such question shall be final and shall not be called in question in any such proceeding.

123[(3) For the purposes of this section "banking company" includes the Reserve Bank, the Development Bank, the Exim Bank, 124[the Reconstruction Bank], 125[the National Housing Bank], the National Bank, 126[the Small Industries Bank] the State Bank of India, a corresponding new bank, a regional rural bank and a subsidiary bank.]

35. Inspection.-(1) Notwithstanding anything to the contrary contained in 127[section 235 of the Companies Act, 1956 (1 of 1956)], the Reserve Bank at any time may, and on being directed so to do by the Central Government shall, cause an inspection to be made by one or more of its officers of any banking company and its books and accounts; and the Reserve Bank shall supply to the banking company a copy of its report on such inspection.

128[(1A) (a) Notwithstanding anything to the contrary contained in any law for the time being in force and without prejudice to the provisions of sub-section (1), the Reserve Bank, at any time, may also cause a scrutiny to be made by any one or more of its officers, of the affairs of any banking company and its books and accounts; and

(b) a copy of the report of the scrutiny shall be furnished to the banking company if the banking company makes a request for the same or if any adverse action is contemplated against the banking company on the basis of the scrutiny.]

(2) It shall be the duty of every director or other officer 129[or employee] of the banking company to produce to any officer making an inspection under sub-section (1) [or a scrutiny under sub-section (1A)] all such books, accounts and other documents in his custody or power and to furnish him with any statements and information relating to the affairs of the banking company as the said officer may require of him within such time as the said officer may specify.

(3) Any person making an inspection under sub-section (1) 130[for a scrutiny under sub-section (1A)] may examine on oath any director or other officer 129[or employee] of the banking company in relation to its business, and may administer an oath accordingly.

(4) The Reserve Bank shall, if it has been directed by the Central Government to cause an inspection to be made, and may, in any other case, report to the Central Government on any inspection 130[or scrutiny] made under this section, and the Central Government, if it is of opinion after considering the report that the affairs of the banking company are being conducted to the detriment of the interests of its depositors, may, after giving such opportunity to the banking company to make a representation in connection with the report as, in the opinion of the Central Government, seems reasonable, by order in writing-

(a) prohibit the banking company from receiving fresh deposits;

(b) direct the Reserve Bank to apply under section 38 for the winding up of the banking company:

Provided that the Central Government may defer, for such period as it may think fit, the passing of an order under this sub-section, or cancel or modify any such order, upon such terms and conditions as it may think fit to impose.

(5) The Central Government may, after giving reasonable notice to the banking company, publish the report submitted by the Reserve Bank or such portion thereof as may appear necessary.

131[Explanation.-For the purpose of this section, the expression "banking company" shall include-

(i) in the case of a banking company incorporated outside India, all its branches in India; and

(ii) in the case of a banking company incorporated in India-

(a) all its subsidiaries formed for the purpose of carrying on the business of banking exclusively outside India; and

(b) all its branches whether situated in India or outside India.]

132[(6) The powers exercisable by the Reserve Bank under this section in relation to regional rural banks may (without prejudice to the exercise of such powers by the Reserve Bank in relation to any regional rural bank whenever it considers necessary so to do) be exercised by the National Sank in relation to the regional rural banks, and accordingly, sub-sections (1) to (5) shall apply in relation to regional rural banks as if every reference therein to the Reserve Bank included also a reference to the National Bank.]

133[35A. Power of the Reserve Bank to give directions.-(1) Where the Reserve Bank is satisfied that-

(a) in the 134[public interest]; or

135[(aa) in the interest of banking policy; or]

(b) to prevent the affairs of any banking company being conducted in a manner detrimental to the interests of the depositors or in a manner prejudicial to the interests of the banking company; or

(c) to secure the proper management of any banking company generally, it is necessary to issue directions to banking companies generally or to any banking company in particular, it may, from time to time, issue such directions as it deems fit, and the banking companies or the banking company, as the case may be, shall be bound to comply with such directions.

(2) The Reserve Bank may, on representation made to it or on its own motion, modify or cancel any direction issued

under sub-section (1), and in so modifying or cancelling any direction may impose such conditions as it thinks fit, subject to which the modification or cancellation shall have effect.

35B. Amendments of provisions relating to appointments of managing directors, etc., to be subject to previous approval of the Reserve Bank.-(1) In the case of a banking company-

(a) no amendment of any provision relating to 136[the maximum permissible number of directors or] the 137[appointment or re-appointment or termination of appointment or remuneration of a chairman, a] 138[managing director or any other director, whole-time or otherwise] or of a manager or a chief executive officer by whatever name called, whether that provision be contained in the company's memorandum or articles of association, or in an agreement entered into by it, or in any resolution passed by the company in general meeting or by its Board of directors shall have effect unless approved by the Reserve Bank;

139[(b) no appointment or re-appointment or termination of appointment of a chairman, a managing or whole-time director, manager or chief executive officer by whatever name called, shall have effect unless such appointment, re-appointment or termination of appointment is made with the previous approval of the Reserve Bank.]

140[Explanation.-For the purpose of this sub-section, any provision conferring any benefit or providing any amenity or perquisite, in whatever form, whether during or after the termination of the term of office 141[of the chairman or the manager] or the chief executive officer by whatever name called or the managing director, or any other director, whole-time or otherwise, shall be deemed to be a provision relating to his remuneration.]

(2) Nothing contained in sections 142[268 and 269, the proviso to sub-section (3) of section 309, sections 310 and 311, the proviso to section 387, and section 388] (in so far as section 388 makes the 143[provisions of sections 269, 310] and 311 apply in relation to the manager of a company) of the Companies Act, 1956 (1 of 1956), shall 144[apply to any matter in respect of which the approval of the Reserve Bank has to be obtained under sub-section (1)].

145[(2A) Nothing contained in section 198 of the Companies Act, 1956 (1 of 1956) shall apply to a banking company and the provisions of sub-section (1) of section 309 and of section 387 of that Act shall, in so far as they are applicable to a banking company, have effect as if no reference had been made in the said provisions to section 198 of that Act.]

(3) No act done by a person 146[as chairman or a managing or whole-time director] or a director not liable to retire by rotation or a manager or a chief executive officer by whatever name called, shall be deemed to be invalid on the ground that it is subsequently discovered that his 147[appointment or reappointment] had not taken effect by reason of any of the provisions of this Act; but nothing in this sub-section shall be construed as rendering valid any act done by such person after his 148[appointment or reappointment] has been shown to the banking company not to have had effect.]

36. Further powers and functions of Reserve Banks.-(1) The Reserve Bank may-

(a) caution or prohibit banking companies or any banking company in particular against entering into any particular transaction or class of transactions, and generally give advice to any banking company;

(b) on a request by the companies concerned and subject to the provision of section 149[44A], assist, as intermediary or otherwise, in proposals for the amalgamation of such banking companies;

(c) give assistance to any banking company by means of the grant of a loan or advance to it underclause (3) of sub-section (1) of section 18 of the Reserve Bank of India Act, 1934 (2 of 1934);

150[(d)151[at any time, if it is satisfied that in the public interest or in me interest of banking policy or for preventing the affairs of the banking company being conducted in a manner detrimental to the interests of the banking company or its depositors it is necessary so to do,] by order in writing and on such terms and conditions as may be specified therein-

(i) require the banking company to call a meeting of its directors for the purpose of considering any matter relating to or arising out of the affairs of the banking company; or require an officer of the banking company to discuss any such matter with an officer of the Reserve Bank;

(ii) depute one or more of its officers to which the proceedings at any meeting of the Board of directors of the banking company or of any committee or of any other body constituted by it; require the banking company to give an opportunity to the officers so deputed to be heard at such meetings and also require such officers to send a report of such proceedings to the Reserve Bank;

(iii) require the Board of directors of the banking company or any committee or any other body constituted by it to give in writing to any officer specified by the Reserve Bank in this behalf at his usual address all notices of, and other communications relating to, any meeting of the Board, committee or other body constituted by it;

(iv) appoint one or more of its officers to observe the manner in which the affairs of the banking company or of its offices or branches are being conducted and make a report thereon;

(v) require the banking company to make, within such time as may be specified in the order, such changes in the management as the Reserve Bank may consider necessary 152[***].]

(2) The Reserve Bank shall make an annual report to the Central Government on the trend and progress of banking in the country, with particular reference to its activities under clause (2) of section 17 of the Reserve Bank of India Act, 1934 (2 of 1934), including in such report its suggestions, if any, for the strengthening of banking business throughout the country.

(3) The Reserve Bank may appoint such staff at such places as it considers necessary for the scrutiny of the returns, statements and information furnished by banking companies under this Act, and generally to ensure the efficient performance of its functions under this Act.

153[36A. Certain provisions of the Act not to apply to certain banking companies.-(1) The provisions of section II, sub-section (1) of section 12, and sections 17, 18, 24 and 25 shall not apply to a banking company-

(a) which, whether before or after the commencement of the Banking Companies (Amendment) Act, 1959 (33 of 1959), has been refused a licence under section 22, or prohibited from accepting fresh deposits by a compromise, arrangement or scheme sanctioned by a court or by any order made in any proceeding relating to such compromise, arrangement or scheme, or prohibited from accepting deposits by virtue of any alteration made in its memorandum; or

(b) whose licence has been cancelled under section 22, whether before or after the commencement of the Banking Companies (Amendment) Act, 1959 (33 of 1959).

(2) Where the Reserve Bank is satisfied that any such banking company as is referred to in sub-section (1) has repaid, or has made adequate provision for repaying all deposits accepted by the banking company, either in full or to the maximum extent possible, the Reserve Bank may, by notice published in the Official Gazette, notify that the banking company has ceased to be a banking company within the meaning of this Act, and thereupon all the provisions of this Act applicable to such banking company shall cease to apply to it, except as respects things done or omitted to be done before such notice.]

CONTROL OVER MANAGEMENT

36AA. Power of Reserve Bank to remove managerial and other persons from office.-(1) Where the Reserve Bank is satisfied that in the public interest or for preventing the affairs of a banking company being conducted in a manner detrimental to the interests of the depositors or for securing the proper management of any banking company it is necessary so to do, the Reserve Bank may, for reasons to be recorded in writing, by order, remove from office, with effect from such date as may be specified in the order, 2[any chairman, director,] chief executive officer (by whatever name called) or other officer or employee of the banking company.

(2) No order under sub-section (1) shall be made 3[unless the chairman, director] or chief executive officer or other officer or employee concerned has been given a reasonable opportunity of making a representation to the Reserve Bank against the proposed order:

Provided that if, in the opinion of the Reserve Bank, any delay would be detrimental to the interests of the banking company or its depositors, the Reserve Bank may, at the time of giving the opportunity aforesaid or at any time thereafter, by order direct that, pending the consideration of the representation aforesaid, if any, 4[the chairman or, as the case may be, director or chief executive officer] or other officer or employee, shall not, with effect from the date of such order-

(a) 5[act as such chairman or director] or chief executive officer or other officer or employee of the banking company;

(b) in any way, whether directly or indirectly, be concerned with, or take part in the management of, the banking company.

(3)(a) Any person against whom an order of removal has been made under subsection (1) may, within thirty days from the date of communication to him of the order, prefer an appeal to the Central Government.

(b) The decision of the Central Government on such appeal, and subject thereto, the order made by the Reserve Bank under sub-section (I), shall be final and shall not be called into question in any court.

(4) Where any order is made in respect of 6[a chairman, director] or chief executive officer or other officer or employee of a banking company under sub-section (1), he shall cease to be 7[a chairman or, as the case may be, a director,] chief executive officer or other officer or employee of the banking company and shall not, in any way, whether directly or indirectly, be concerned with, or take part in the management of, any banking company for such period not exceeding five years as may be specified in the order.

(5) If any person in respect of whom an order is made by the Reserve Bank under sub-section (1) or under the proviso to sub-section (2) contravenes the provisions of this section, he shall be punishable with fine which may extend to two hundred and fifty rupees for each day during which such contravention continues.

(6) Where an order under sub-section (1) has been made, the Reserve Bank may, by order in writing, appoint a suitable person in place of 8[the chairman or director], or chief executive officer or other officer or employee who has been removed from his office under that sub-section, with effect from such date as may be specified in the order.

(7) Any person appointed as 9[chairman, director or chief executive officer] or other officer or employee under this section shall,-

(a) hold office during the pleasure of the Reserve Bank and subject thereto for a period not exceeding three years or such further periods not exceeding three years at a time as the Reserve Bank may specify;

(b) not incur any obligation or liability by reason only of his being a 9[chairman, director or chief executive officer] or other officer or employee or for anything done or omitted to be done in good faith in the execution of the duties of his office or in relation thereto.

(8) Notwithstanding anything contained in any law or in any contract, memorandum or articles of association, on the removal of a person from office under this section, that person shall not be entitled to claim any compensation for the loss or termination of office.

12[36AAA. Supersession of Board of directors of a multi-State co-operative bank.-(1) Where the Reserve Bank is satisfied that in the public interest or for preventing the affairs of a multi-State co-operative bank being conducted in a manner detrimental to the interest of the depositors of the multi-State co-operative bank or for securing the proper management of the multi-State co-operative bank, it is necessary so to do, the Reserve Bank may, for reasons to be recorded in writing, by order, supersede the Board of directors of such multi-State co-operative bank for a period not exceeding five years as may be specified in the order, which may be extended from time to time, so, however, that total period shall not exceed five years.

(2) The Reserve Bank may, on supersession of the Board of directors of the multi-State co-operative bank under sub-section (1) appoint an administrator for such period as it may determine.

(3) The Reserve Bank may issue such directions to the Administrator as it may deem appropriate and the Administrator shall be bound to follow such directions.

(4) Upon making the order of supersession of the Board of directors of a multi-State co-operative bank,-

(a) The Chairman, managing director and other directors as from the date of supersession of the Board shall vacate their offices as such;

(b) All the powers, functions and duties which may, by or under the provisions of the Multi-State Co-operative Societies Act, 2002 or this Act or any other law for the time being in force, be exercised and discharged by or on behalf of the Board of directors of such a multi-State Co-operative bank or by a resolution passed in general meeting of such co-operative bank, shall, until the Board of directors of such co-operative bank is reconstituted, be exercised and discharged by the Administrator appointed by the Reserve Bank under sub-section (2):

Provided that the power exercised by the Administrator shall be valid not withstanding that such power is exercisable by a resolution passed in the general meeting of such multi-State co-operative bank.

(5) (a) The Reserve Bank may constitute a committee of three or more persons who have experience in law, finance, banking, administration or accountancy to assist the Administrator in discharge of his duties.

(b) The committee shall meet at such times and places and observe such rules of procedure as may be specified by the Reserve Bank.

(6) The salary and allowances to the Administrator and the members of the committee constituted by the Reserve Bank shall be such as may be specified by the Reserve Bank and may be payable by the concerned multi-State co-operative bank.

(7) On and before expiration of period of supersession of the Board of directors as specified in the order issued under sub-section (1), the Administrator of the multi-State co-operative bank shall call the general meeting of the society to elect new directors.

(8) Notwithstanding anything contained in any other law or in any other contract, or bye-laws of a multi-State co-operative bank, no person shall be entitled to claim any compensation for the loss or termination of his office.

(9) The Administrator appointed under sub-section (2) shall vacate office immediately after the board of directors of the multi-State co-operative society has been constituted.]

13 [36AAB. Order of winding up of multi-State co-operative bank to be final in certain cases,-Where a multi-State co-operative bank, being an eligible co-operative bank, has been registered under section 13A of the Deposit Insurance and Credit Guarantee Corporation Act, 1961, as an insured bank, and subsequently-

(a) in pursuance of a scheme prepared with the previous approval of the Reserve Bank under section 18 of the Multi-State Co-operative Societies Act, 2002, an order sanctioning a scheme of compromise and arrangement or reorganisation or reconstruction has been made; or

(b) on requisition by the Reserve Bank, an order for winding up of the multi-State co-operative bank has been made under section 87 of the Multi-State Co-operative Societies Act, 2002; or

(c) an order for the supersession of the Board the appointment of an administrator therefor has been made under section 36AAA,

Such order for sanctioning the scheme of compromise and arrangement or reorganisation or reconstruction under clause (a) or the winding up of the mult-State Co-operative Bank under clause (b) or any order for the supersession of the Board and the appointment of an administrator under clause (c) shall not be liable to be called in question in any manner.]

14 36AAC. Reimbursement to Deposit Insurance Corporation by liquidator or transferee bank-Where a multi-State co-operative bank, being an insured bank within the meaning of the Deposit Insurance and Credit Guarantee Corporation Act, 1961, is wound up and the Deposit Insurance Corporation has become liable to the depositors' of the insured bank under subsection (1) or subsection (2) of section 16 of the Act, the Deposit Insurance Corporation shall be reimbursed by the liquidator or such other person in the circumstances, to the extent and in the manner provided in section 21 of the Act.

36AB. Power of Reserve Bank to appoint additional directors,-(1) If the Reserve Bank is of 10[opinion that in the interest of banking policy or in the public interest or] in the interests of the banking company or its depositors it is necessary so to do, it may, from time to time by order in writing, appoint, with effect from such date as may be specified in the order; one or more persons to hold office as additional directors of the banking company:

11[***]

(2) Any person appointed as additional director in pursuance of this section-

(a) shall hold office during the pleasure of the Reserve Bank and subject thereto for a period not exceeding three years or such further periods not exceeding three years at a time as the Reserve Bank may specify;

(b) shall not incur any obligation or liability by reason only of his being a director or for any thing done or omitted to be done in good faith in the execution of the duties of his office or in relation thereto; and

(c) shall not be required to hold qualification-shares in the banking company.

(3) For the purpose of reckoning any proportion of the total number of directors of the banking company, any additional director appointed under this section shall not be taken into account.

36AC. Part IIA to override other laws.-Any appointment or removal of a director, chief executive officer or other officer or employee in pursuance of section 36AA or section 36AB shall have effect notwithstanding anything to the contrary contained in the Companies Act, 1956 (1 of 1956) or any other law for the time being in force or in any contract or any other instrument.]

1. Part IIA (Sections 36AA to 36AC) Indicated by Act 55 of 1963, Section 18 w.e.f. 1-2-1964.

2. Substituted by Act 58 of 1968, Section 13, for "any director" w.e.f. 1-2-1969.

3. Substituted by Act 58 of 1968, Section 13, for "unless the director" w.e.f. 1-2-1969.

4. Substituted by Act 58 of 1968, Section 13, for "the director or, as the case may be, chief executive officer" w.e.f. 1-2-1969.

5. Substituted by Act 58 of 1968, Section 13, for "act as such director" w.e.f. 1-2-1969.

6. Substituted by Act 58 of 1968, Section 13, for "a director" w.e.f. 1-2-1969.

7. Substtituted by Act 58 of 1968, Section 13, for "a direetor or as the case may be" w.e.f. 1-2-1969.

8. Substituted by Act 58 of 1968, Section 13, for "the director" w.e.f. 1-2-1969.

9. Substituted by Act 58 of 1968, Section 13, for "director or chief executive officer" w.e.f. 1-2-1969.

10. Substituted by Act 58 of 1968, Section 14, for "opinion that" w.e.f. 1-2-1969.

11. Proviso omitted by Act 1 of 1984, Section 31 w.e.f. 15-2-1984.

12.Inserted by Act 24 of 2004.

13. Inserted by Act 24 Of 2004.

14. Inserted by Act 24 of 2004.

PROHIBITION OF CERTAIN ACTIVITIES IN RELATION TO BANKING COMPANIES

36AD. Punishments for certain activities in relation to banking companies.-

(1) No person shall-

(a) obstruct any person from lawfully entering or leaving any office or place of business of a banking company or from carrying on any business there, or

(b) hold, within the office or place of business of any banking company, any demonstration which is violent or which prevents, or is calculated to prevent, the transaction of normal business by the banking company, or

(c) act in any manner calculated to undermine the confidence of the depositors in the banking company.

(2) Whoever contravenes any provision of sub-section (1) without any reasonable excuse shall be punishable with imprisonment for a term which may extend to six months, or with fine which may extend to one thousand rupees, or with both.

2[(3) [*****] <![endif]>

ACQUISITION OF THE UNDERTAKINGS OF BANKING COMPANIES IN CERTAIN CASES

36AE. Power of Central Government to acquire undertakings of banking companies in certain cases.-(1) If, upon receipt of a report from the Reserve Bank, the Central Government is satisfied that a banking company-

(a) has, no more than one occasion, failed to comply with the directions given to it in writing under section 21 or section 35A, in so far as such directions relate to banking policy, or

(b) is being managed in a manner detrimental to the interests of its depositors, and that-

(i) in the interests of the depositors of such banking company, or

(ii) in the interest of banking policy, or

(iii) for the better provision of credit generally or of credit to any particular section of the community or in any particular area, it is necessary to acquire the undertaking of such banking company, the Central Government may, after such consultation with the Reserve Bank as it thinks fit, by notified order, acquire the undertaking of such company (hereinafter referred to as the acquired bank) with effect from such date as may be specified in this behalf by the Central Government (hereinafter referred to as the appointed day):

Provided that no undertaking of any banking company shall be so acquired unless such banking company has been given a reasonable opportunity of showing cause against the proposed action.

Explanation.-In this Part,-

(a) "notified order" means an order published in the Official Gazette;

(b) "undertaking", in relation to a banking company incorporated outside India, means the undertaking of the company in India.

(2) Subject to the other provisions contained in this Part, on the appointed day, the undertaking of the acquired bank and all the assets and liabilities of the acquired bank shall stand transferred to, and vest in, the Central Government.

(3) The undertaking of the acquired bank and its assets and liabilities shall be deemed to include all rights, powers, authorities and privileges and all property, whether movable or immovable, including, in particular, cash balances, reserve funds, investments, deposits and all other interests and rights in, or arising out of, such property as may be in the possession of or held by, the acquired bank immediately before the appointed day and all books, accounts and documents relating thereto, and shall also be deemed to include all debts, liabilities and obligations, of whatever kind, then existing of the acquired bank.

(4) Notwithstanding anything contained in sub-section (2), the Central Government may, if it is satisfied that the undertaking of the acquired bank and its assets and liabilities should, instead of vesting in the Central Government, or continuing to so vest, vest in a company established under any scheme made under this Part or in any corporation (hereinafter in this Part and in the Fifth Schedule referred to as the transferee bank) that Government may, by order, direct that the said undertaking, including the assets and liabilities thereof, shall vest in the transferee bank either on the publication of the notified order or on such other date as may be specified in this behalf by the Central Government.

(5) Where the undertaking of the acquired bank and the assets and liabilities thereof vest in the transferee bank under sub-section (4), the transferee bank, shall, on and from the date of such vesting, be deemed to have become the transferee of the acquired bank and all the rights and liabilities in relation to the acquired bank shall, on and from the date of such vesting, be deemed to have been the rights and liabilities of the transferee bank.

(6) Unless otherwise expressly provided by or under this Part, all contracts, deeds, bonds, agreements, powers of attorney, grants of legal representation and other instruments of whatever nature subsisting or having effect immediately before the appointed day and to which the acquired bank is a party or which are in favour of the acquired bank shall be of as full force and effect against or in favour of the Central Government, or as the case may be, of the transferee bank, and may be enforced or acted upon as fully and effectually as if in the place of the

acquired bank the Central Government or the transferee bank had been a party thereto or as if they had been issued in favour of the Central Government or the transferee bank, as the case may be.

(7) If, on the appointed day, any suit, appeal or other proceeding of whatever nature is pending by or against the acquired bank, the same shall not abate, be discontinued or be, in any way, prejudicially affected by reason of the transfer of the undertaking of the acquired bank or of anything contained in this Part, but the suit, appeal or other proceeding may be continued, prosecuted and enforced by or against the Central Government or the transferee bank as the case may be.

36AF. Power of the Central Government to make scheme.- (1) The Central Government may, after consultation with the Reserve Bank, make a scheme for carrying out the purposes of this Part in relation to any acquired bank.

(2) In particular, and without prejudice to the generality of the foregoing power, the said scheme may provide for all or any of the following matters, namely:-

(a) the corporation, or the company incorporated for the purpose, to which the undertaking including the property, assets and liabilities of the acquired bank may be transferred, and the capital, constitution, name and office thereof;

(b) the constitution of the first Board of management (by whatever name called) of the transferee bank, and all such matters in connection therewith or incidental thereto as the Central Government may consider to be necessary or expedient;

(c) the continuance of the services of all the employees of the acquired bank (excepting such of them as, not being workmen within the meaning of the Industrial Disputes Act, 1947(14 of 1947), are specifically mentioned in the scheme] in the Central Government or in the transferee bank, as the case may be, on the same terms and conditions so far as may be, as are specified in clauses (i) and (j) of sub-section (5) of section 45;

(d) the continuance of the right of any person who, on the appointed day, is entitled to or is in receipt of, a pension or other superannuation or compassionate allowance or benefit, from the acquired bank or any provident, pension or other fund or any authority administering such fund, to be paid by, and to receive from, the Central Government or the transferee bank, as the case may be, or any provident, pension or other fund or any authority administering such fund, the same pension, allowance or benefit so long as he observes the conditions on which the pension, allowance or benefit was granted, and if any question arises whether he has so observed such conditions, the question shall be determined by the Central Government and the decision of the Central Government thereon shall be final;

(e) the manner of payment of the compensation payable in accordance with the provisions of this Part to the shareholders of the acquired bank, or where the acquired bank is a banking company incorporated outside India, to the acquired bank in full satisfaction of their, or as the case may be, its claims;

(f) the provision, if any, for completing the effectual transfer to the Central Government or the transferee bank of any asset or any liability which forms part of the undertaking of the acquired bank in any country outside India;

(g) such incidental, consequential and supplemental matters as may be necessary to secure that the transfer of the business, property, assets and liabilities of the acquired bank to the Central Government or transferee bank, as the case may be, is effectual and complete.

(3) The Central Government may, after consultation with the Reserve Bank, by notification in the Official Gazette, add to, amend or vary any scheme made under this section.

(4) Every scheme made under this section shall be published in the Official Gazette.

(5) Copies of every scheme made under this section shall be laid before each House of Parliament as soon as may be after it is made.

(6) The provisions of this Part and of any scheme made there under shall have effect notwithstanding anything to the contrary contained in any other provisions of this Act or in any other law or any agreement, award or other instrument for the time being in force.

(7) Every scheme made under this section shall be binding on the Central Government or, as the case may be, on the

transferee bank and also on all members, creditors, depositors and employees of the acquired bank and of the transferee bank and on any other person having any right, liability, power or function in relation to, or in connection with, the acquired bank or the transferee bank, as the case may be.

36AG. Compensation to be given to shareholders of the acquired bank.-(I) Every person who, immediately before the appointed day, is registered as a holder of shares in the acquired bank or, when the acquired bank is a banking company incorporated outside India, the acquired bank, shall be given by the Central Government, or the transferee bank, as the case may be, such compensation in respect of the transfer of the undertaking of the acquired bank as it determined in accordance with the principles contained in the Fifth Schedule.

(2) Nothing contained in sub-section (1) shall affect the rights inter se between the holder of any share in the acquired bank and any other person who may have any interest in such shares and such other person shall be entitled to enforce his interest against the compensation awarded to the holder of such share, but not against the Central Government, or the transferee bank.

(3) The amount of compensation to be given in accordance with the principles contained in the Fifth Schedule shall be determined in the first instance by the Central Government, or the transferee bank, as the case may be, in consultation with the Reserve Bank, and shall be offered by it to all those to whom compensation is payable under sub-section (1) in full satisfaction thereof.

(4) If the amount of compensation offered in terms of sub-section (3) is not acceptable to any person to whom the compensation is payable, such person may, before such date as may be notified by the Central Government in the Official Gazette, request the Central Government in writing, to have the matter referred to the Tribunal constituted under section 36AH.

(5) If, before the date notified under sub-section (4), the Central Government receives requests, in terms of that sub-section, from not less than one-fourth in number of the shareholders holding not less than one-fourth in value of the

paid-up share capital of the acquired bank, or, where the acquired bank is a banking company incorporated outside India, from the acquired bank, the Central Government shall have the matter referred to the Tribunal for decision.

(6) If, before the date notified under sub-section (4), the Central Government does not receive requests as provided in that sub-section, the amount of compensation offered ' under sub-section (3), and where a reference has been made to the Tribunal, the amount determined by it, shall be the compensation payable under sub-section (!) and shall be final and binding on all parties concerned.

36AH. Constitution of the Tribunal.-(1) The Central Government may, for the purpose of this Part, constitute a Tribunal which shall consist of a Chairman and two other members.

(2) The Chairman shall be a person who is, or has been, a Judge of a High Court or of the Supreme Court, and, of the two other members, one shall be a person, who, in the opinion of the Central Government, has had experience of commercial banking and the other shall be a person who is a chartered accountant within the meaning of the Chartered Accountants' Act, 1949 (38 of 1949).

(3) If, for any reason, a vacancy occurs in the office of the Chairman or any other member of the Tribunal, the Central Government may fill the vacancy by appointing another person thereto in accordance with the provisions of sub-section (2), and any proceeding may be continued before the Tribunal, so constituted, from the stage at which the vacancy occurred.

(4) The Tribunal may, for the purpose of determining any compensation payable under this part, choose one or more persons having special knowledge or experience of any relevant matter to assist it in the determination of such compensation.

36AI. Tribunal to have powers of a civil court.-(1) The Tribunal shall have the powers of a civil court, while trying a suit, under the Code of Civil Procedure,, 1908 (5 of 1908) in respect of the following matters, namely:-

(a) summoning and enforcing the attendance of any person and examining him on oath;

(b) requiring the discovery and production of documents;

(c) receiving evidence on affidavits;

(d) issuing commissions for the examination of witnesses or documents.

(2) Notwithstanding anything contained in sub-section (1), or in any other law for the time being in force, the Tribunal shall not compel the Central Government or the Reserve Bank,-

(a) to produce any books of account or other documents which the Central Government, or the Reserve Bank, claims to be of a confidential nature;

(b) to make any such books or documents part of the record of the proceedings before the Tribunal; or

(c) to give inspection of any such books or documents to any party before it or to any other person.

36AJ. Procedure of the Tribunal.-(1) The Tribunal shall have power to regulate its own procedure.

(2) The Tribunal may hold the whole or any part of its inquiry in camera

(3) Any clerical or arithmetical error in any order of the Tribunal or any error arising therein from any accidental slip or omission may, at any time, be corrected by the Tribunal either of its own motion or on the application of any of the parties.]

SUSPENSION OF BUSINESS AND WINDING UP OF BANKING COMPANIES

1[2[36B. High Court defined.-In this Part and in Part IIIA "High Court", in relation to a banking company, means the High Court exercising jurisdiction in the place where the registered office of the banking company is situated or, in the case of a banking company incorporated outside India, where its principal place of business in India is situated.

37. Suspension of business.-(1) The 3[High Court] may on the application of a banking company which is temporarily unable to meet its obligations make an order (a copy of which it shall cause to be forwarded to the Reserve Bank) staying the commencement or continuance of all actions and proceedings against the company for a fixed period of time on such terms

and conditions as it shall think fit and proper, and may from time to time extend the period so however that the total period of moratorium shall not exceed six months.

(2) No such application shall be maintainable unless it is accompanied by a report of the Reserve Bank indicating that in the opinion of the Reserve Bank the banking company will be able to pay its debts if the application is granted:

Provided that the 3[High Court] may, for sufficient reasons, grant relief under this section even if the application is not accompanied by such report, and where such relief is granted, the 3[High Court] shall call for a report from the Reserve Bank on the affairs of the banking company on receipt of which it may either rescind any order already passed or pass such further orders thereon as may be just and proper in the circumstances.

4[(3) When an application is made under sub-section (1), the High Court may appoint a special officer who shall forthwith take into his custody or under his control all the assets, books, documents, effects and actionable claims to which the banking company is or appears to be entitled and shall also exercise such other powers as the High Court may deem fit to confer on him, having regard to the interests of the depositors of the banking company.]

5[(4) Where the Reserve Bank is satisfied that the affairs of a banking company in respect of which an order under sub-section (1) has been made, are being conducted in a manner detrimental to the interests of the depositors, it may make an application to the High Court for the winding up of the company, and where any such application is made, the High Court shall not make any order extending the period for which the commencement or continuance of all actions and proceedings against the company were stayed under that sub-section.]

6[38. Winding up by High Court.-(1) Notwithstanding anything contained in section 391, section 392, section 433 and section 583 of the Companies Act, 1956 (1 of 1956), but without prejudice to its powers under sub-section (1) of section 37 of this Act, the High Court shall order the winding up of a banking company-

(a) if the banking company is unable to pay its debts; or

(b) if an application for its winding up has been made by the Reserve Bank under section 37 or this section.

(2) The Reserve Bank shall make an application under this section for the winding up of a banking company if it is directed so to do by an order under clause (b) of sub-section (4) of section 35.

(3) The Reserve Bank may make an application under this section for the winding up of a banking company-

(a) if the banking company-

(i) has failed to comply with the requirements specified in section 11; or

(ii) has by reason of the provisions of section 22 become disentitled to carry on banking business in India; or

(iii) has been prohibited from receiving fresh deposits by an order under clause (a) of sub-section (4) of section 35 or under clause (b) of sub-section (3A) of section 42 of the Reserve Bank of India Act, 1934 (2 of 1934); or

(iv) having failed to comply with any requirement of this Act other than the requirements laid in section 11, has continued such failure, or, having contravened any provision of this Act continued such contravention beyond such period or periods as may be specified in that behalf by the Reserve Bank from time to time, after notice in writing of such failure or contravention has been conveyed to the banking company; or

(b) if in the opinion of the Reserve Bank-

(i) a compromise or arrangement sanctioned by a court in respect of the banking company cannot be worked satisfactorily with or without modifications; or

(ii) the returns, statements or information furnished to it under or in pursuance of the provisions of this Act disclose that the banking company is unable to pay its debts; or

(iii) the continuance of the banking company is prejudicial to the interests of its depositors.

(4) Without prejudice to the provisions contained in section 434 of the Companies Act, 1956 (I of 1956) a banking company shall be deemed to be unable to pay its debts if it has refused to meet any lawful demand made at any of its offices or branches

within two working days, if such demand is made at a place where there is an office, branch or agency of the Reserve Bank, or within five working days, if such demand is made elsewhere, and if the Reserve Bank certifies in writing that the banking company is unable to pay its debts.

(5) A copy of every application made by the Reserve Bank under sub-section (1) shall be sent by the Reserve Bank to the registrar.]

7[38A. Court liquidator.-(1) There shall be attached to every High Court a Court liquidator to be appointed by the Central Government for the purpose of conducting all proceedings for the winding up of banking companies and performing such other duties in reference thereto as the High Court may impose.

8[***]

(4) Where having regard to the number of banking companies wound up and other circumstances of the case, the Central Government is of opinion that it is not necessary or expedient to attach for the time being a Court liquidator to a High Court, it may, from time to time, by notification in the Official Gazette, direct that this section shall not have effect in relation to that High Court.]

9[39. Reserve Bank to be official liquidator.-10[(1)] Notwithstanding anything contained in section 38A of this Act or in section 448 or section 449 of the Companies Act, 1956(1 of 1956), where in any proceeding for the winding up by the High Court of a banking company, an application is made by the Reserve Bank in this behalf, the Reserve Bank, the State Bank of India or any other bank notified by the Central Government in this behalf or any individual, as stated in such application shall be appointed as the official liquidator of the banking company in such proceeding and the liquidator, if any, functioning in such proceeding shall vacate office upon such appointment.]

11[(2) Subject to such directions as may be made by the High Court, the remuneration of the official liquidator appointed under this section, the cost and expenses of this establishment and the cost and expenses of the winding up shall be met out of the assets of the banking company which is being wound up, and notwithstanding anything to the contrary contained in any other law for the time being in force, no fees shall be payable to the Central Government, out of the assets of the banking company.]

12[39A. Application of Companies Act to liquidators.-(1) All the provisions of the Companies Act, 1956 (1 of 1956), relating to a liquidator, in so far as they are not inconsistent with this Act, shall apply to or in relation to a liquidator appointed under section 38A or section 39.

(2) Any reference to the "official liquidator" in this Part and Part IIIA shall be construed as including a reference to any liquidator of a banking company.]

40. Stay of proceedings.-Notwithstanding anything to the contrary contained in 13[section 466 of the Companies Act, 1956 (1 of 1956)], the 14[High Court] shall not make any order staying the proceedings in relation to the winding up of a banking company, unless the 14[High Court] is satisfied that an arrangement has been made whereby the company can pay its depositors in full as their claims accrue.

15[41. Preliminary report by official liquidator.-Notwithstanding anything to for the contrary contained in section 455 of the Companies Act, 1956 (1 of 1956), where a winding up order has been made in respect of a banking company whether before or after the commencement of the Banking Companies (Second Amendment) Act, 1960 (37 of 1960), the official liquidator shall submit a preliminary report to the High Court within two months from the date of the winding up order or where the winding up order has been made before such commencement, within two months from such commencement, giving the information required by that section so far as it is available to him and also stating the amount of assets of the banking company in cash which are in his custody or under his control on the date of the report and the amount of its assets which are likely to be collected in cash before the expiry of that period of two months in order that such assets may be applied speedily towards the making of preferential payments under section 530 of the Companies Act, 1956, and in the discharge, as far as possible, of the liabilities and obligations of the banking company to its depositors and other creditors in accordance with the provisions hereinafter contained; and the official liquidator shall make for the purposes aforesaid every endeavour to collect in cash as such of the assets of the banking company as practicable.

41A. Notice to preferential claimants and secured and unsecured creditors.-Within fifteen days from the date of the winding up order of a banking company or where the winding up order has been made before the commencement of the Banking Companies (Second Amendment) Act, 1960 (37 of 1960), within one month from such commencement, the official liquidator shall, for the purpose of making an estimate of the debts and liabilities of the banking company (other that its liabilities and obligations to its depositors), by notice served in such manner as the Reserve Bank may direct, call upon-

(a) every claimant entitled to preferential payment under section 530 of the Companies Act, 1956(1 of 1956), and

(b) every secured and every unsecured creditor, to send to the official liquidator within one month from the date of the service of the notice a statement of the amount claimed by him.

(2) Every notice under sub-section (1) sent to a claimant having a claim under section 530 of the Companies Act, 1956 (1 of 1956), shall state that if a statement of the claim is not sent to the official liquidator before the expiry of the period of one month from the date of the service, the claim shall not be treated as a claim entitled to be paid under section 530 of the Companies Act, 1956, in priority to all other debts but shall be treated as an ordinary debt due by the banking company.

(3) Every notice under sub-section (1) sent to a secured creditor shall require him to value his security before the expiry of the period of one month from the date of the service of the notice and shall state that if a statement of the claim together with the valuation of the security is not sent to the official liquidator before the expiry of the said period, then, the official liquidator shall himself value the security and such valuation shall be binding on the creditor.

(4) If a claimant fails of comply with the notice sent to him under sub-section (1), his claim will not be entitled to be paid under section 530 of the Companies Act, 1956 (1 of 1956), in priority to all other debts but shall be treated as an ordinary debt due by the banking company; and if a secured creditor fails

to comply with the notice sent to him under sub-section (1), the official liquidator shall himself value the security and such valuation shall be binding on the creditor.]

42. Power to dispense with meetings of creditors, etc.- Notwithstanding anything to the contrary contained in 16[17[section 460] of the Companies Act, 1956 (1 of 1956)], the 18[High Court] may, in the proceedings for winding up a banking company, dispense with any meetings of creditors or contributories 19[***] if it considers that no object will be secured thereby sufficient to justify the delay and expense.

20[43. Booked depositors' credits to be deemed proved.-In any proceeding for the winding up of a banking company, every depositor of the banking company shall be deemed to have filed his claim for the amount shown in the books of the banking company as standing to his credit and, notwithstanding anything to the contrary contained in 21[section 474 of the Companies Act, 1956 (1 of 1956)], the High Court shall presume such claims to have been proved, unless the official liquidator shows that there is reason for doubting its correctness.]

22[43A. Preferential payments to depositors.-(1) In every proceeding for the winding up of a banking company where a winding up order has been made, whether before or after the commencement of the Banking Companies (Second Amendment) Act, 1960, (37 of 1960) within three months from the date of the winding up order or where the winding up order has been made before such commencement, within three months therefrom, the preferential payments referred to in section 530 of the Companies Act, 1956 (1 of 1956), in respect of which statements of claims have been sent within one month from the date of the service of the notice referred to in section 41 A, shall be made by the official liquidator or adequate provision for such payments shall be made by him.

(2) After the preferential payments as aforesaid have been made or adequate provision has been made in respect thereof, there shall be paid within the aforesaid period of three months-

(a) in the first place to every depositor in the savings bank account of the banking company a sum of two hundred and fifty rupees or the balance at his credit, whichever is less; and thereafter;

(b) in the next place, to every other depositor of the banking company a sum of two hundred and fifty rupees or the balance at his credit, whichever is less, in priority to all other debts from out of the remaining assets of the banking company available for payment to general creditors:

Provided that the sum total of the amounts paid under clause (a) and clause (b) to any one person who in his own name (and not jointly with any other person) is a depositor in (he savings bank account of the banking company and also a depositor in any other account, shall not exceed the sum of two hundred and fifty rupees.

(3) Where within the aforesaid period of three months full payment cannot be made of the amounts required to be paid under clause (a) or clause (b) of sub-section (2) with the assets in cash, the official liquidator shall pay within that period to every depositor under clause (a) or, as the case may be, clause (b) of that sub-section on a pro rata basis so much of the amount due to the depositor under that clause as the official liquidator is able to pay with those assets; and shall pay the rest of that amount to every such depositor as and when sufficient assets are collected by the official liquidator in cash.

(4) After payments have been made first to depositors in the savings bank account and then to the other depositors in accordance with the foregoing provisions, the remaining assets of the banking company available for payment to general creditors shall be utilised for payment on a pro rata basis of the debts of the general creditors and of the further sums, if any, due to the depositors; and after making adequate provision for payment on a pro rata basis as aforesaid of the debts of the general creditors, the official liquidator shall, as and when the assets of the company are collected in cash, make payment on a pro rata basis as aforesaid, of the further sums, if any, which may remain due to the depositors referred to in clause (a) and clause (b) of sub-section (2).

(5) In order to enable the official liquidator to have in his custody or under his control in cash as much of the assets of the banking company as possible, the securities given to every secured creditor may be redeemed by the official liquidator-

(a) where the amount due to the creditor is more than the value of the securities as assessed by him or, as the case may be, as assessed by the official liquidator, on payment of such value; and

(b) where the amount due to the creditor is equal to or less than the value of the securities as so assessed, on payment of the amount due: Provided that where the official liquidator is not satisfied with the valuation made by the creditor, he may apply to the High Court for making a valuation,

(6) When any claimant, creditor or depositor to whom any payment is to be made in accordance with 23[the provisions of this section], cannot be found or is not readily traceable, adequate provision shall be made by the official liquidator for such payment.

(7) For the purposes of this section, the payments specified in each of the following clauses shall be treated as payments of a different class, namely:-

(a) payments to preferential claimants under section 530 of the Companies Act, 1956 (1 of 1956);

(b) payments under clause (a) of sub-section (2) to the depositors in the savings bank account;

(c) payments under clause (b) of sub-section (2) to the other depositors;

(d) payments to the general creditors and payments to the depositors in addition to those specified in clause (a) and clause (b) of sub-section (2).

(8) The payments of each different class specified in sub-section (7) shall rank equally among themselves and be paid in full unless the assets are insufficient to meet them, in which case they shall abate in equal proportion.]]

24[(9) Nothing contained in sub-sections (2), (3), (4), (7) and (8) shall apply to a banking company in respect of the depositors of which the Deposit Insurance Corporation is liable under section 16 of the Deposit Insurance Corporation Act, 1961, (47 of 1961).

(10) After preferential payments referred to in sub-section (1) have been made or adequate provision has been made in respect thereof, the remaining assets of the banking company

referred to in sub-section (9) available for payment to general creditors shall be utilised for payment on pro rata basis of the debts of the general creditors and of the sums due to the depositors:

Provided (hat where any amount in respect of any deposit is to be paid by the liquidator to the Deposit Insurance Corporation under section 21 of the Deposit Insurance Corporation Act, 1961 (47 of 1961), only the balance, if any, left after making the said payment shall be payable to the depositor.]

25[44. Powers of High Court in voluntary winding up.-(1) Notwithstanding anything to the contrary contained in section 484 of the Companies Act, 1956 (1 of 1956), no banking company may be voluntarily wound up unless the Reserve Bank certifies in writing that the company is able to pay in full all its debts to its creditors as they accrue.

(2) The High Court may, in any case where a banking company is being wound up voluntarily, make an order that the voluntary winding up shall continue, but subject to the supervision of the court.

(3) Without prejudice to the provisions contained in sections 441 and 521 of the Companies Act, 1956 (1 of 1956), the High Court may of its own motion and shall on the application of the Reserve Bank, order the winding up of a banking company by the High Court in any of the following cases, namely:-

(a) where the banking company is being wound up voluntarily and at any stage during the voluntary winding up proceedings the company is not able to meet its debts as they accrue; or

(b) where the banking company is being wound up voluntarily or is being wound up subject to the supervision of the court and the High Court is satisfied that the voluntary winding up or winding up subject to the supervision of the court cannot be continued without detriment to the interests of the depositors.]

26[44A. Procedure for amalgamation of banking companies.-(1) Notwithstanding anything contained in any law for the time being in force, no banking company shall be amalgamated with another banking company, unless a scheme containing the terms of such amalgamation has been placed in draft before the shareholders of each of the banking companies concerned separately, and approved by a resolution passed by a majority in number representing two-thirds in value of the shareholders of each of the said companies, present either in person or by proxy at a meeting called for the purpose.

(2) Notice of every such meeting as is referred to in sub-section (1) shall be given to every shareholder of each of the banking companies concerned in accordance with the relevant articles of association indicating the time, place and object of the meeting, and shall also be published atleast once a week for three consecutive weeks in not less than two newspapers which circulate in the locality or localities where the registered offices of the banking companies concerned are situated, one of such newspapers being in a language commonly understood in the locality or localities.

(3) Any shareholder, who has voted against the scheme of amalgamation at the meeting or has given notice in writing at or prior to the meeting of the company concerned or to the presiding officer of the meeting that he dissents from the scheme of amalgamation, shall be entitled, in the event of the scheme being sanctioned by the Reserve Bank, to claim from the banking company concerned, in respect of the shares held by him in that company, their value as determined by the Reserve Bank when sanctioning the scheme and such determination by the Reserve Bank as to the value of the shares (o be paid to the dissenting shareholder shall be final for all purposes.

(4) If the scheme of amalgamation is approved by the requisite majority of shareholders in accordance with the provisions of this section, it shall be submitted to the Reserve Bank for sanction and shall, if sanctioned by the Reserve Bank by an order in writing passed in this behalf, be binding on the banking companies concerned and also on all the shareholders thereof.

27[***]

(6) On the sanctioning of a scheme of amalgamation by the Reserve Bank, the properly of the amalgamated banking company shall, by virtue of the order of sanction, be transferred to and vest in, and the liabilities of the said company shall, by virtue of the said order be transferred to, and become the

liabilities of, the banking company which under the scheme of amalgamation is to acquire the business of the amalgamated banking company, subject in all cases to 28[the provisions of the scheme as sanctioned.]

29[(6A) Where a scheme of amalgamation is sanctioned by the Reserve Bank under the provisions of this section, the Reserve Bank may, by a further order in writing, direct that on such date as may be specified therein the banking company (hereinafter in this section referred to as the amalgamated banking company) which by reason of the amalgamation will cease to function, shall stand dissolved and any such direction shall take effect notwithstanding anything to the contrary contained in any other law.

(6B) Where the Reserve Bank directs a dissolution of the amalgamated banking company, it shall transmit a copy of the order directing such dissolution to the Registrar before whom the banking company has been registered and on receipt of such order the Registrar shall strike off the name of the company.

(6C) An order under sub-section (4) whether made before or after the commencement of section 19 of the Banking Laws (Miscellaneous Provisions) Act, 1963 (55 of 1963) shall be conclusive evidence that all the requirements of this section relating to amalgamation have been complied with, and a copy of the said order certified in writing by an officer of the Reserve Bank to be a true copy of such order and a copy of the scheme certified in the tike manner to be a true copy thereof shall, in all legal proceedings (whether in appeal or otherwise and whether instituted before or after the commencement of the said section 19), be admitted as evidence to the same extent as the original order and the original scheme.]

30[(7) Nothing in the foregoing provisions of this section shall affect the power of the Central Government to provide for the amalgamation of two or more banking companies 31[***] under section 396 of the Companies Act, 1956 (1 of 1956):

Provided that no such power shall be exercised by the Central Government except after consultation with the Reserve Bank.]

32[33[44B.] Restriction on compromise or arrangement between banking company and creditors.-34[(1)]

Notwithstanding anything contained in any law for the time being in force, no 35[High Court] shall sanction a compromise or arrangement between a banking company and its creditors or any class of them or between such company and its members or any class of them 36[or sanction any modification in any such compromise or arrangement unless the compromise or arrangement or modification, as the case may be,] is certified by the Reserve Bank 37[in writing as not being incapable of being worked and as not being detrimental to the interests of the depositors of such banking company.]

38[(2) Where an application under 39[section 39 of the Companies Act, 1956 (1 of 1956)], is made in respect of a banking company, the High Court may direct the Reserve Bank to make an inquiry in relation to the affairs of the banking company and the conduct of its directors and when such direction is given, the Reserve Bank shall make such inquiry and submit its report to the High Court.]

40[45. Power of Reserve Bank to apply to Central Government for suspension of business by a banking company and to prepare scheme of reconstitution of amalgamation.-(1) Notwithstanding anything contained in the foregoing provisions of this Part or in any other law or 41[any agreement or other instrument], for the time being in force, where it appears to the Reserve Bank that there is good reason so to do, the Reserve Bank may apply to the Central Government for an order of moratorium in respect of 42[a banking company].

(2) The Central Government, after considering the application made by the Reserve Bank under sub-section (1), may make an order of moratorium staying the commencement or continuance of all actions and proceedings against the company for a fixed period of time on such terms and conditions as it thinks fit and proper and may from time to time extend the period so however that the total period of moratorium shall not exceed six months.

(3) Except as otherwise provided by any directions given by the Central Government in the order made by it under sub-section (2) or at any time thereafter the banking company shall not during the period of moratorium make any payment to any depositors or discharge any liabilities or obligations to any other creditors.

43[(4) During the period of moratorium, if the Reserve Bank is satisfied that-

(a) in the public interest; or

(b) in the interests of the depositors; or

(c) in order to secure the proper management of the banking company; or

(d) in the interests of the banking system of the country as a whole, it is necessary so to do, the Reserve Bank may prepare a scheme-

(i) for the reconstruction of the banking company, or

(ii) for the amalgamation of the banking company with any other banking institution (in this section referred to as "the transferee bank").

(5) The scheme aforesaid may contain provisions for all or any of the following matters, namely:

(a) the constitution, name and registered office, the capital, assets, powers, rights, interests, authorities and privileges, the liabilities, duties and obligations of the banking company on its reconstruction or as the case may be, of the transferee bank;

(b) in the case of amalgamation of the banking company, the transfer to the transferee bank of the business, properties, assets and liabilities of the banking company on such terms and conditions as may be specified in the scheme;

(c) any change in the Board of directors, or the appointment of a new Board of directors, of the banking company on its reconstruction or, as the case may be, of the transferee bank and the authority of whom, the manner in which, and the other terms and conditions on which, such change or appointment shall be made and in the case of appointment of a new Board of directors or of any director the period for which such appointment shall be made;

(d) the alteration of the memorandum and articles of association of the banking company on its reconstruction or, as the case may be, of the transferee bank for the purpose of altering the capital thereof or for such other purposes as may be necessary to give effect to the reconstruction or amalgamation;

(e) subject to the provisions of the scheme, the continuation by or against the banking company on its reconstruction or, as

the case may be, the transferee bank, of any actions or proceedings pending against the banking company immediately before the date of the order of moratorium;

(f) the reduction of the interest or rights which the members, depositors and other creditors have in or against the banking company before its reconstruction or amalgamation to such extent as the Reserve Bank considers necessary in the public interest or in the interest of the members, depositors and other creditors or for the maintenance of the business of the banking company;

(g) the payment in cash or otherwise to depositors and other creditors in full satisfaction of their claim-

(i) in respect of their interest or rights in or against the banking company before its reconstruction or amalgamation; or

(ii) where their interest or rights aforesaid in or against the banking company has or have been reduced under clause (f), in respect of such interest or rights as so reduced;

(h) the allotment to the members of the banking company for shares held by them therein before its reconstruction or amalgamation [whether their interest in such shares has been reduced under clause (f) or not], of shares in the banking company on its reconstruction or, as the case may be, in the transferee bank and where any members claim payment in cash and not allotment of shares, or where it is not possible to allot shares to any members, the payment in cash to those members in full satisfaction of their claim-

(i) in respect of their interest in shares in the banking company before its reconstruction or amalgamation; or

(ii) where such interest has been reduced under clause (f) in respect of their interest in shares as so reduced;

(i) the continuance of the services of all the employees of the banking company (excepting such of them as not being workmen within the meaning of the Industrial Disputes Act, 1947 (14 of 1947), are specifically mentioned in the scheme) in the banking company itself on its reconstruction or, as the case may be, in the transferee bank at the same remuneration and on the same terms and conditions of service, which they were getting, or as the case may be, by which they were being governed, immediately before the date of the order of moratorium:

Provided that the scheme shall contain a provision that-

(i) the banking company shall pay or grant not later than the expiry of the period of three years from the date on which the scheme is sanctioned by the Central Government, to the said employees the same remuneration and the same terms and conditions of service 44[as are, at the time of such payment or grant, applicable] to employees of corresponding rank or status of a comparable banking company to be determined for this purpose by the Reserve Bank (whose determination in this respect shall be final);

(ii) the transferee bank shall pay or grant not later than the expiry of the aforesaid period of three years, to the said employees the same remuner-ation and the same terms and conditions of service44[as are, at the time of such payment or grant, applicable] to the other employees corresponding rank or status of the transferee bank subject to the qualifications and experience of the said employees being the same as or equivalent to those of such other employees of the transferee bank:

Provided further that if in any case under clause (ii) of the first proviso any doubt or difference as to whether the qualification and experience of any of the said employees are the same as or equivalent to the qualifications and experience of the other employees of corresponding rank or status of the transferee bank 45[the doubt or difference shall be referred, before the expiry of a period of three years from the date of the payment or grant mentioned in that clause,] to the Reserve Bank whose decision thereon shall be final;

(j) notwithstanding anything contained in clause (i) where any of the employees of the banking company not being workmen within the meaning of the Industrial Disputes Act, 1947 (14 of 1947), are specifically mentioned in the scheme under clause (i) or where any employees of the banking company have by notice in writing given to the banking company, or, as the case may be, the transferee bank at any time before the expiry of the one month next following the date on which the scheme is sanctioned by the Central Government, intimated their intention of not becoming employees of the banking company on its reconstruction or, as the case may be, of the transferee bank, the payment to such employees of compensation, if any, to which they are entitled under the Industrial Disputes Act, 1947, and such pension, gratuity, provident fund and other retirement benefits ordinarily admissible to them under the rules or authorisations of the banking company immediately before the date of the order of moratorium;

(k) any other terms and conditions for the reconstruction or amalgamation of the banking company;

(l) such incidental, consequential and supplemental matters as are necessary to secure that the reconstruction or amalgamation shall be fully and effectively carried out.

(6)(a) A copy of the scheme prepared by the Reserve Bank shall be sent in draft to the banking company and also to the transferee bank and any other banking company concerned in the amalgamation, for suggestions and objections, if any, within such period as the Reserve Bank may specify for this purpose.

(b) The Reserve Bank may make such modifications, if any, in the draft scheme as it may consider necessary in the light of the suggestions and objections received from the banking company and also from the transferee bank, and any other banking company concerned in the amalgamation and from any members, depositors or other creditors of each of those companies and the transferee bank.

(7) The scheme shall thereafter be placed before the Central Government for its sanction and the Central Government may sanction the scheme without any modifications or with such modifications as it may consider necessary, and the scheme as sanctioned by the Central Government shall come into force on such date as the Central Government may specify in this behalf:

Provided that different dates may be specified for different provisions of the scheme.

46[(7A) The sanction accorded by the Central Government under sub-section (7), whether before or after the commencement of section 21 of the Banking Laws (Miscellaneous Provisions) Act, 1963 (55 of 1963) shall be conclusive evidence that all that requirements of this section relating to reconstruction, or, as the case may be, amalgamation have been complied with and a copy of the sanctioned scheme certified in writing by an officer of the Central Government to be a true copy thereof, shall, in all legal proceedings (whether in appeal or otherwise and whether instituted before or after the commencement of the said section 21), be admitted as evidence to the same extent. as the original scheme.]

(8) On and from the date of the coming into operation of the scheme or any provision thereof, the scheme or such provision shall be binding on the banking company, or, as the case may be, on the transferee bank and any other banking company concerned in the amalgamation and also on all the members, depositors and other creditors and employees of each of those companies and of the transferee bank, and on any other person having any right or liability in relation to any of those companies or the transferee bank 47[including the trustees or other persons managing, or connected in any other manner with, any provident fund or other fund maintained by any of those companies or the transferee bank].

(9)48[On and from the date of the coming into operation or, or as the case may be, the date specified in this behalf in, the scheme], the properties and assets of the banking company shall, by virtue of and to the extent provided in the scheme, stand transferred to, and vest in, and the liabilities of the banking company shall, by virtue of and to the extent provided in the scheme, stand transferred to, and become the liabilities of the transferee bank.

(10) If any difficulty arises in giving effect to the provisions of the scheme, the Central Government may by order do anything not inconsistent with such provisions which appears to it necessary or expedient for the purpose of removing the difficulty.

(11) Copies of the scheme or of any order made under sub-section (10) shall be laid before both Houses of Parliament, as soon as may be, after the scheme has been sanctioned by the Central Government, or, as the case may be, the order has been made.

(12) Where the scheme is a scheme for amalgamation of the banking company, any business acquired by the transferee bank under the scheme or under any provision thereof shall,

after the coming into operation of the scheme or such provision, be carried on by the transferee bank in accordance with the law governing the transferee bank, subject to such modifications in that law or such exemptions of the transferee bank from the operation of any provisions thereof as the Central Government on the recommendation of the Reserve Bank may, by notification in the Official Gazette, make for the purpose of giving full effect to the scheme: Provided that no such modification or exemption shall be made so as to have effect for a period of more than seven years from the date of the acquisition of such business.

(13) Nothing in this section shall be deemed to prevent the amalgamation with a banking institution by a single scheme of several banking companies in respect of each of which an order of moratorium has been made under this section.

(14) The provisions of this section and of any scheme made under it shall have effect notwithstanding anything to the contrary contained in any other provisions of this Act or in any other law or any agreement, award or other instrument for the time being in force.

(15) In this section, "banking institution" means any banking company and includes the Stale Bank of India or 49[a subsidiary bank or a corresponding new bank].

50[Explanation.-References in this section of the terms and conditions of service as applicable to an employee shall not be construed as extending to the rank and status of such employee.]

SPECIAL PROVISIONS FOR SPEEDY DISPOSAL OF WINDING UP PROCEEDINGS

45A. Part III A to override other laws.-The provisions of this Part and the rules made thereunder shall have effect notwithstanding anything inconsistent therewith contained in the 2[Companies Act, 1956 (1 of 1956)] or the Code of Civil Procedure, 1908 (5 of 1908), or the 3[Code of Criminal

Procedure, 1973 (2 of 1974) or any other law for the time being in force or any Instrument having effect by virtue of any such law; but the provisions of any such law or Instrument Insofar as the same are not varied by, or inconsistent with, the provisions of this Part or rules made thereunder shall apply to all proceedings under this Part.

45B. Power of High Court to decide all claims in respect of banking companies.-The High Court shall, save as otherwise expressly provided in section 45C, have exclusive jurisdiction to entertain and decide any claim made by or against a banking company which is being wound up (including claims by or against any of its branches in India) or any application made under 4[section 391 of the Companies Act, 1956 (1 of 1956)] by or in respect of a banking company or any question of priorities or any other question whatsoever, whether of law or fad, which may relate to or arise in the course of the winding up of a banking company, whether such claim or question has arisen or arises or such application has been made or is made before or after the date of the order for the winding up of the banking company or before or after the commencement of the Banking Companies (Amendment) Act, 1953 (52 of 1953).

45C. Transfer of pending proceedings.-(1) Where a winding up order is made or has been made in respect of a banking company, no suit or other legal proceeding, whether civil or criminal, in respect of which the High Court has jurisdiction under this Act and which is pending in any other court immediately before the commencement of the Banking Companies (Amendment) Act, 1953 (52 of 1953), or the date of the order for the winding up of the banking company, whichever is later, shall be proceeded with except in the manner hereinafter provided.

(2) The official liquidator shall, within three months from the date of the winding up order or the commencement of the Banking Companies (Amendment) Act, 1953 (52 of 1953), whichever is later, or such further time as the High Court may allow, submit to the High Court a report containing a list of all such pending proceedings together with particulars thereof.

(3) On receipt of a report under sub-section (2), the High Court may, if it so thinks fit, give the parties concerned an opportunity to show cause why the proceedings should not be transferred to itself and after making an inquiry in such manner as may be provided by rules made under section 45U, it shall make such order as it deems fit transferring to itself all or such of the pending proceedings as may be specified in the order and such proceedings shall thereafter be disposed of by the High Court.

(4) If any proceedings pending in a court is not so transferred to the High Court under sub-section (3), such proceeding shall be continued in the court in which the proceeding was pending.

(5) Nothing in this section shall apply to any proceeding pending in appeal before the Supreme Court or a High Court.

45D. Settlement of list of debtors.-(1) Notwithstanding anything to the contrary contained in any law for the time being in force, the High Court may settle in the manner hereinafter provided a list of debtors of a banking company which is being wound up.

(2) Subject to any rules that may be made under section 52, the official liquidator shall, within six months from the date of the winding up order or the commencement of the Banking Companies (Amendment) Act, 1953 (52 of 1953), whichever is later, from time to time, file to the High Court lists of debtors containing such particulars as are specified in the Fourth Schedule:

Provided that such lists may, with the leave of the High Court, be filed after the expiry of the said period of six months.

(3) On receipt of any list under sub-section (2), the High Court shall, wherever necessary, cause notices to be issued on all persons affected and after making an inquiry in such manner as may be provided by rules made under section 45U, it shall make an order settling the list of debtors:

Provided that nothing in this section shall debar the High Court from settling any such list in part as against such of the persons whose debts have been settled without settling the debts of all the persons placed on the list.

(4) At the time of the settlement of any such list, the High Court shall pass an order for the payment of the amount due by each debtor and make such further orders as may be necessary in respect of the relief claimed, including reliefs against any guarantor or in respect of the realisation of any security.

(5) Every such order shall, subject to the provisions for appeal, be final and binding for all purposes as between the banking company on the one hand and the person against whom the order is passed all persons claiming through or

under him on the other hand, and shall be deemed to be a decree in a suit.

(6) In respect of every such order, the High Court shall issue a certificate specifying clearly the reliefs granted and the names and descriptions of the parties against whom such reliefs have been granted, the amount of costs awarded and by whom, and out of what funds and in what proportions, such costs are to be paid; and every such certificate shall be deemed to be a certified copy of the decree for all purposes including execution.

(7) At the time of settling the list of debtors or at any other time prior or subsequent thereto, the High Court shall have power to pass any order in respect of a debtor on the application of the official liquidator for the realisation, management, protection, preservation or sale of any property given as security to the banking company and to give such powers to the official liquidator to carry out the aforesaid directions as the High Court thinks fit.

(8) The High Court shall have power to sanction a compromise in respect of any debt and to order the payment of any debt by Instalments.

(9) In any case in which any such list is settled ex parte as against any person, such person may, within thirty days from the date of the order settling the list, apply to the High Court for an order to vary such list, so far as it concerns him, and if the High Court is satisfied that he was prevented by any sufficient cause from appearing on the date fixed for the settlement of such list and that he has a good defence to the claim of the banking company on merits, the High Court may vary the list and pass such orders in relation thereto as it thinks fit: Provided that the High Court may, if it so thinks fit, entertain the application after the expiry of the said period of thirty days.

(10) Nothing in this section shall-

(a) apply to a debt which has been secured by a mortgage of immovable property, if a third party has any interest in such immovable property; or

(b) prejudice the rights of the official liquidator to recover any debt due to a banking company under any other law for the time being in force.

45E. Special provisions to make calls on contributories.- Notwithstanding that the list of the contributories has not been settled under 5[section 467 of the Companies Act, 1956 (1 of 1956)], the High Court may, if it appears to it necessary or expedient so to do, at any time after making a winding up order, make a call on and order payment thereof by any contributory under sub-section (1) of 6[section 470 of the Companies Act, 1956 (1 of 1956)], if such contributory has been placed on the list of contributories by the official liquidator and has not appeared to dispute his liability.

45F. Documents of banking company to be evidence.-(1) Entries in the books of account or other documents of a banking company which is being wound up shall be admitted in evidence in all 7[legal

proceedings]; and all such entries may be proved either by the production of the books of account or other documents of the banking company containing such entries or by the production of a copy of the entries, certified by the official liquidator under his signature and stating that it is a true copy of the original entries and that such original entries are contained in the books of account or other documents of the banking company in his possession.

(2) Notwithstanding anything to the contrary contained in the Indian Evidence Act, 1872 (1 of 1872), all such entries in the books of account or other documents of a banking company shall, as against the directors, 8[officers and other employees] of the banking company in respect of which the winding up order has been made 9[***], by prima facie evidence of the truth of all matters purporting to be therein recorded.

45G. Public examination of directors and auditors.-(1) Where an order has been made for the winding up of a banking company, the official liquidator shall submit a report whether in his opinion any loss has been caused to the banking company since its formation by any act or omission (whether or not a fraud has been committed by such ' act or omission) of any person in the promotion or formation of the banking company or of any director or auditor of the banking company.

(2) If, on consideration of the report submitted under sub-section(1), the High Court is of opinion that any person who

has taken part in the promotion or formation of the banking company or has been a director or an auditor of the banking company should be publicly examined, it should hold a public sitting on a date to be appointed for that purpose and direct that such person, director or auditor shall attend there at and shall be publicly examined as to the promotion or formation or the conduct of the business of the banking company, or as to his conduct and dealings, Insofar as they relate to the affairs of the banking company:

Provided that no such person shall be publicly examined unless he has been given an opportunity to show cause why he should not be so examined.

(3) The official liquidator shall take part in the examination and for that purpose may, if specially authorized by the High Court in that behalf, employ such legal assistance as may be sanctioned by the High Court.

(4) Any creditor or contributory may also take part in the examination either personally or by any person entitled to appear before the High Court.

(5) The High Court may put such questions to the person examined as it thinks fit.

(6) The person examined shall be examined on oath and shall answer all such questions as the High Court may put or allow to be put to him.

(7) A person ordered to be examined under this section may, at his own cost, employ any person entitled to appear before the High Court who shall be at liberty to put to him such questions as the High Court may deem just for the purpose of enabling him to explainer qualify any answer given by him: Provided that if he is, in the opinion of the High Court, exculpated from any charges made or suggested against him, the High Court may allow him such costs in its discretion as it may deem fit.

(8) Notes of the examination shall be taken down in writing, and shall be read over to or by, and signed by, the person examined and may thereafter be used in evidence against him in any proceeding, civil or criminal, and shall be open to the Inspection of any creditor or contributory at all reasonable limes.

(9) Where on such examination, the High Court, is of opinion (whether a fraud has been committed or not)-

(a) that a person, who has been a director of the banking company, is not fit to be a director of a company, or

(b) that a person, who has been an auditor of the banking company or a partner of a firm acting as such auditor, is not fit to act as an auditor of a company or to be a partner of a firm acting as such auditor, the High Court may make an order that person shall not, without the leave of the High Court, be a director of, or in any way, whether directly or indirectly, be concerned or take part in the management of an company or, as the case may be, act as an auditor of, or be a partner of firm acting as auditors of any company for such period not exceeding five years as may be specified in the order.

45H. Special provisions for assessing damages against delinquent directors, etc.-(1) Where an application is made to the High Court under 10[section 543 of the Companies Act, 1956(1 of 1956)], against any promoter, director, manager, liquidator or officer of a banking company for repayment or restoration of any money or property and the applicant makes out a prima facie case against such person, the High Court shall make an order against such person to repay and restore the money or property unless he proves that he is not liable to make the repayment or restoration either wholly or in part:

Provided that where such an order is made jointly against two or more such persons, they shall be jointly and severally liable to make the repayment or restoration of the money or property.

(2) Where an application is made, to the High Court under 10[section 543 of the Companies Act, 1956 (I of 1956)], and the High Court has reason to believe that a property belongs to any promoter, director, manager, liquidator or officer of the banking company, whether the property stands in the name of such person or any other person at an ostensible owner, then the High Court may, at any time, whether before or after making an order under sub-section (1), direct the attachment of such property, or such portion thereof, as it thinks fit and the property so attached shall remain subject to attachment unless the ostensible owner can prove to the satisfaction of the High Court

that he is the real owner and the provisions of the Code of Civil Procedure, 1908 (5 of 1908), relating to attachment of property shall, as far as may be, apply to such attachment,

45I. Duty of directors and officers of banking company to assist in the realisation or property.-Every director or other officer of a banking company which is being wound up shall give such assistance to the official liquidator as he may reasonably require in connection with the realisation and distribution of the property of the banking company.

45J. Special provisions for punishing offences in relation to banking companies being wound up.-(1) The High Court may, if it thinks fit, take cognizance of and try in a summary way and offence alleged to have been committed by any person who has taken part in the promotion or formation of the banking company which is being wound, up or by any director, manager or officer thereof: Provided that the offence is one punished under this Act or under the 11[Companies Act, 1956(1 of 1956)].

(2) When trying any such offence as aforesaid, the High Court may also try any other offence not referred to in sub-section (1) which is an offence with which the accused may, under the 12[Code of Criminal Procedure, 1973 (2 of 1974)], be charged at the same trial.

(3) In any case tried summarily under sub-section (1), the High Court-

(a) need not summon any witness, if it is satisfied that the evidence of such witness will not be material;

(b) shall not be bound to adjourn a trial for any purpose unless such adjournment is, in the opinion of the High Court, necessary in the interests of justice;

(c) shall, before passing any sentence, record judgment embodying the substance of the evidence and also the particulars specified in section 263 of the 12[Code of Criminal Procedure, 1973 (2 of 1974)], so far as that section may be applicable, and nothing contained in sub-section (2) of section 262 of the [Code of Criminal Procedure, 1973 (2 of 1974)], shall apply to any such trial.

(4) All offences in relation to winding up alleged to have been committed by any person specified in sub-section (1) which

are punishable under this Act or under the 11[Companies Act, 1956(1 of 1956)], and which are not tried in a summary way under ' sub-section (1) shall, notwithstanding anything to the contrary in that Act or the 12[Code of Criminal Procedure, 1973 (2 of 1974)], or in any other law for the time being in force, be taken cognizance of and tried by a Judge of the High Court other than the Judge for the time being dealing with the proceedings for the winding up of the banking company.

(5) Notwithstanding anything to the contrary contained in the 13[Code of Criminal Procedure, 1973 (2 of 1974)], the High Court may take cognizance of any offence under this section, without the accused being committed to it for trial 14[***].

45K. Power of High court to enforce schemes of arrangements, etc.-[Rep. by the Banking Companies (Amendment) Act, 1959, Section 31 (w.e.f. 1-10-1959).]

45L. Public examination of directors and auditors, etc., in respect of a banking company under schemes of arrangement.- (1) Where an application for sanction a compromise or arrangement in respect of a banking company is made under 15[section 39] of the Companies Act, 1956 (1 of 1956)], or where such sanction has been given and the High Court is of opinion, whether on a report of the Reserve Bank or otherwise, that any ' person who has taken part in the promotion or formation of the banking company or has been a director or auditor of the banking company should be publicly examined, it may direct such examination of such person and the provisions of section 45G shall, as far as may be, apply to the banking company as they apply to a banking company which is being wound up.

(2) Where a compromise or arrangement is sanctioned under 15[section 391 of the Companies Act, 1956 (1 of 1956)], in respect of a banking company, the provisions of 16[section 543 of the said Act] and of section 45H of this Act shall, as far as may be, apply to the banking company as they apply to a banking company which is being wound up as if the order sanctioning the compromise or arrangement were an order for the winding up of the banking company.

17[(3) Where 18[a scheme of reconstruction or amalgamation of a banking company] has been sanctioned by the Central Government under section 45 and the Central Government is of opinion that any person who has taken part in the promotion or formation of the banking company or has been a director or auditor of the banking company should be publicly examined, that Government may apply to the High Court for the examination of such person and if on such examination the High Court finds (whether a fraud has been committed or not) that that person is not fit to be a director of a company or to act as an auditor of a company or to be a partner of a firm acting as such auditors, the Central Government shall make an order that that person shall not, without the leave of the Central Government, be a director of, or in any way, whether directly or indirectly, be concerned or take part in the management of any company or, as the case may be, act as an auditor of, or be a partner of a firm acting as auditors of, any company for such period not exceeding five years as may be specified in the order.

(4) Where 19[a scheme of reconstruction or amalgamation of a banking company] has been sanctioned by the Central Government under section 45, the provisions of section 543 of the Companies Act, 1956 (1 of 1956), and of section 45H of this Act shall, as far as may be, apply to the banking company as they apply to a banking company which is being wound up as if the order sanctioning the scheme of reconstruction or amalgamation, as the case may be, were an order for the winding up of the banking company; and any reference in the said section 543 to the application of the official liquidator shall be construed as a reference to the application of the Central Government.]

45M. Special provisions for banking companies working under schemes of arrangement at the commencement of the Amendment Act.-Where any compromise or arrangement sanctioned in respect of a banking company under 20[section 391 of the Companies Act, 1956 (1 of 1956)] is being worked at the commencement of the Banking Companies (Amendment) Act, 1953 (52 of 1953) the High Court may, if it so thinks fit, on the application of such banking company,-

(a) excuse any delay in carrying out any of the provisions of the compromise or arrangement; or

(b) allow the banking company to settle the list of its debtors in accordance with the provisions of section 45D and in such a case, the provisions of the said section shall, as far as may be, apply to the banking company as they apply to a banking company which is being wound up as if the order sanctioning the compromise or arrangement were an order for the winding up of the banking company.

45N. Appeals.-(1) An Appeal shall lie from any order or decision of the High Court in a civil proceeding under this Act when the amount or value of the subject-matter of the claim exceeds five thousand rupees.

(2) The High Court may by rules provide for an appeal against any order made under section 45J and the conditions subject to which any such appeal would lie.

(3) Subject to the provisions of sub-section (1) and sub-section (2)and notwithstanding anything contained in any other law for the time being in force, every order or decision of the High Court shall be final and binding for all purposes as between the banking company on the one hand, and all persons who are parties thereto and all persons claiming through or under them or any of them, on the other hand.

45O. Special period of limitation.-(1) Notwithstanding anything to the contrary contained in the Indian Limitation Act, 1908 (9 of 1908) or in any other law for the time being in force, in computing the period of limitation prescribed for a suit or application by a banking company which is being wound up, the period commencing from the date of the presentation of the petition for the winding up of the banking company shall be excluded.

(2) Notwithstanding anything to the contrary contained in the Indian Limitation Act, 1908 (9 of 1908) or 21[section 543 of the Companies Act, 1956(1 of 1956)] or in any other law for the time being in force, there shall be no period of limitation for the recovery of arrears of calls from any director of a banking company which is being wound up or for the enforcement by the banking company against any of its directors of any claim based on a contract, express or implied; and in respect of all other claims by the banking company against its directors, the period of limitation shall be twelve years from the date of the accrual of such claims 22[or five years from the date of the first appointment of the liquidator, whichever is longer].

(3) The provisions of this section, Insofar as they relate to banking companies being wound up, shall also apply to a banking company in respect of which a petition for the winding up has been presented before the commencement of the Banking Companies (Amendment) Act, 1953 (52 of 1953).

45P. Reserve Bank to tender advice in winding up proceeding.-Where in any proceeding for the winding up of a banking company in which any person other than the Reserve Bank has been appointed as the official liquidator and the High Court has directed the official liquidator to obtain the advice of the Reserve Bank on any matter (which it is hereby empowered to do), it shall be lawful for the Reserve Bank to examine the record of any such proceeding and tender such advice on the matter as it may think fit.

45Q. Power to Inspect.-(1) The Reserve Bank shall, on being directed so to do by the Central Government or by the High Court, cause an Inspection to be made by one or more of its officers of a banking company which is being wound up and its books and accounts.

(2) On such Inspection, the Reserve Bank shall submit its report to the Central Government and the High Court.

(3) If the Central Government, on consideration of the report of the Reserve Bank, is of opinion that there has been a substantial irregularity in the winding up proceedings, it may bring such irregularity to the notice of the High Court for such action as the High Court may think fit.

(4) On receipt of the report of the Reserve Bank under sub-section (2) or on any irregularity being brought to its notice by the Central Government under sub-section (3), the High Court may, if it deems fit, after giving notice to and hearing the Central Government in regard to the report, give such directions as it may consider necessary.

45R. Power to call for returns and information.-The Reserve Bank may, at any time by a notice in writing, require the liquidator of a banking company to furnish it, within such time as may be specified in the notice or such further time as the Reserve Bank may allow, any statement or information relating to or connected with the winding up of the banking company;

and it shall be the duty of every liquidator to comply with such requirements.

Explanation.-For the purposes of this section and section 45Q, a banking company working under a compromise or arrangement but prohibited from receiving fresh deposits, shall, as far as may be, deemed to be banking company which is being wound up.

45S. Chief Presidency Magistrate and District Magistrate to assist official liquidator in taking charge of property of banking company being wound up-(1) For the purpose of enabling the official liquidator or the special officer appointed under sub-section (3) of section 37 to take into his custody or under his control, all property, effects and actionable claims to which a banking company 23[***] is or appears to be entitled, the official liquidator or the special officer, as the case may be, may request in writing the 24[Chief Metropolitan Magistrate or the Chief Judicial Magistrate], within whose jurisdiction any property, books of accounts or other documents of such banking company may be situate or be found, to take possession thereof, and the 24[Chief Metropolitan Magistrate or the Chief Judicial Magistrate], as the case may be, shall, on such request being made to him,-

25[(a)take possession of such property, books of accounts or other documents, and

(b) forward them to the official liquidator or the special officer.]

26[(2) Where any such property and effects are in the possession of the 24[Chief Metropolitan Magistrate or the Chief Judicial Magistrate], as the case may be, such Magistrate shall, on request in writing being made to him by the official liquidator or the special officer referred to in sub-section (1), sell such property and effects and forward the net proceeds of the sole to the official liquidator or the special officer:

Provided that such sale shall, as far as practicable, be effected by public auction.

(3) For the purpose of securing compliance with the provisions of sub-section (1), the 24[Chief Metropolitan Magistrate or the Chief Judicial Magistrate] may take or cause

to be taken such steps and use of cause to be used such fore as may, in his opinion, be necessary.

(4) No act of the 24[Chief Metropolitan Magistrate or the Chief Judicial Magistrate] done in pursuance of this section shall be called in question in any court or before any authority.]

45T. Enforcement of orders and decisions of High Court.- (1) All orders made in any civil proceeding by a High Court may be enforced in the same manner in which decrees of such court made in any suit pending therein may be enforced.

(2)Notwithstanding anything to the contrary contained in the Code of Civil Procedure, 1908(5 of 1908), a liquidator may apply for the execution of a decree by a court, other than the one which made it on production of a certificate granted under subsection (6) of section 45D and on his certifying to such other court in writing the amount remaining due or relief remaining unenforced under the decree.

(3) Without prejudice to the provisions of sub-section (1) or sub-section (2), any amount found due to the banking company by an order or decision of the High Court, may, with the leave of the High Court, be recovered 27[by the liquidator in the same manner as an arrear of land revenue and for the purpose of such recovery the liquidator may forward to the Collector within whose jurisdiction the property of the person against whom any order or decision of the High Court has been made is situate, a certificate under his signature specifying the amount so due and the person by whom it is payable].

28[(4) On receipt of a certificate under sub-section (3), the Collector shall proceed to recover from such person the amount specified therein as if it were an arrear of land revenue:

Provided that without prejudice to any other powers of the Collector, he shall, for the purposes of recovering the said amount, have all the powers which, under the Code of Civil Procedure, 1908 (5 of 1908), a civil court has for the purpose of the recovery of an amount due under a decree.]

45U. Power of High Court to make rules.-The High Court may make rules consistent with this Act and the rules made under section 52 prescribing-

(a) the manner in which inquiries and proceedings under Part III or Part IIIA may be held;

(b) the offences which may be tried summarily;

(c) the authority to which, and the conditions subject to which, appeals may be preferred and the manner in which such appeals may be filed and heard;

(d) any other matter for which provision has to be made for enabling the High Court to effectively exercise its functions under this Act.

45V. References to directors, etc., shall be construed as including references to past directors, etc.-For the removal of doubts it is hereby declared that any reference in this Part to a director, manager, liquidator, officer or auditor of a banking company shall be construed as including a reference to any past or present director, manager, liquidator, officer or auditor of the banking company.

45W. Part II not to apply to banking companies being wound up.-Nothing contained in Part II shall apply to a banking company which is being wound up.

45X. Validation of certain proceedings.-Notwithstanding anything contained in section 45B or any other provision of this Part or in section 11 of the Banking Companies (Amendment) Act, 1950 (20 of 1950), no proceeding held, judgment delivered or decree or order made before the commencement of the Banking Companies (Amendment) Act, 1953 (52 of 1953), by any court other than the High Court in respect of any matter over which the High Court has jurisdiction under this Act shall be invalid or be deemed ever to have been invalid merely by reason of the fact that such proceeding, judgment, decree or order was held, delivered or made by a court other man the High Court.]

PROVISIONS RELATING TO CERTAIN OPERATIONS OF BANKING COMPANIES

45Y. Power of Central Government to make rules for the preservation of records.-The Central Government may, after consultation with the Reserve Bank and by notification in the Official Gazette, make rules specifying the periods for which-

(a) a banking company shall preserve its books, accounts and other documents; and

(b) a banking company shall preserve and keep with itself different instruments paid by it.

45Z. Return of paid instruments to customers.-(1) Where a banking company is required by its customer to return to him a paid instrument before the expiry of the period specified by rules made under section 45 Y, the banking company shall not return the instrument except after making and keeping in its possession a true copy of all relevant parts of such instrument, such copy being made by a mechanical or other process which in itself ensures the accuracy of the copy.

(2) The banking company shall be entitled to recover from the customer the cost of making such copies of the instrument.

Explanation.-In this section, "customer" includes a Government department and a corporation incorporated by or under any law.

45ZA. Nomination for payment of depositors' money.-(1) Where a deposit is held by a banking company to the credit of one or more persons, the depositor or, as the case may be, all the depositors together, may nominate, in the prescribed manner, one person to whom in the event of the death of the sole depositor or the death of all the depositors, the amount of deposit may be returned by the banking company.

(2) Notwithstanding anything contained in any other law for the time being in force or in any disposition, whether testamentary or otherwise, in respect of such deposit, where a nomination made in the prescribed manner purports to confer on any person the right to receive the amount of deposit from the banking company, the nominee shall, on the death of the sole depositor or, as the case may be, on the death of all the depositors, become entitled to all the rights of the sole depositor or, as the case may be, of the depositors, in relation to such deposit to the exclusion of all other persons, unless the nomination is varied or cancelled in the prescribed manner.

(3) Where the nominee is a minor, it shall be lawful for the depositor making the nomination to appoint in the prescribed manner any person to receive the amount of deposit in the event of his death during the minority of the nominee.

(4) Payment by a banking company in accordance with the provisions of this section shall constitute a full discharge to the banking company of its liability in respect of the deposit: Provided that nothing contained in this sub-section shall affect

the right or claim which any person may have against the person to whom any payment is made under this section.

45ZB. Notice of claims of other persons regarding deposits not receivable.-No notice of the claim of any person, other than the person or persons in whose name a deposit is held by a banking company, shall be receivable by the banking company, nor shall the banking company be bound by any such notice though even expressly given to it:

Provided that where any decree, order, certificate or other authority from a court of competent jurisdiction relating to such deposit is produced before a banking company, the banking company shall take due note of such decree, order, certificate or other authority.

45ZC. Nomination for return of articles kept in safe custody with banking company.-(1) Where any person leaves any article in safe custody with a banking company, such person may nominate, in the prescribed manner, on person to whom, in the event of the death of the person leaving the article in safe custody, such article may be returned by the banking company.

(2) Where the nominee is a minor, it shall be lawful for the person making the nomination to appoint in the prescribed manner any person to receive the article deposited in the event of his death during the minority of the nominee.

(3) The banking company shall, before returning any articles under this section to the nominee or the person appointed under sub-section (2), prepare, in such manner as may be directed by the Reserve Bank from time to time, an inventory of the said articles which shall be signed by such nominee or person and shall deliver a copy of the inventory so prepared to such nominee or person.

(4) Notwithstanding anything contained in any other law for the time being in force or in any disposition, whether testamentary or otherwise, in respect of such article, where a nomination made in the prescribed manner purports to confer on any person the right to receive the article from the banking company, the nominee shall, on the death of the person leaving the article in safe custody, become entitled to the return of the article to the exclusion of all other persons, unless the nomination is varied or cancelled in the prescribed manner:

Provided that nothing contained in this section shall affect the right or claim which any person may have against the person to whom the article is returned in pursuance of this sub-section.

45ZD. Notice of claims of other persons regarding articles not receivable.-No notice of the claim of any person, other than the person or persons in whose name any article is held by a banking company in safe custody, shall be receivable by the banking company, nor shall the banking company be bound by any such notice even though expressly given to it:

Provided that where any decree, order, certificate or other authority from a court of competent jurisdiction relating to such article is produced before a banking company, the banking company shall take due note of such decree, order, certificate or other authority.

45ZE. Release of contents of safety lockers.-(1) Where an individual is the sole hirer of a locker from a banking company, whether such locker is located in the safe deposit vault of such banking company or elsewhere, such individual may nominate one person to whom, in the event of the death of such individual, the banking company may give access to the locker and liberty to remove the contents of the locker.

(2) Where any such locker is hired from a banking company by two or more individuals jointly and under the contract of hire, the locker is to be operated under the joint signatures of two or more of such hirers, such hirers may nominate one or more persons to whom, in the event of the death of such joint hirer or hirers, the banking company may give, jointly with the surviving joint hirer or joint hirers, as the case may be, access to the locker and liberty to remove the contents of such locker.

(3) Every nomination under sub-section (1) or sub-section (2) shall be made in the prescribed manner.

(4) The banking company shall, before permitting the removal of the contents of any locker by any nominee or jointly by any nominee and survivors as aforesaid, prepare, in such manner as may be directed by the Reserve Bank from time to time, an inventory of the contents of the locker which shall be signed by such nominee or jointly by such nominee and survivors and shall deliver a copy of the inventory so prepared to such nominee or nominee and survivors.

(5) On the removal of the contents of any locker by any nominee or jointly by any nominee and survivors as aforesaid, the liability of the banking company in relation to the contents of the locker shall stand discharged.

(6) No suit, prosecution or other legal proceedings shall lie against a banking company for any damage caused or likely to be caused, for allowing access to any locker, and liberty to remove the contents of such locker, in pursuance of the provisions of subsection (1) or sub-section (2) as the case may be.

45ZF. Notice of claims of oilier persons regarding safety lockers not receivable.-No notice of the claim of any person, other than hirer or hirers of a locker, shall be receivable by a banking company nor shall the banking company be bound by any such notice even though expressly given to it:

Provided that where any decree, order, certificate or other authority from a court of competent jurisdiction relating to the locker or its contents is produced before the banking company, the banking company shall take due note of such decree, order, certificate or other authority.]

MISCELLANEOUS

46. Penalties.-

(1) Whoever in any return, balance-sheet or other document 1[or in any information required or furnished] by or under or for the purposes of any provision of this Act, wilfully makes a statement which is false in any material particular, knowing it to be false, or wilfully omits to make a material statement, shall be punishable with imprisonment for a term which may extend to three years and shall also be liable to fine.

(2) If any person fails to produce any book, account or other document or to furnish any statement or information which under sub-section (2) of section 35 it is his duty to produce or furnish, or to answer any question relating to the business of a banking company which is asked by 2[an officer making an inspection or scrutiny under that section.] he shall be punishable with a fine which may extend to 3[two thousand rupees] in respect of each offence, and if he persists in such refusal, to a further fine which may extend to 4[one hundred rupees] for every day during which the offence continues.

(3) If any deposits are received by a banking company in contravention of an order under clause (a)of sub-section (4) of section 35, every director or other officer of the banking company, unless he proves that the contravention took place without his knowledge or that he exercised all due diligence to prevent it shall be deemed to be guilty of such contravention and shall be punishable with a fine which may extend to twice the amount of the deposits so received.

5[6[7[(4) If any other provision of this Act is contravened or if any default is made in-

(i) complying with any requirement of this Act or of any order, rule or direction made or condition imposed thereunder, or

(ii) carrying out the terms of, or the obligations under, a scheme sanctioned under sub-section (7) of section 45, by any person, such person shall be punishable with fine which may extend to 8[fifty thousand rupees or twice the amount involved in such contravention or default where such amount is quantifiable, whichever is more, and where a contravention or default is a continuing one, with a further fine which may extend to two thousand and five hundred rupees] for every day, during which the contravention or default continues.]

(5) Where a contravention or default has been committed by a company, every person who, at the time the contravention or default was committed, was in charge of, and was responsible to, the company, for the conduct of the business of the company, as well as the company, shall be deemed to be guilty of the contravention or default and shall be liable to be proceeded against and punished accordingly:

Provided that nothing contained in this sub-section shall render any such person liable to any punishment provided in this Act if he proves that the contravention or default was committed without his knowledge or that he exercised all due diligence to prevent the contravention or default.

(6) Notwithstanding anything contained in sub-section (5), where a contravention or default has been committed by a company, and it is proved that the same was committed with the consent or connivance of, or is attributable to any gross negligence on the part of, any director, manager, secretary or

other officer of the company, such director, manager, secretary or other officer shall also be deemed to be guilty of that contravention or default and shall be liable to be proceeded against and punished accordingly.

Explanation.-For the purposes of this section,-

(a) "company" means any body corporate and includes a firm or other association of individuals, and

(b) "direction", in relation to a firm, means a partner in the firm.]

9[***]

10[46A. Chairman, director, etc., to be public servants for the purposes of Chapter IX of the Indian Penal Code.-11[Every Chairman who is appointed on a whole-time basis, managing director, director, auditor] liquidator, manager and any other employee of a banking company shall be deemed to be a public servant for the purposes of Chapter IX of the Indian Penal Code (45 of 1860).]

47. Cognizance of offences.-No court shall take a cognizance of any offence punishable under 12[sub-section (5)of section 36AA or] section 46 except upon complaint in writing made by an officer of 13[the Reserve Bank or, as the case may be, the National Bank] generally or specially authorised in writing in this behalf by 14[the Reserve Bank, or as the case may be, the National Bank] and 15[no court other than that of a Metropolitan Magistrate or a Judicial Magistrate of the first class or any court superior thereto] shall try any such offence.

16[47A. Power of Reserve Bank to impose penalty.-(1)Notwithstanding anything contained in section 46, if a contravention or default of the nature referred to in subsection (3) or sub-section (4) of section 46, as the case may be, is made by a banking company, then, the Reserve Bank may impose on such banking company-

(a) where the contravention is of the nature referred to in sub-section (3) of section 46, a penalty not exceeding twice the amount of the deposits in respect of which such contravention was made;

(b) where the contravention or default is of the nature referred to in sub-section (4) of section 46, a penalty not exceeding 17[five lakh rupees or twice the amount involved in such contravention or default where such amount is quantifiable, whichever is more, and where such the contravention or default is a continuing one, a further penalty which may extend to twenty-five thousand rupees] for every day, after the first, during which the contravention of default continues.

18[(2) For the purpose of adjudging the penalty under sub-section (1), the Reserve Bank shall serve notice on the banking company requiring it to show cause why the amount specified in the notice should not be imposed and a reasonable opportunity of being heard shall also be given to such banking company.]

(4) No complaint shall be filed against any banking company in any court of law in respect of any contravention or default in respect of which any penalty has been imposed by the Reserve Bank under this section.

(5) Any penalty imposed by the Reserve Bank under this section shall be payable within a period of fourteen days from the date on which notice issued by the Reserve Bank demanding payment of the sum is served on the banking company and in the event of failure of the banking company to pay the sum within such period, may be levied on a direction made by the principal civil court having jurisdiction in the area where the registered office of the banking company is situated; or, in the case of a banking company incorporated outside India, where its principal place of business in India is situated:

Provided that no such direction shall be made except on an application made to the court by the Reserve Bank or any officer authorised by that Bank in this behalf.

(6) The court which makes a direction under sub-section (5) shall issue a certificate specifying the sum payable by the banking company and every such certificate shall be enforceable in the same manner as if it were a decree made by the court in a civil suit.

(7) Where any complaint has been filed against any banking company in any court in respect of the contravention or default of the nature referred to in sub-section (3) or, as the case may be, sub-section (4) of section 46, then, no proceedings for the imposition of any penalty on the banking company shall be taken under this section.]

48. Application of fines.-A court imposing any fine under this Act may direct that the whole or any part thereof shall be applied in or towards payment of the costs of the proceedings, or in or towards the rewarding of the person on whose information the fine is recovered.

49. Special provisions for private banking companies.-The exemptions, whether express or implied, in favour of a private company in 19[sections 90, 165, 182, 204 and 255, clauses (a) and (b) of sub-section (1) of section 293 and sections 300, 388A and 416 of the Companies Act, 1956 (1 of 1956)], shall not operate in favour of a private company which is a banking company.

20[49A. Restriction on acceptance of deposits withdrawable by cheque.-No person other than a banking company, the Reserve Bank, the State Bank of India or any other 21[banking institution, firm or other person notified by the Central Government in this behalf on the recommendation of the Reserve Bank] shall accept from the public deposits of money withdrawable by cheque: Provided that nothing contained in this section shall apply to any savings bank scheme run by the Government.

49B. Change of name by a banking company.-Notwithstanding anything contained in section 21 of the Companies Act, 1956 (1 of 1956), the Central Government shall not signify its approval to the change of name of any banking company unless the Reserve Bank certifies in writing that it has no objection to such change.

49C. Alteration of memorandum of a banking company.-Notwithstanding anything contained in the Companies Act, 1956 (1 of 1956), no application for the confirmation of the alteration of the memorandum of a banking company shall be maintainable unless the Reserve Bank certifies that there is no objection to such alteration.]

50. Certain claims for compensation barred.-No person shall have any right, whether in contract or otherwise, to any compensation for any loss incurred by reason of the operation of any of the provisions 22[contained in sections 10, 12A, 16, 35A, 35B, 23[36, 43A and 45] or by reason of the compliance by a banking company with any order or direction given to it under this Act].

24[51. Application of certain provisions to the State Bank of India and other notified banks.-25[(1)] Without prejudice to the provisions of the State Bank of India Act, 1955(23 of 1955) or any other enactment, the provisions of sections 10, 13 to 15, 17, 26[19 to 21A, 23 to 28, 29] excluding sub-section (3) 27[sub-section (1B), (1C) and (2) of sections 30, 31,] 34, 35, 35A, 36 [excluding clause(a) of sub-section(1)] 45Y to 45ZF, 46 to 48] 50, 52 and 53 shall also apply; so far as may be, to and in relation to the State Bank of India 28[or any corresponding new bank or a Regional Rural Bank or any subsidiary bank] as they apply to and in relation to banking companies:

29[Provided that-

(a) nothing contained in clause (c) of sub-section (1) of section 10 shall apply to the chairman of the State Bank of India or to a 30[managing director] of any subsidiary bank insofar as the said clause precludes him from being a director of, or holding an office in, any institution approved by the Reserve Bank;

31[(b) nothing contained in sub-clause (iii) of clause (b) of sub-section (!) of section 20 shall apply to any bank referred to in sub-section (1), insofar as the said sub-clause (iii) of clause (b) precludes that bank from entering into any commitment for granting any loan or advance to or on behalf of a company (not being a Government company) in which not less than forty per cent of the paid-up capital is held (whether singly or taken together) by the Central Government or the Reserve Bank or a corporation owned by that bank; and

(c) nothing contained in section 46 or in section 47A shall apply to,-

(i) an officer of the Central Government or the Reserve Bank, nominated or appointed as director of the State Bank of India or any corresponding new bank or a Regional Rural Bank or any subsidiary bank or a banking company; or

(ii) an officer of the State Bank of India or a corresponding new bank or a Regional Rural Bank or a subsidiary bank nominated or appointed as director of any of the said banks (not being the bank of which he is an officer) or of a banking company.;]

32[***]

33[(2) References to a banking company in any rule or direction relating to any provision of this Act referred to in sub-section (1) shall, except where such rule or direction provides otherwise, be construed as referring also to the State Bank of India, a corresponding new bank, a Regional Rural Bank and a subsidiary bank.]

52. Power of Central Government to make rules.-(1) The Central Government may, after consultation with the Reserve Bank, make rules to provide for all matters for which provision is necessary or expedient for the purpose of giving effect to the provisions of this Act and all such rules shall be published in the Official Gazette.

(2) In particular, and without prejudice to the generality of the foregoing power, such rules may provide for the details to be included in the returns required by (his Act and the manner in which such returns shall be submitted 34[and the form in which the official liquidator may file lists of debtors to the court having jurisdiction under Part III or Part IIIA and the particulars which such lists may contain and any other matter which has to be, or may be, prescribed].

35[***]

34[(4) The Central Government may by rules made under this section annul, alter or add to, all or any of the provisions of the Fourth Schedule.]

36[(5) Every rule made by the Central Government under this Act shall be laid, as soon as may be after it is made, before each House of Parliament, while it is in session, for a total period of thirty days which may be comprised in one session or in two or more successive sessions, and if, before the expiry of the session immediately following the session or the successive sessions aforesaid, both Houses agree in making any modification in the rule or both Houses agree that the rule should not be made, the rule shall thereafter have effect only in such modified form or be of no effect, as the case may be; so, however, that any such modification or annulment shall be without prejudice to the validity of anything previously done under that rule.]

53. Power to exempt in certain cases.-The Central Government may, on the recommendation of the Reserve Bank,

declare, by notification in the Official Gazette, that any or all of the provisions of this Act shall not apply to any banking company 37[or institution] or to any class of banking companies either generally or for such period as may be specified.

54. Protection of action taken under Act.-(1) No suit or other legal proceeding shall be lie against the Central Government, the Reserve Bank or any officer for anything which is in good faith done or intended to be done in pursuance of this Act.

(2) Save as otherwise expressly provided by or under this Act, no suit or other legal proceeding shall lie against the Central Government, the Reserve Bank or any officer for any damage caused or likely to be caused by anything in good faith done or intended to be done in pursuance of this Act.

55. Amendment of Act 2 of 1934.-The Reserve Bank of India Act, 1934 shall be amended in the manner specified in the fourth column of the First Schedule, and the amendments to section 18 thereof as specified in the said Schedule shall be deemed to have had effect on and from the 20th day of September, 1947.

38[55A. Power to remove difficulties.-If any difficulty arises in giving effect to the provisions of this Act, the Central Government may, by order, as occasion requires, do anything (not inconsistent with the provisions of this Act) which appears to it to be necessary for the purpose of removing the difficulty:

Provided that no such power shall be exercised after the expiry of a period of three years from the commencement of section 20 of the Banking Laws (Amendment) Act, 1968 (58 of 1968).]

APPLICATION OF THE ACT TO CO-OPERATIVE BANKS

56. Act to apply to co-operative societies subject to modifications.-The provisions of this Act, as in force for the time being, shall apply to, or in relation to, cooperative societies as they apply to, or in relation to banking companies subject to the following modifications, namely:-

(a) throughout this Act, unless the context otherwise requires,-

(i) references to a "banking company" or "the company" or "such company" shall be construed as references to a co-operative bank;

(ii) reference to "commencement of this Act" shall be construed as reference to commencement of the Banking Laws(Application to Co-operative Societies) Act, 1965 (23 of 1965);

(b) in section 2, the words and figures "the Companies Act, 1956 (1 of 1956) and" shall be omitted;

(c) in section 5,-

1[(i) after clause (cc), the following clauses shall be inserted, namely:-

(cci) "Co-operative bank" means a state co-operative bank, a central co-operative bank and a primary co-operative bank;

(ccii) "co-operative credit society" means a co-operative society, the primary object of which is to provide financial accommodation to its members and includes a co-operative land mortgage bank;

36(cciia) "co-operative society" means a society registered or deemed to have been registered under any Central Act for the time being in force relating to the multi-State Co-operative Societies, or any other Central or State law relating to Co-operative Societies for the time being in force;';

(cciii) "director" in relation to a co-operative society, includes a member of any committee or body for the time being vested with the management of the affairs of that society;

37(cciiia) "multi-State co-operative bank" means a multi-State co-operative society which is a primary co-operative bank;

38(cciiib) "multi-State co-operative society" means a multi-State co-operative society registered as such under any Central Act for the time being in force relating to the multi-State co-operative societies but does not include a national co-operative society and a federal co-operative;';

cciv) "primary agricultural credit society" means a co-operative society,-

(1) the primary object or principal business of which is to provide financial accommodation to its members for agricultural

purposes or for purposes connected with agricultural activities (including the marketing of crops); and

(2) the bye-laws of which do not permit admission of any other co-operative society as member:

Provided that this sub-clause shall not apply to the admission of a co-operative bank as a member by reason of such co-operative bank subscribing to the share capital of such co-operative society out of funds provided by the State Government for the purpose;

(ccv) "primary co-operative bank" means a co-operative society, other than a primary agricultural credit society,-

(1) the primary object or principal business of which is the transaction of banking business;

(2) the paid-up share capital and reserves of which are not less than one lakh of rupees; and

(3) the bye-laws of which do not permit admission of any other co-operative society as a member:

Provided that this sub-clause shall not apply to the admission of a co-operative bank as a member by reason of such co-operative bank subscribing to the share capital of such co-operative society out of funds provided by the State Government for the purpose;

(ccvi) "primary credit society" means a co-operative society, other than a primary agricultural credit society,-

(1) the primary object or principal business of which is the transaction of banking business;

(2) the paid-up share capital and reserves of which are less than one lakh of rupees; and

(3) the bye-laws of which do not permit admission of any other co-operative society as a member;

Provided that this sub-clause shall not apply to the admission of a co-operative bank as a member by reason of such co-operative bank subscribing to the share capital of such co-operative society out of funds provided by the State Government for the purpose.

Explanation.-If any dispute arises as to the primary object or principal business of any co-operative society referred to in clauses (cciv), (ccv) and (ccvi), a determination thereof by the Reserve Bank shall be final;

(ccvii) "central co-operative bank", "39[***]", "primary rural credit society" and "state co-operative bank" shall have the meaning respectively assigned to them in the National Bank for Agriculture and Rural Development Act, 1981;]

2[(ii) clauses (ff), (h) and (nb) shall be omitted;]

(d) for section 5A, the following section shall be substituted, namely:-

"5A. Act to override bye-laws, etc.-(1) The provisions of 3[this Act] shall have effect, notwithstanding anything to the contrary contained in the bye-laws of a co-operative society, or in any agreement executed by it, or in any resolution passed by it in general meeting, or by its Board of Directors or other body entrusted with the management of its affairs, whether the same be registered, executed or passed; as the case may be before or after the commencement of the Banking Laws (Application to Co-operative Societies Act, 1965 (23 of 1965).

(2) Any provision contained in the bye-laws, agreement or resolution aforesaid shall, to the extent to which it is repugnant to the provisions of 2[this Act,] become or be void, as the case may be.";

(e) in section 6, in sub-section (1),-

(i) in clause (b), the words, "but excluding the business of a managing agent or secretary and treasurer of company" shall be omitted;

(ii) in clause (d), after the word "company", the words "co-operative society" shall be inserted;

(iii) in clause (m), after the word "company", the words "or co-operative society" shall be inserted;

4[(f) for section 7, the following section shall be substituted, namely:-

"7. Use of words "bank", "banker" or "banking".-(1)No co-operative society other than a co-operative bank shall use as part of its name or in connection with its business any of the words "bank", "banker" or "banking", and no co-operative society shall carry on the business of banking in India unless it uses as part of its name at least of such words.

(2) Nothing in this section apply to-

(a) a primary credit society, or

(b) a co-operative society formed for the protection of the mutual interest of co-operative banks or co-operative land mortgage banks, or

(c) any co-operative society, not being a primary credit society, formed by the employees of-

(i) a banking company or the State Bank of India or a corresponding new bank or a subsidiary bank of such banking company, State Bank of India or a corresponding new bank, or

(ii) a co-operative bank or a primary credit society or a co-operative land mortgage bank, insofar as the word "bank", "banker" or "banking" appears as part of the name of the employer bank, or as the case may be, of the bank whose subsidiary the employer bank is."];

5[(fi) in section 8, for the proviso, the following proviso shall be substituted, namely:

"Provided that this section shall not apply-

(a) to any such business as aforesaid which was in the course of being transacted on the commencement of clause (iii) of section 42 of the Banking Laws

(Amendment) Act, 1983, so, however, that the said business shall be completed before the expiry of one year from such commencement; or

(b) to any business as is specified in pursuance of clause (o) of sub-section (1) of section 6;";

(fii) in section 9, for the second proviso, the following provisos shall be substituted, namely:-

"Provided further that in the case of a primary credit society which becomes a primary co-operative bank after the commencement of clause (iii) of section 42 of the Banking Laws (Amendment) Act, 1983, the period of seven years shall commence from the day it so becomes a primary co-operative bank:

Provided also that the Reserve Bank may, in any particular case, extend the aforesaid period of seven years by such period

as it may consider necessary where it is satisfied that such extension would be in the interests of the depositors of the co-operative bank."];

(g) 6[sections 10, 10A, 7[10B, 10BB, 10C], and 10D] shall be omitted;

(h) for section 11, the following section shall be substituted, namely:-

"11. Requirement as to minimum paid-up capital and reserves.-(1) Notwithstanding any law relating to co-operative societies for the time being in force, no co-operative bank shall commence or carry on the business of banking in India unless the aggregate value of its paid-up capital and reserves is not less than one lakh of rupees:

Provided that nothing in this sub-section shall apply to-

(a) any such bank which is carrying on such business at the commencement of the Banking Laws (Application to Co-operative Societies) Act, 1965 (23 of 1965), for a period of three years from such commencement; or

(b) to a primary credit society which becomes a primary co-operative bank after such commencement, for a period of two years from the date it so becomes a primary co-operative bank or for such further period not exceeding one year, the Reserve Bank, having regard to the interests of the depositors of the primary co-operative bank, may think fit in any particular case to allow.

(2) For the purpose of this section, "value" means the real or exchangeable value and not the nominal value which may be shown in the books of the co-operative bank concerned.

(3) If any dispute arises in computing the aggregate value of the paid-up capital and reserves of any co-operative bank, a determination thereof by the Reserve Bank shall be final for the purposes of this section;]

(i) sections 12, !2A, 13 and 15 to 17 shall be omitted;

6[(j)) For section 18, the following section shall be substituted, namely:-

18. Cash reserve.-(1) Every co-operative bank, not being a State cooperative bank for the time being included in the Second Schedule to the Reserve Bank of India

Act, 1934 (hereinafter referred to as a "scheduled State Co-operative Bank"), shall maintain in India by way of cash reserve with itself or by way of balance in a current account with the Reserve Bank or the State co-operative bank of the State concerned or by way of net balance in current accounts, or, in the case of a primary co-operative bank, with the central cooperative bank of the district concerned, or in one or more of the aforesaid ways, a sum equivalent to at least three per cent of the total of its demand and time liabilities in India, as on the last Friday of the second preceding fortnight and shall submit to the Reserve Bank before the fifteenth day of every month a return showing the amount so held on alternate Fridays during a month with particulars of its demand and time liabilities in India on such Fridays or if any such Friday is a public holiday under the Negotiable Instruments Act, 1881 (26 of 1881) at the close of business on the preceding working day.

Explanation.-In this section and in section 24-

(a) "liabilities in India" shall not include-

(i) the paid-up capital or the reserves or any credit balance in the profit and loss account of the co-operative bank;

(ii) any advance taken from a State Government, the Reserve Bank, the Development Bank, the Exim Bank, 7[the Reconstruction Bank,] 8[the National Housing Bank] the National Bank 9[the Small Industries Bank] or from the National Co-operative Development Corporation established under section 3 of the National Co-operative Development Corporation Act, 1962 (26 of 1962), by the bank;

(iii) in the case of a State or Central co-operative bank, also any deposit of money with it representing the reserves fund or any part thereof maintained with it by any other co-operative society within its area of operation, and in the case a Central co-operative bank, also an advance taken by it from the State co-operative bank of the State concerned;

(iv) in the case of a primary co-operative bank, also any advance taken by it from the State co-operative bank of the State concerned or the Central cooperative bank of the district concerned;

(v) in the case of any co-operative bank, which has granted an advance against any balance maintained with it, such balance to the extent of the amount outstanding in respect of such advance; and

(vi) in the case of any co-operative bank, the amount of any advance or other credit arrangement drawn and availed of against approved securities;

(b) "fortnight" shall mean the period from Saturday to the second following Friday, both days inclusive;

(c) "net balance in current accounts" shall, in relation to a co-operative bank, mean the excess, if any, of the aggregate of the credit balances in current account maintained by that co-operative bank with the State Bank of India or a subsidiary bank or a corresponding new bank, over the aggregate of the credit balances in current accounts held by the said banks with such co-operative bank;

(d) for the purpose of computation of liabilities, the aggregate of the liabilities of a co-operative bank to the State Bank of India, a subsidiary bank, a corresponding new bank, a Regional Rural bank, a banking company or any other financial institution notified by the Central Government in this behalf shall be reduced by the aggregate of the liabilities of all such banks and institutions to the cooperative bank;

(e) any cash with a co-operative bank or any balance held by a co-operative bank with another bank, shall not, to the extent such cash or such balances represents the balance in, or investment of, Agricultural Credit Stabilisation Fund of such co-operative bank, be deemed to be cash maintained in India.

(2) The Reserve Bank may, for the purposes of this section and section 24, specify from time to time, with reference to any transaction or class of transactions, that such transaction or transactions shall be regarded as liability in India of a co-operative bank, and, if any question arises to whether any transaction or class of transactions shall be regarded for the purposes of this section and section24, as liability in India of a co-operative bank, the decision of the Reserve Bank thereon, shall be final."];

(k) for section 19, the following section shall be substituted, namely:-

"19. Restriction on holding shares in other co-operative societies.-No co-operative bank shall hold shares in any other co-operative society except to such extent and subject to such conditions as the Reserve Bank may specify in that behalf:

Provided that nothing contained in this section shall apply to-

(i) shares acquired through funds provided by the State Government for that purpose;

(ii) in the case of a Central co-operative bank, the holding of shares in the State co-operative bank to which it is affiliated;

(iii) in the case of a primary co-operative bank, the holding of shares in the Central co-perative bank to which it is affiliated or in the State cooperative bank of the State in which it is registered:

Provided further that where any shares are held by a co-operative bank in contravention of this section at the commencement of the Banking Laws (Application to Co-operative Societies) Act, 1965 (23 of 1965), the co-operative bank shall without delay report the matter to the Reserve Bank and shall, notwithstanding anything contained in this section, be entitled to hold the shares for such period and on such conditions as the Reserve Bank may specify"

10[(1) for section 20 of the principal Act, the following section shall be substituted, namely:

"20. Restrictions on loans and advances.-(1) No co-operative bank shall-

(a) make any loans or advances on the security of its own shares; or

(b) grant unsecured loans or advances-

(i) to any of its directors; or

(ii) to firms or private companies in which any of its directors is interested as partner of managing agent or guarantor or to individuals in cases where any of its directors is a guarantor; or

(iii) to any company in which the chairman of the Board of directors of the co-operative bank (where the appointment of a chairman is for a fixed term) is interested as its managing agent, or where there is no managing agent, as its chairman or managing director:

Provided that nothing in clause (b) shall apply to the grant of unsecured loans or advances-

(a) made by a co-operative bank-

(i) against bills for supplies or services made or rendered to government or bills of exchange arising out of bona fide commercial or trade transactions, or

(ii) in respect whereof trust-receipts are furnished to the co-operative bank;

(b) made by a primary co-operative bank to any of its directors or to any other person within such limits and on such terms and conditions as may be approved by the Reserve Bank in this behalf.

(2) Every co-operative bank shall, before the close of the month succeeding that to which the return relates, submit to the Reserve Bank a return in the prescribed form and manner showing all unsecured loans and advances granted by it to companies in cases [other than those in which the co-operative bank is prohibited under sub-section (1) to make unsecured loans and advances] in which any of its directors is interested as director or managing agent or guarantor.

(3) If, on examination of any return submitted under sub-section (2), it appears to the Reserve Bank that any loans or advances referred to in that subsection are being granted to the detriment of the interests of the depositors of the co-operative bank, the Reserve Bank may, by order in writing prohibit the co-operative bank from granting any such further loans or advances or impose such restrictions on the grant thereof as it thinks fit, and may by like order direct the co-operative bank to secure the re-payment of such loans or advance within such time as may be specified in the order";

11[(m) in section 20A, in sub-section (1).-

(i) the words and figures "Notwithstanding anything to the contrary contained in section 293 of the Companies Act, 1956 (1 of 1956)," shall be omitted;

(ii) in clause (a), for the words "any of its directors", the words "any of its past or present directors" shall be substituted;]

(n) in section 21, in sub-section (2), in clauses (c) and (d), for the words "any one company, firm, association of persons or individuals", the words "any one party" shall be substituted;

(o) in section 22,-

(i) for sub-sections(1) and (2) the following sub-sections shall be substituted, namely:-

"(1) Save as hereinafter provided, no co-operative society shall carry on banking business in India unless-

(a) it is a primary credit society, or

(b) it is a co-operative bank and holds a licence issued in that behalf by the Reserve Bank, to such conditions, if any, as the Reserve Bank may deem fit to impose:

Provided that nothing in this sub-section shall apply to a co-operative society, not being a primary credit society or a co-operative bank carrying on banking business at the commencement of the Banking Laws (Application to Co-operative

Societies) Act, 1965 (23 of 1965), for a period of one year from such commencement.

12[(2) Every co-operative society carrying on business as a co-operative bank at the commencement of the Banking Laws (Application to Co-operative Societies) Act, 1965 (23 of 1965) shall before the expiry of three months from the commencement, every co-operative bank which comes into existence as a result of the division of any other co-operative society carrying on business as a co-operative bank, or the amalgamation of two or more co-operative societies carrying on banking business shall, before the expiry of three months from its so coming into existence, every primary credit society which becomes a primary co-operative bank after such commencement shall before the expiry of three months from the date on which it so becomes a primary co-operative bank and every co-operative society other than a primary credit society shall before commencing banking Business in India, apply in writing to the Reserve Bank for a licence under this section: Provided that nothing in clause (b) of sub-section (1) shall be deemed to prohibit-

(i) a co-operative society carrying on business as a co-operative bank at the commencement of the Banking Law

(Application to Co-operative Societies) Act, 1965 (23 of 1965); or

(ii) a co-operative bank which has come into existence as a result of the division of any other co-operative society carrying on business as a cooperative bank, or the amalgamation of two or more co-operative societies carrying on banking business at the commencement of the Banking Laws (Application to Co-operative Societies) Act, 1965 (23 of 1965) or at any time thereafter; or

(iii) a primary credit society which becomes a primary Co-operative bank after such commencement, from carrying on banking business until it is granted a licence in pursuance of this section or is, by a notice in writing notified by the Reserve Bank that the licence cannot be granted to it.]"

13[(ii) sub-section (3A) shall be omitted;

(iii) in sub-section (4) in clause (iii)the words, brackets, figures and letter "and sub-section (3A)" shall be omitted;]

22A Validation of licences granted by Reserve Bank to multi-State co-operative societies.--Notwithstanding anything contained in any law or, judgment delivered or decree or order of any court made,--

(a) no licence, granted to a multi-

14[(p) in section 23,-

(i) for sub-section (1), the following sub-section shall be substituted, namely:-]

"(1) Without obtaining the prior permission of the Reserve Bank, no co-operative bank shall open a new place of business or change otherwise than within the same city, town or village, the location of an existing place of business:

Provided that nothing in this sub-section shall apply to-

(a) the opening for a period not exceeding one month of temporary place of business within a city, town or village or the environs thereof within which the co-operative bank already has a place of business, for the purpose of affording banking facilities to the public on the occasion of an exhibition, a conference or a mela or any like occasion;

(b) the 15[opening or changing the location of branches] by a Central cooperative bank within the area of its operation";

16(ii) after sub-section (4), the following sub-section shall be inserted, namely:-

"(4A) Any co-operative bank other than a primary co-operative bank requiring the permission of the Reserve Bank under this section shall forward its application to the Reserve Bank through the National Bank which shall give its comments on the merits of the application and sent it to the Reserve Bank:

Provided that the co-operative bank shall also send an advance copy of the application directly to the Reserve Bank."];

17[(q) in section 24,-

(i) in sub-section (1) the words "After the expiry of two years from the commencement of this Act" shall be omitted;

(ii) for sub-section (2) and (2A), the following sub-sections shall be substituted, namely:-

"(2) In computing the amount for the purposes of sub-section (1),-

(a) any balances maintained in India by a co-operative bank in current account with the Reserve Bank or by way of net balance in current accounts, and in the case of a scheduled State Co-operative Bank, also the balance required under section 42 of the Reserve Bank of India Act, 1934 (2 of 1934), to be so maintained,

(b) any balances maintained by a Central co-operative bank with the State co-operative bank of the State concerned, and

(c) any balances maintained by a primary co-operative bank with Central co-operative bank of the district concerned or with the State cooperative bank of the State concerned, shall be deemed to be cash maintained in India.

(2A)(a) Notwithstanding anything contained in sub-section (1) or in sub-section (2), after the expiry of two years from the commencement of the Banking Laws (Application to Co-operative Societies) Act, 1965(23 of 1965), or of such further period not exceeding one year as the Reserve Bank, having regard to the interests of the co-operative bank concerned, may think fit in any particular case to allow:-

(i) a scheduled State co-operative bank, in addition to the average daily balance which it is or may be, required to maintain under section 42 of the Reserve Bank of India Act, 1934 (2 of 1934), and

(ii) every other co-operative bank, in addition to the cash reserve which is required to maintain under section 18, shall maintain in India, in cash, or in gold valued at a price not exceeding the current market price or in unencumbered approved securities valued at a price determined in accordance with such one or more of, or combination of, the following methods of valuation namely, valuation with reference to cost price, market price, book value or face value, as may be specified by the Reserve Bank from time to time, an amount which shall not, at the close of business on any day, be less than twenty-five per cent or such other percentage not exceeding four per cent as the Reserve Bank may, from time to time, by notification in the Official Gazette, specify, of the total of its demand and time liabilities in India, as on the last Friday of the second preceding fortnight.

(b) In computing the amount for the purpose of clause (a), the following shall be deemed to be cash maintained in India, namely:-

(i) any balance maintained by scheduled State co-operative bank with the Reserve Bank in excess of the balance required to be maintained by it under section 42 of the Reserve Bank of India Act, 1934 (2 of 1934);

(ii) any cash or balances maintained in India by a co-operative bank, other than a scheduled State co-operative bank, with itself or with the State co-operative bank of the State concerned, or in current account with the Reserve Bank or by way of net balance in current accounts and, in the case of a primary co-operative bank, also any balances maintained with the Central co-operative bank of he district concerned, in excess of the aggregate of the cash or balances required to be maintained under section 18;

(iii) any net balance in current accounts.

Explanation.-For the purposes of this sub-section-

(a) approved securities or a portion thereof, representing investment of monies of Agricultural Credit Stabilisation Fund of a co-perative bank shall not be deemed to be unencumber approved securities;

(b) in case a co-operative bank has taken an advance against any balance maintained with the State co-operative bank of the State concerned or with the Central co-operative bank of the district concerned, such balance to the extent to which it has been drawn against or availed of shall not be deemed to be cash maintained in India.

(c) for the purpose of clause (a), the market price of an approved security shall be the price as on the date of the issue of the notification or as on any earlier or later date as may be notified from time to time by the Reserve Bank in respect of any class or classes of securities;"

(iii) in sub-section (3) for the proviso, the following proviso shall be substituted, namely:-

"Provided that every co-operative bank, other than a primary cooperative bank, shall also furnish within the said period, a copy of the said return to the National Bank.";

(iv) in sub-section (6), in clause (a), for the words "fourteen days", the words "the thirty days" shall be substituted;]

18[(qq) after section 24, the following section shall be inserted, namely:-

"24A. Power to exempt.-Without prejudice to the provisions of section 53, the Reserve Bank may, by notification in the Official Gazette, declare that, for such period and subject to such conditions as may be specified in such notification the whole or any part of the provisions of section 18 or section 24, as may be specified therein, shall not apply to any co-operative bank or class of co-operative banks, with reference to all or any of the offices of such co-operative bank or banks, or with reference to the whole or any part of the assets and liabilities of such co-operative bank or banks."]

(r) section 25 shall be omitted;

19[(ri) in the second proviso to section 26, for the expression "regional rural Bank" the expression "co-operative bank, other than a primary co-operative bank" shall be substituted;

(rii) in section 27, for sub-section (3)the following sub-section shall be substituted, namely:-

"(3) Every co-operative bank, other than a primary co-operative bank, shall submit a copy of the return which it submits to the Reserve Banks, under sub-section (1) also to the National Bank and the powers exercisable by the Reserve Bank under sub-section (2) may also be exercised by the National Bank in relation to co-operative banks, other than primary co-operative banks.]

(s) for sections 29 and 30, the following section shall be substituted namely:-

"29. Accounts and Balance Sheet.-(1) At the expiration of eacn year ending with the 30th days of June, 20[or at the expiration of a period of twelve months ending with such date as the Central Government may, by notification in the Official Gazette, specify in this behalf] every co-operative bank, in respect of all business transacted by it, shall prepare with reference to that year 20[or the period] a balance sheet and profit and loss account as on the last working day of the year 20[or the period] in the Forms set out in the Third Schedule as near there to as circumstances admit:

20[Provided that with a view to facilitating the transition from one period of accounting to another period of accounting under this sub-section, the Central Government may, by order published in the Official Gazette, make such provisions as it considers necessary or expedient for me preparation of, or for other matters relating to, the balance-sheet or profit and loss account in respect of the concerned year or period, as the case may be].

(2) The balance-sheet and profit and loss account shall be signed by the manager or the principal officer of the bank and where there are more than three directors of the bank, by at least three of those directors, or where there are not more than three directors, by all the directors.

(3) The Central Government, after giving not less than there months' notice of its intention so to do by a notification in the Official Gazette, may from time to time by a like notification amend the Forms set out in the Third Schedule."

21[(t) in section 31,-

(i) for the words "within three months" and "of three months', the words "within six months" and "of six months" shall, respectively, be substituted;

(ii) for the second proviso, the following proviso shall be substituted, namely:

"Provided further that a co-operative bank, other than a primary cooperative bank, shall furnish such returns also to the National Bank.";]

(u) sections 32 to 34 shall be omitted;

(v) in section 34A, sub-section (3) shall be omitted;

(w) in section 35,-

(i) in sub-section (1),-

(a) for the words and figures "section 235 of the Companies Act, 1956(1 of 1956)", the words "any law relating to co-operative societies for the time being in force" shall be substituted;

22[(b) the following proviso shall be inserted at the end, namely:-

"Provided that the Reserve Bank may, if it considers it necessary or expedient so to do, cause an inspection to be made of a primary co-operative bank under this sub-section by one or more officers of a State co-operative bank in the State in which such primary cooperative bank is registered."];

(ii) in sub-section (4), clause (b) shall be omitted.

23[(iii) after sub-section (4), the following sub-section shall be inserted, namely:-

"(4A) Without prejudice to the provisions of sub-section (4), the Reserve Bank may, if it considers it necessary or expedient so to do supply a copy of the report on any inspection or scrutiny to the State co-operative bank and the Registrar of co-operative societies of the State in which the bank which has been inspected or whose affairs have been scrutinised is registered."];

24[(iv) in sub-section (6), for the expressions "regional rural banks' and "regional rural bank", wherever they occur, the expressions "co-operative banks other than primary cooperative bank" shall, respectively, be substituted.]

25[(v)] the Explanation shall be omitted;

(x) in section 35A, in sub-section (1), in clause (c), for the words "any banking company", the words "the banking business of any co-operative bank" shall be substituted;

(y) section 35B shall be omitted;

26[(z) in section 36, in sub-section (1),-

(a) clause (b) shall be omitted;

(b) for clause (d), the following clause shall be substituted, namely:-

(d) at any time, if it is satisfied that for the reorganisation or expansion of co-operative credit on sound lines it is necessary so to do by an order in writing and on such terms and conditions as may be specified therein,-

(i) depute one or more of its officers to watch the proceedings at any meeting of the Board of directors of the co-operative bank or of any other body constituted by it and require the co-operative bank to give an opportunity to the officer so deputed to be heard at such meetings and to offer such advice on such matters as the officer may consider necessary or proper for the reorganisation and expansion of co-operative credit on sound lines, and also require such officer to send a report of such proceedings to the Reserve Bank;

(ii) appoint one or more of its officers to observe the manner in which the affairs of the co-operative bank or its offices or branches are being conducted and make a report thereon;"];

(za) in section 36A,-

(i) for sub-section (1), the following sub-section shall be substituted, namely:-

"(1) The provisions of section 11, section 18 and section 24 shall not apply to a co-operative bank which has been refused a licence under section 22 of whose licence has been cancelled under that section or which is or has been prohibited or precluded from accepting deposits by virtue of any order made under this Act or of any alteration made in its bye-laws.";

(ii) after sub-section (2), the following sub-section shall be inserted, namely:-

"(3) Subject to the provisions of sub-sections (1) and (2), a co-operative society carrying on business as a primary co-operative bank at the commencement of the Banking Laws (Application to Co-operative Societies) Act, 1965 (23 of 1965), or a co-operative society which becomes a primary co-operative bank after such commencement shall, notwithstanding that it does not at any time thereafter satisfy the requirements of the definition of primary co-operative bank 27[in clause (ccv) of section 5], continue to be a primary co-operative bank within the meaning of this Act, and may, with the approval of the Reserve Bank and subject to such terms and conditions as the Reserve Bank may specify in that behalf, continue to carry on the business of banking.";

28[(zaa)in section 35AD, sub-section (3) shall be omitted;"]

(zb) 40[Part II A except sections 36AAA, 36AAB and 36AAC], 29[Part IIC], Part III, except sub-sections (1), (2) and (3) of section 45,and Part IIIA except section 45W shall be omitted;

30[(zc) in section 46,-

(i) in sub-section (4) the word "or" occurring at the end of clause (i) and clause (ii) shall be omitted;

(ii) in clause (a) of the Explanation, after the words "includes a", the words "co-operative society" shall be inserted;]

(zd) in section 47, the words brackets, figures and letters "sub-section (5) of section 36AA or" shall be omitted;

(ze) section 49 shall be omitted;

(zf) in section 49A, for the proviso, the following proviso shall be substituted, namely:-

"Provided that nothing contained in this section shall apply to-

(a) a primary credit society-

(b) any other co-operative society accepting such deposits at the commencement of the Banking Laws (Application to Co-operative Societies) Act, 1965 (23 of 1965), for a period of one year from the date of such commencement; and

(c) any savings bank scheme run by the Government";

(zg) sections 49B and 49C shall be omitted;

(zh) in section 50, the figures and letters "10,12A, 16", "35B", and "43A" shall be omitted;

(zi) section 51 shall be omitted;

(zj) in section 52,-

(i) in sub-section (2) the words, figures and letter "and the form in which official liquidator may file lists of debtors to the court jurisdiction under Part III or Part IIIA and the particulars which such lists may contain" shall be omitted;

(ii) sub-section (4) shall be omitted;

31[(zji) in section 54, after the expression "Reserve Bank", wherever it occurs, the expression "or the National Bank" shall be inserted;]

(zk) For section 65 and the First Schedule, the following section shall be substituted, namely:-

"55, Act 18 of 1891 and Act 46 of 1949 to apply in relation to co-operative banks.-(1) The Bankers' Books Evidence Act, 1891 shall apply in relation to a co-operative bank as it applies in relation to a bank as defined in section 2 of that Act.

(2) The Banking Companies (Legal Practitioners' Clients' Accounts) Act, 1949 shall apply in relation to a co-operative bank as it applies in relation to a banking company as defined in section 2 of that Act.";

(zl) for the third Schedule and the Fourth Schedule, the following Schedule shall be substituted, namely:-

"THE THIRD SCHEDULE

(see section 29)

FORM A

Form of Balance-sheet

CAPITAL AND LIABILITIES

PROPERTY AND ASSETS

Rs. P. Rs. P.

Rs. P. Rs. P.

1. CAPITAL:

(i) Authorised Capital

.....shares of Rs.....each

.....shares of Rs..... each

....

(ii) Subscribed Capital

.....shares of Rs..... each

.....shares of Rs..... each

(iii) Amount called up

On.....shares of Rs..... each less class unpaid

On..... shares of Rs..... each less calls unpaid of (iii) above, held by

(a) Individuals

(b) Co-operative institutions

(c) State Government

1. CASH:

In hand and with Reserve Bank 31[National Bank] State Bank of India, State Co-operative Bank and Central Co-operative Bank

2. BALANCES WITH OTHER BANKS:

(i) Current deposits

(ii) Savings bank deposits

(iii) Fixed deposits

3. MONEY AT CALL AND SHORT NOTICE:

4. Investments:

(i) In Central and State Government securities (at book value)

____

____

Face value Rs.

Market value Rs.

(ii) Other Trustee securities

(iii) Shares in co-operative institutions other than in item (5) below

(iv) other investments (to be specified)

2. RESERVE FUND AND OTHER RESERVES

(i) Statutory Reserve

(ii) Agricultural (Credit stabilization fund)

(iii) Building Fund

(iv) Dividend Equalization Fund

(v) Special Bad Debts Reserve

(vi) Bad and Doubtful Debts Reserve

(vii) Investment and Depreciation Reserve

5. INVESTMENT OUT OF THE PRINCIPAL SUBSIDIARY STATE PARTNERSHIP FUNDS

In shares of:

(i) Central Co-operative Banks

(ii) Primary agricultural credit societies

(iii) Other societies

6. ADVANCES†:

(viii) Other Funds and Reserves (to be specified)

(i) Short-term loans, cash credits, overdrafts and bills discounted

Of which secured against:

(a) Government and other

3. PRINCIPAL/SUBSIDIARY STATE PARTNERSHIP FUND ACCOUNT:

For share capital of:

(i) Central co-operative banks

(ii) Primary agricultural credit societies

(iii) other societies approved securities

(b) Other tangible securities @

Of the advances, amount due from individuals

Of the advances, amount overdue Considered bad and doubtful of recovery

(ii) Medium-term loans Of which secured against:

4. DEPOSITS AND OTHER ACCOUNTS:

(i) Fixed deposits*

(a) Individuals**

(b) Central co-operative banks

(c) Other societies

(ii) Savings Bank Deposits

(a) Individuals**

(b) Central co-operative banks

(a) Government and other approved securities

(b) Other tangible securities @

Of the advances, amount due from individuals

Of the advances, amount overdue considered bad and doubtful of recovery

(ii) Long-term loans Of which secured against

(c) Other societies

(iii) Current deposits

(a) individuals**

(b) Central co-operative bank

(c) Other societies

(iv) Money at call and short notice____________

(a) Government and other approved securities

(b) Other tangible securities @

5. BORROWINGS:

(i) From the Reserve Bank of India 32[the National Bank] State/Central co-operative Bank:

(a) Short-term loans, cash, credits and overdrafts

(A) Government and other approved secu rities

(B) Other tangible securities @

(b) Medium term loans

Of which secured against

(A) Government and other approved securities

(B) Other tangible Securities @

Of the advances, amount due from individuals

Of the advances, amount over due

Considered bad and doubtful of recovery____________

7. INTEREST RECEIVABLE

Of which overdue Considered bad and doubtful of recovery

(A)

(B)

(ii)

(A)

(B)

(A)

(B)

(A)

(B)

(c) Long-term loans Of which secured against:

Government and other approved securities

Other tangible securities @

From the State Bank of India

(a) Short-term loans, cash-credits and over drafts

Of which secured against:

Government and other approved securities

Other tangible securities @

(b) Medium term-loans

Of which secured against:

Government and other approved securities:

Other tangible securities @

(c) Long-term loans:

Of which secured against:

Government and other approved securities

Other tangible securities @

8. BILLS RECEIVABLE BEING BILLS FOR COLLECTION

As per contra ____________

9. BRANCH ADJUSTMENT __________

10. PREMISES LESS ____________

DEPRECIATION

11. FURNITURE AND FIXTURES LESS

DEPRECIATION ____________

12. OTHER ASSETS

(to be specified)

13. NON-BANKING ASSETS ACQUIRED IN SATISFACTION OF CLAIMS

(standing mode of valuation) ____________

(iii)

(A)

(B)

(A)

(B)

(A)

(B)

(iv)

From the State Government

(a) Short-term loans Of which secured against:

Government and other approved securities

Other tangible securities @

(d) Medium term loans

Of which secured against:

Government and other approved securities

Other tangible securities @

(c) Long-term loans

Of which secured against:

Government and other

approved securities

Other tangible securities @

Loans from other sources

(source and security to be specified rule)

14. PROFIT AND LOSS

6. BILL FOR COLLECTION BEING BILLS RECEIVABLE

As per contra ___________

7. BRANCH ADJUSTMENTS ___________

8. OVERDUE INTEREST RESERVE

____

9. INTEREST PAYABLE

____

10. OTHER LIABILITIES

(i) Bills payable

(ii) Unclaimed dividends

(iii) Suspense

(iv) Sundries

11. PROFIT AND LOSS

Profit as per last balance-sheet

Less appropriations

Add profit for the year brought from the Profit and Loss Account

---

Total

Total ______

CONTINGENT LIABILITIES

(i) Outstanding liabilities for guarantees issued

(ii) Others

Total ______

Total ______

FORM B

Form of Profit and Loss Account

Profit and Loss Account for the year ended-

EXPENDITURE INCOME

Rs. P. Rs. P.

Rs. P. Rs. P.

1. Interest on deposits, borrowings, etc.

2. Salaries and allowances and provident fund

3. Directors and local committee members' fees and allowances

4. Rent, taxes, insurance, lighting, etc.

5. Law charges

6. Postage, telegrams and telephonic charges

7. Auditor's fees

8. Depreciation on and repairs in property

1. Interest and discount

2. Commission, exchange and brokerage

3. Subsidies and donations

4. Income from non-banking assets and profit from sale of or dealing with such assets

5. Other receipts

6. Loss (if any)

9. Stationery, printing and advertisement, etc.

10. Loss from sale of or dealing with non-banking assets

11. Other expenditure

12. Balance of profit ___________

Total ___________

____

Total ___________

General Instructions-The corresponding figures (to the nearest rupee, if so desired for the year immediately preceding the year to which the profit and loss account relates should be shown in separate columns."

THE FIRST SCHEDULE

(See section 55)

AMENDMENTS

Year	No.	Short title	Amendments
1	2	3	4
1934	2	The reserve Bank	of India Act, 1934

(1) In section 17, to clause (15A), the following shall be added, namely:-

"and under the Banking Companies Act, 1949."

(2) (a) Section 18 shall be renumbered as sub-section (1) of that section and in sub-section (1) as so renumbered,-

(i) in clause (3) after the words "of that section", the following worlds shall be added, namely:

"or when the loan or advance, is made to banking company as defined in the Banking Companies Act, 1949, against such other form of security as the Bank may consider sufficient";

(ii) for the worlds "under this section" wherever the occur, the words "under this sub-section" shall be substituted;

(b) after sub-section (1) as so renumbered, the following sub-section shall be inserted, namely:-

"(2) Where a banking company to which a loan or advance has been made under the provisions of clause (3) of sub-section (1) is wound up, any sums due to the Bank in respect of such loan or advance, shall subject only to the claims, if any, of any other banking company in respect of any prior loan or advance made by such banking company against any security, be a first charge on the assets of the banking company."

(3) In section 42, for sub-section (6) the following sub-section shall be substituted, namely:-

"(6) The bank shall, save as hereinafter provided, by notification in the Gazette of India,-

(a) direct the inclusion in the Second Schedule of any bank not already so included which carries on the business of banking in any Province of India and which-

(i) has a paid-up capital and reserves of an aggregate value of not less than five lakhs of rupees, and

(ii) satisfies the Bank that its affairs are not being conducted in a manner detrimental to the interests of its depositors; and

(iii) is a company as defined in clause (2) of section 2 of the Indian Companies Act, 1913 (7 of 1913) or a corporation or a company incorporated by or under any law in force in any place outside the Provinces of India;

(b) direct the exclusion from that Schedule of any scheduled bank-

(i) the aggregate value of whose paid-up capital and reserves becomes at any time less than five lakhs of rupees, or

(ii) which is, in the opinion of the Bank after making an inspection under section 35 of the Banking Companies Act, 1949, conducting its affairs to the detriment of the interests of its depositors, or

(iii) which goes into liquidation or otherwise ceases to carry on banking business:

Provided that the Bank may, on application of the scheduled bank concerned and subject to such conditions, if any, as it may impose, defer the making of a direction under sub-clause (i) or sub-clauses (ii) of clause (b) for such period as the bank considers reasonable to give the scheduled bank and opportunity of increasing the aggregate value of its paid-up capital and reserves to not less than five lakhs of rupees or, as the case may be, of removing the defects in the conduct of its affairs;

(c) alter the description is that Schedule whenever any scheduled bank changes its name.

Explanation-In this sub-section the expre-ssion 'value' means the real or exchangeable value and not the nominal value which may be shown in the books of the bank concerned; and if any dispute arises in computing the aggregate value of the paid up capital and reserves of a bank, a determination thereof by the Bank shall be final for the purposes of this sub-section.

THE SECOND SCHEDULE-Repeals.-[Rep. by Repealing and Amending Act, 1957 (36 of 1957), Section 52 and Schedule 1]

THE THIRD SCHEDULE

(See section 29)

33[Form A

Form of Balance Sheet

Balance Sheet of________________(here enter name of the Banking Company)

Balance Sheet as on 31st March______________(Year)

(000'somitted)

Capital and Liabilities

Schedule

As on 31-3-.... (current year)

As on 31-3-.... (previous year)

1

2

3

4

5

Capital

Reserves and surplus

Deposits

Borrowings

Other liabilities and provisions

Total

ASSETS

Cash and Balances with Reserve

Bank of India

Balances with Banks and money at call and short notice

Investments

Advances

Fixed Assets

Other Assets

Total

Contingent liabilities 12 Bill for collection

6

7

8

9

10

11

SCHEDULE I

Capital

As on 31-3.... (current year)

As on 31-3.... (previous year)

I. For Nationalised Banks Capital (Fully owned by Central Government)

II. For Banks incorporated outside India Capital

(i) (The amount brought in by banks by way of Start-up capital as prescribed

by RBI should be shown under this head)

(ii) Amount of deposit kept with the RBI Under section 11(2) of the Banking Regulation Act, 1949.

Total

III. For other Banks

Authorised Capital (Shares of Rs..... each)

Issued Capital (Shares of Rs..... each)

Subscribed Capital (Shares of Rs..... each)

Called-up Capital (Shares of Rs..... each)

Less: Calls unpaid

Add: Forfeited shares

SCHEDULE 2

Reserves and Surplus

As on 31-3.... (current year)

As on 31-3.... (previous year)

I. Statutory Reserves

Opening Balance

Additions during the year

Deductions during the year

II. Capital Reserves

Opening Balance

Additions during the year

Deductions during the year

III. Share premium

Opening Balance

Additions during the year

Deductions during the year

IV. Revenue and other Reserves

Opening Balance

Additions during the year

Deductions during the year

V. Balance of Profit and Loss Account

__________ __________

Total (I, II, III, IV and V) __________ __________

SCHEDULE 3

Deposits

As on 31-3.... (current year)

As on 31-3.... (previous year)

A.I. Demand Deposits

(i) From Banks

(ii) From others

II. Savings Bank Deposits

III. Term Deposits

(i) From Banks

(ii) From others

__________ __________

Total (I, II, III) __________ __________

B. (i) Deposits of branches in India

(ii) Deposits of branches outside India

__________ __________

Total __________ __________

SCHEDULE 4

Borrowings

As on 31-3... (current year)

As on 31-3.... (previous year)

I. Borrowing in India

(i) Reserve Bank of India

(ii) Other Banks

(iii) Other institutions and agencies

II. Borrowings outside India

__________ __________

Total: (I and II) __________ __________

Secured borrowings included in 1 and
II above-Rs.

SCHEDULE 5

Other Liabilities and Provisions

As on31-3.... (current year)

As on 31-3.... (previous year)

I. Bills payable

II. Inter-office adjustments (net)

III. Interests accrued

IV. Others (Including provisions)

__________ __________

Total: __________ __________

SCHEDULE 6

Cash and Balances with Reserve Bank of India

As on 31-3.... (current year)

As on 31-3.... (previous year)

I. Cash in hand

(Including foreign currency notes)

II. Balance with Reserve Bank of India

(i) in Current Account

(ii) in other Accounts

__________ __________

Total: __________ __________ (I and II)

SCHEDULE 7

Balances with banks and Money at Call and short Notice

As on 31-3.... (current year)

As on 31-3.... (previous year)

I. In India

(i) Balances with banks

(a) In Current Accounts

(b) In Other Deposit Accounts

(ii) Money at call and short notice

(a) With banks

(b) With other institutions

__________ __________

Total: __________ __________ (I and II)

II. Outside India

(i) in Current Accounts

(ii) in Other Deposit Accounts

(iii) Money at call and short notice

__________ __________

Total: __________ __________ (I, II and III)

__________ __________

Grant Total: __________ __________

(I and II)

SCHEDULE 8

Investments

As on 31-3.... (current year)

As on 31-3.... (previous year)

I. Investments in India in

(i) Government Securities

(ii) Other approved securities

(iii) Shares

(iv) Debentures and Bonds

(v) Subsidiaries and/or joint ventures

(vi) Others (to be specified)

__________ __________

Total: __________ __________

II. Investments outside India in

(i) Government securities (Including local authorities)

(ii) Subsidiaries and/or joint ventures abroad

(iii) Other investments (to be specified)

__________ __________

Total: __________ __________

Grand Total (I and II)

SCHEDULE 9

Advances

As on 31-3.... (current year)

As on 31-3.... (previous year)

A. (i) Bills purchased and discounted

(ii) Cash credits, overdrafts and loans repayable on demand

(iii) Term loans

__________ __________

Total: __________ __________

B. (i) Secured by tangible assets

(ii) Covered by Bank/Government Guarantees

(iii) Unsecured

Total: __________ __________ C.I. Advances in India (i) Priority sectors (ii) Public sector (iii) Banks (iv) Others

Total: __________ __________

II. Advances Outside India

(i) Due from banks (ii) Due from others

(a) Bills purchased and discounted

(b) Syndicated loans

(c) Others

Total: __________ __________ __________ __________

Grand Total; (C.I. & C.II) __________ __________

SCHEDULE 10

Fixed Assets

As on 31-3.... (current year)

As on 31-3.... (previous year)

I. Premises

At cost as on 31st March of the preceding year

Additions during the year

Deductions during the year

Depreciation to date

II. Other Fixed Assets (including furniture and fixtures)

At cost as on 31st March of the preceding year

Additions during the year

Deductions during the year

Depreciation to date

__________ __________

Total: (I and II) __________ __________

SCHEDULE 11

Other Assets

As on 31-3.... (current year)

As on 31-3.... (previous year)

I. Inter-office adjustment (net)

II. Interest accrued

III. Tax paid in advance/tax deducted at source

IV. Stationery and stamps

V. Non-banking assets acquired in satisfaction of claims

VI. Others*

__________ __________

Total: __________ __________

SCHEDULE 12

Contingent Liabilities

As on 31-3.... (current year)

As on 31-3.... (previous year)

I. Claims against the bank not acknowledged as debts

II. Liability for partly paid investments

III. Liability on account of outstanding forward exchange contracts

IV. Guarantees given on behalf of constituents

(a) In India

(b) Outside India

V. Acceptances, endorsements and other obligations

VI. Other items for which the bank is contingently liable

__________ __________

Total: __________ __________

FORM 'B': Form of Profit and Loss Account for the year ended 31st March (year)

Schedule

No.

Year ended 31-3..... (current year)

Year ended 31-3..... (previous year)

I. Income

Interest earned 13 Other Income 14

__________ __________

Total: __________ __________

II. Expenditure

Interest expended 15

Operating expenses 16 Provisions and contingencies

__________ __________

Total: __________ __________

III. Profit/Loss

Net Profit/Loss (-) for the year

Profit/Loss (-) brought forward

__________ __________

Total: __________ __________

IV. Appropriations

Transfer to statutory reserves

Transfer to other reserves

Transfer to Government/proposed dividend

Balance carried over to balance sheet

__________ __________

Total: __________ __________

SCHEDULE 13

Interest Earned

Year ended on

31-3 .... (current year)

Year ended on

31-3 .... (previous year)

I. Interest/discount on advance/bills

II. Income on investments

III. Interest on balances with Reserve Bank of India and other inter-bank funds

IV. Others

__________ __________

Total: __________ __________

SCHEDULE 14

Other Income

Year ended on

31-3......... (current year)

Year ended on

31-3......... (previous year)

I. Commission, exchange and brokerage

II. Profit on sale of investments

Less: Loss on sale of investments

III. Profit on revaluation of investments

Less: Loss on revaluation of investments

IV. Profit on sale of land, buildings and other assets

Less: Loss on sale of land, buildings and other assets

V. Profit on exchange transactions

Less: Loss on exchange transactions

VI. Income earned by way of dividends etc. from subsidiaries/ companies and/or joint ventures abroad/in India

VII. Miscellaneous Income

__________ __________

Total: __________ __________

SCHEDULE 15

Interest Expended

Year ended on

31-3.......... (current year)

Year ended on

31-3........ (previous year)

I. Interest on deposits

II. Interest on Reserve Bank of India/Inter-back borrowings

III. Others

Total:

SCHEDULE 16

Operating Expenses

Year ended on

31-3........ (current year)

Year ended on

31-3........ (previous year)

I. Payments to and provisions for employees

II. Rent, taxes and lighting

III. Printing and stationery

IV. Advertisement and publicity

V. Depreciation on Bank's property

VI. Director's fees, allowances and expenses

VII. Auditors' fees and expenses (Including branch auditors)

VIII. Law charges

IX. Postages. Telegrams, Telephones, etc.

X. Repairs and maintenance

XI. Insurance

XII. Other expenditure

Total:

34[THE FOURTH SCHEDULE

[See section 45D(2)]

List of Debtors

1. The official liquidator shall from time to time submit list of debtors to the High Court, each list being verified by an affidavit.

2. Every such list shall contain the following particulars:

(a) names and addresses of the debtors;

(b) amount of debt due to the banking company by each debtor;

(c) rate of interest, if any, and the date up to which such interest has been calculated in the case of each debtor;

(d) description of papers, writings, and documents, if any, relating to each debt;

(e) relief or reliefs claimed against each debtor.

3. (a) In every such list, the official liquidator shall distinguish between the debts for which the banking company holds and security other than a personal security and the debts for which no security or only a personal security is given;

(b) In the case of secured debts, particulars of the securities claimed by the ban king company, and whenever possible their estimated value, and the names and addresses of person or persons, if any, having an interest in the securities or the right of redemption therein;

(c) In case the debt is guaranteed by any person or persons, the name and address of the guarantor or guarantors with particulars as to the extent to which the debt is guaranteed and description of documents, papers or writings in support of such guarantee.

4. If the debtor is adjudged insolvent either before or after he has been included in any such list, but before such list is settled, the name and address of the assignee or the receiver of his estate, as the case may be, should be stated in, or added to, the list.

5. If the original debtor dies either before or after he has been included in any such list, but before such list is settled, there shall be substituted in his place the names and addresses of his legal representatives as far as the official liquidator is able to ascertain.]

THE FIFTH SCHEDULE

Principles of Compensation

1. The compensation to be given under section 36AG shall be an amount equal to the value of the assets of the acquired bank as on the day immediately before the appointed day, computed in accordance with the provisions of Part I of this

Schedule less the total amount of liabilities thereof computed in accordance with the provisions of Part II of this Schedule.

Part I-Assets

For the purposes of this Part "assets" means the total of the following:-

(a) the amount of cash in hand and with the Reserve Bank and the State Bank of India (including foreign currency notes which shall be converted at the market rate of exchange);

(b) the amount of balances with any bank, whether on deposit or current account, and money at call and short notice, balance held outside India being converted at the market rate of exchange:

Provided that any balance which are not realisable in full shall be deemed to be debts and valued accordingly;--

(c) the market value, as on the day immediately before the appointed day, of any securities, shares debentures, bonds and other investments, held by the bank concerned.

Explanation.-For the purposes of this clause,-

(i) securities of the Central and State Governments [other than the securities specified in sub-clauses (ii) and (iii) of this Explanation] maturing for redemption, within five years from the appointed day shall be valued at the face value or the market value, whichever is higher;

(ii) securities of the Central Government, such as Post Office Certificates and Treasury Savings Deposit Certificates and any other securities or certificates issued or to be issued under the Small Savings Scheme of the Central Government, shall be valued at their face valuc or the encashable value of the market value, as on the day immediately before the appointed day, whichever is higher;

(iii) where the market value of any Government security such as the zamindari abolition bonds or other similar security in respect of which the principal is payable in instalment, is not ascertain able or is, for any reason, not considered as reflecting the fair value thereof or as otherwise appropriate, the security shall be valued at such an amount as is considered reasonable having ' regard to the instalments of principal and interest remaining to be paid, the period during which such instalments are payable, the yield of any security, issued by the Government to which the security pertains and having the same or approximately the same maturity, and other relevant factors;

(iv) where the market value of any security, share, debenture, bond or other investment is not considered reasonable by reason of its having been affected by abnormal factors, the investment may be valued on the basis of its average market value over any reasonable period;

(v) where the market value of any security, share, debenture, bond or other investment is not ascertainable, only such value, if any, shall be taken into account as is considered reasonable having regard to the financial position of the issuing concern, the dividend paid by it during the preceding five years and other relevant factors;

(d) the amount of advances (including loans, cash, credits, overdrafts, bills purchased and discounted), and other debts, whether secured or unsecured, to the extent to which they are reasonably considered recoverable, having regard to the value of the security, if any, the operations on the account, the reported worth and respectability of the borrower, the prospects of realisation and other relevant considerations;

(e) the value of any land or buildings;

(f) the total amount of premia paid, in respect of all leasehold properties, reduced in the case of each such premium by an amount which bears to such premium the same proportion as the expired term of the lease in respect of which such premium shall have been paid bears to the total term of the lease;

(g) the written down value as per books, or the realisable value, as may be considered reasonable, of all furniture, fixture and fittings;

(h) the market or realisable value, as may be a appropriate, of the other assets appearing on the books of the bank, no value being allowed for capitalised expenses, such as share selling commission, organisational expenses and brokerage, losses incurred and similar other items.

Liabilities

For the purpose of the Part "liabilities" means the total amount of all outside liabilities existing on the appointed day, and all contingent liabilities which the Central Government or the transferee bank may reasonably be expected to be required to be out of its own resources on or after the appointed day and where the acquired bank is a banking company incorporated outside India, includes the liabilities of the offices and branches in India of the acquired bank to its offices and branches outside India.

2. If the acquired bank is not incorporated in India, the assets or, as the case may be, the liabilities of the bank shall be, for the purposes of Part 1 and Part 11, and subject to the other provisions therein, the assets and liabilities of the offices of the bank situated in India.

COMPENSATION PAYABLE TO SHAREHOLDERS

3. Every shareholder of the acquired bank to whom the compensation is payable, shall be given such amount as compensation, as bears to the total compensation, calculated in accordance with the provisions of paragraph 1, the same proportion as the amount of paid-up capital of the shares held by the shareholder bears to the total-up capital of the acquired bank.

CERTAIN DIVIDENDS NOT TO BE TAKEN INTO ACCOUNT

4. No separate compensation shall be payable for any profits or any dividends in respect of any period immediately preceding the appointed day, for which, in the ordinary course, profits would have been transferred or dividend declared after the appointed day.]

6

Amendments to the Banking Regulation Act, 1949

Amendment of Section 56 of Act 10 of 1949: In Part V of the Banking Regulation Act, 1949 (hereafter referred to as the principal Act), in the provisions of the principal Act as applied to, or in relation to, co-operative societies, by section 56,--

(I) in section 5 of the principal Act, as amended by sub-clause (i) of clause (c) of the said section 56,-

(A) after clause (ccii), the following clause shall be inserted and shall be deemed to have been inserted with effect from the 1st day of March, 1966, namely:-

'(cciia) "co-operative society" means a society registered or deemed to have been registered under any Central Act for the time being in force relating to the multi-State co-operative societies, or any other Central or State law relating to co-operative societies for the time being in force;

(B) after clause (cciii), the following clauses shall be inserted and shall be deemed to have been inserted with effect from the 1st day of March, 1966, namely:-

'(cciiia) "multi-State co-operative bank" means a multi-State co-operative society which is a primary co-operative bank;'

'(cciiib) "multi-State co-operative society" means a multi-State co-operative society registered as such under any Central Act for the time being in force relating to the multi-State co-operative societies but does not include a national co-operative society and a federal co-operative;'

(C) in clause (ccvii), the words "co-operative society" shall be omitted and shall be deemed to have been omitted with effect from the 1st day of March, 1966;

(II) after section 22 of the principal Act, as amended by clause (o) of said section 56, the following section shall be inserted, namely:-

"22A Validation of licences granted by Reserve Bank to multi state co-operative societies. Notwithstanding anything contained in any law or, judgment delivered or decree or order of any court made,--

(a) no licence, granted to a multi-State co-operative society by the Reserve Bank under section 22, which was subsisting on the date of commencement of the Banking Regulation (Amendment) and Miscellaneous Provisions Act, 2004, shall be invalid or be deemed ever to have been invalid merely by the reason of such judgment, decree or order;

(b) every licence, granted to a multi-State co-operative society by the Reserve Bank under section 22, which was subsisting on the date of commencement of the Banking Regulation (Amendment) and Miscellaneous Provisions Act, 2004, shall be valid and be deemed always to have been validly granted in accordance with law;

(c) a multi-State co-operative society whose application for grant of licence for carrying on banking business was pending with the Reserve Bank on the date of commencement of the Banking Regulation (Amendment) and Miscellaneous Provisions Act, 2004 shall be eligible to carry on banking business until it is granted a licence in pursuance of section 22 or is, by a notice in writing notified by the Reserve Bank that the licence cannot be granted to it;";

(III) for clause (zaa) of the said section 56, the following clauses shall be substituted, namely:-

'(zaa) after section 36AA of the principal Act, the following sections shall be inserted, namely:-

"36AAA Supersession of Board of directors of a multi-state co-operative bank. (1) Where the Reserve Bank is satisfied that in the public interest or for preventing the affairs of a multi-State co-operative bank being conducted in a manner detrimental to the interest of the depositors or of the multi-State co-operative bank or for securing the proper management of the multi-State co-operative bank, it is necessary so to do, the Reserve Bank may, for reasons to be recorded in writing, by order, supersede the Board of directors of such multi-State co-operative bank for a period not exceeding five years as may be specified in the order, which may be extended from time to time, so, however, that total period shall not exceed five years.

(2) The Reserve Bank may, on supersession of the Board of directors of the multi-State co-operative bank under sub-section (1) appoint an Administrator for such period as it may determinc.

(3) The Reserve Bank may issue such directions to the Administrator as it may deem appropriate and the Administrator shall be bound to follow such directions.

(4) Upon making the order of supersession of the Board of directors of a multi-State co-operative bank,--

(a) the chairman, managing director and other directors as from the date of supersession of the Board shall vacate their offices as such;

(b) all the powers, functions and duties which may, by or under the provisions of the Multi-State Co-operative Societies Act, 2002 (39 of 2002) or this Act or any other law for the time being in force, be exercised and discharged by or on behalf of the Board of directors of such a multi-State co-operative bank or by a resolution passed in general meeting of such co-operative bank, shall, until the Board of directors of such co-operative bank is reconstituted, be exercised and discharged by the Administrator appointed by the Reserve Bank under sub-section (2):

Provided that the power exercised by the Administrator shall be valid notwithstanding that such power is exercisable by a resolution passed in the general meeting of such multi-State co-operative bank.

(5) (a) The Reserve Bank may constitute a committee of three or more persons who have experience in law, finance, banking, administration or accountancy to assist the Administrator in discharge of his duties.

(b) The committee shall meet at such times and places and observe such rules of procedure as may be specified by the Reserve Bank.

(6) The salary and allowances to the Administrator and the members of the committee constituted by the Reserve Bank

shall be such as may be Specified by the Reserve Bank and be payable by the concerned multi-State co-operative bank.

(7) On and before expiration of period of supersession of the Board of directors as specified in the order issued under sub-section (1), the Administrator of the multi-State co-operative bank shall call the general meeting of the society to elect new directors.

(8) Notwithstanding anything contained in any other law or in any contract, or bye-laws of a multi-State co-operative bank, no person shall be entitled to claim any compensation for the loss or termination of his office.

(9) The Administrator appointed under sub-section (2) shall vacate office immediately after the Board of directors of the multi-State co-operative society has been constituted.

36AAB Order of winding up multi-State co-operative bank to be final in certain cases. Where a multi-State co-operative bank, being an eligible cooperative bank, has been registered under section 13A of the Deposit Insurance and Credit Guarantee Corporation Act, 1961 (47 of 1961), as an insured bank, and subsequently-

(a) in pursuance of a scheme prepared with the previous approval of the Reserve Bank under section 18 of the Multi-State Co-operative Societies Act, 2002 (39 of 2002), an order sanctioning a scheme of compromise and arrangement or reorganisation or reconstruction has been made; or

(b) on requisition by the Reserve Bank, an order for winding up of the multi-State co-operative bank has been made under section 87 of the Multi-State Co-operative Societies Act, 2002 (39 of 2002); or

(c) an order for the supersession of the Board and the appointment of an Administrator therefor has been made under section 36AAA,

such order for sanctioning the scheme of compromise and arrangement or reorganisation or reconstruction under clause (a) or the winding up of the multi-State co-operative bank under clause (b) or an order for the supersession of the Board and the appointment of an Administrator under clause (c) shall not be liable to be called in question in any manner.

36AAC Reimbursement to the Deposit Insurance Corporation by liquidator or transferee bank. Where a multi-State co-operative bank, being an insured bank within the meaning of the Deposit Insurance and Credit Guarantee Corporation Act, 1961 (47 of 1961), is wound up and the Deposit Insurance Corporation has become liable to the depositors of the insured bank under sub-section (1) or sub-section (2) of section 16 of that Act, the Deposit Insurance Corporation shall be reimbursed by the liquidator or such other person in the circumstances, to the extent and in the manner provided in section 21 of that Act".

(zab) in section 36AD, sub-section (3) shall be omitted;",

(IV) in clause (zb) of the said section 56, for the word, figures and letter "Part IIA", the words, figures and letters "Part IIA except sections 36AAA, 36AAB and 36AAC", shall be substituted.

AMENDMENTS TO THE DEPOSIT INSURANCE AND CREDIT GUARANTEE CORPORATION ACT, 1961

3. Amendment of section 2 of Act 47 of 1961: In the Deposit Insurance and Credit Guarantee Corporation Act, 1961, in section 2,-

(a) in clause (q), the words "co-operative society" shall be omitted and shall be deemed to have been omitted with effect from the 1st day of March, 1966;

(b) in clause (r), for the words "primary co-operative bank", the words "co-operative society", "primary co-operative bank" shall be substituted and shall be deemed to have been substituted with effect from the 1st day of March, 1966.

REPEAL AND SAVING

4. Repeal and saving:

(1) The Banking Regulation (Amendment) and Miscellaneous Provisions Ordinance, 2004 (Ordinance 3 of 2004) is hereby repealed.

(2) Notwithstanding such repeal, anything done or any action taken under the Banking Regulation Act, 1949 (10 of 1949) and Deposit Insurance and Credit Guarantee Corporation Act, 1961, (47 of 1961) as amended by the said Ordinance shall

be deemed to have been done or taken under the corresponding provisions of those Acts, as amended by this Act.

ANNEXURE: EXTRACT FROM THE BANKING REGULATION ACT, 1949

(10 OF 1949)

* * * * *

APPLICATION OF THE ACT TO CO-OPERATIVE BANKS

56. Act to Apply to Co-operative Societies Subject to Modifications: The provisions of this Act, as in force for the time being, shall apply to, or in relation to, co-operative societies as they apply to, or in relation to, banking companies subject to the following modifications, namely:--

* * * * *

(c) in section 5,--

(i) after clause (cc), the following clauses shall be inserted, namely:--

* * * * *

(ccvii) "central co-operative bank", "co-operative society", "primary rural credit society" and "state co-operative Bank" shall have the meanings respectively assigned to them in the National Bank for Agriculture and Rural Development Act, 1981(61 of 1981);

* * * * *

(zaa) in section 36AD, sub-section (3) shall be omitted.

* * * * *

(zb) Part IIA, Part IIC, Part III, except sub-sections (1), (2) and (3) of section 45, and Part IIIA except section 45W, shall be omitted;

* * * * *

EXTRACT FROM THE DEPOSIT INSURANCE AND CREDIT GUARANTEE CORPORATION ACT, 1961

(47 OF 1961)

* * * * *

2. Definitions:

In this Act, unless the context otherwise requires,--

* * * * *

(q) the expressions "central co-operative bank", "co-operative society" and "State co-operative bank" shall have the meanings respectively assigned to them in the National Bank for Agriculture and Rural Development Act, 1981(61 of 1981);

(r) the expressions "primary co-operative bank" and "primary credit society" shall have the meanings respectively assigned to them in Part V of the Banking Regulation Act, 1949(10 of 1949);

* * * * *

CORRIGENDA

In the National Commission for Minority Educational Institutions Ordinance, 2004 (Ord. 6 of 2004) as published in the Gazette of India, Extraordinary, Part II, Section 1, dated the 11the November, 204 (Issue No. 35),--

At page 1, in the long title, line 2, for "therewtih", read "therewith".

At page 3,--

(a) in line 23, for "assinged", read "assigned";

(b) in line 26, for "Commision", read "Commission.";

At Page 6,--

(a) in line 2, for "emplopyee", read "employee";

(b) in line 29, for "House", read "Houses".

BANKING REGULATION ACT, 1949

PRELIMINARY

1. Short title, extent and commencement

(1) This Act may be called the Banking 2[Regulation] Act, 1949.

3[(2) It extends to the whole of India 4[* * *]

(3) It shall come into force on such date5 as the Central Government may, by notification in the Official Gazette, appoint in this behalf.

2. Application of other laws not barred

The provisions of this Act shall be in addition to, and not, save as hereinafter expressly provided, in derogation of the

6[Companies Act, 1956 (1 of 1956)], and any other law for the time being in force.

7[3. Act to apply to co-operative societies in certain cases

Nothing in this Act shall apply to-

(a) a primary agricultural credit society;

(b) a co-operative land mortgage bank; and

(c) any other co-operative society, except in the manner and to the extent specified in Part V.]

4. Power to suspend operation of Act

(1) The Central Government, if on a representation made by the Reserve Bank in this behalf it is satisfied that it is expedient so to do, may by notification in the Official Gazette, suspend for such period, not exceeding sixty days, as may be specified in the notification, the operation of all or any of the provisions of this Act, either generally or in relation to any specified banking company.

(2) In a case of special emergency, the Governor of the Reserve Bank, or in his absence a Deputy Governor of the Reserve Bank nominated by him in this behalf may, by order in writing, exercise the powers of the Central Government under sub-section (1) so however that the period of suspension shall not exceed thirty days, and where the Governor or the Deputy Governor, as the case may be, does so, he shall report the matter to the Central Government forthwith, and the order shall, as soon as may be, be published in the Gazette of India.

(3) The Central Government may, by notification in the Official Gazette, extend from time to time the period of any suspension ordered under sub-section (1) or sub-section (2) for such period, not exceeding sixty days at any one time, as it thinks fit so however that the total period does not exceed one year.

(4). A copy of any notification issued under sub-section (3) shall be laid on the table of 8[Parliament] as soon as may be after it is issued.

5. Interpretation

9[In this Act], unless there is anything repugnant in the subject or context,-

10[(a) "approved securities" means-

(i) securities in which a trustee may invest money under clause (a), clause (b), clause (bb), clause (c) or clause (d) of section 20 of the Indian Trust Act, 1882 (2 of 1882);

(ii) such of the securities authorised by the Central Government under clause (f) of section 20 of the Indian Trust Act, 1882 (2 of 1882), as may be prescribed];

(b) "banking" means the accepting, for the purpose of lending or investment, of deposits of money from the public, repayable on demand or otherwise, and withdrawable by cheque, draft, order or otherwise.

(c) "banking company" means any company which transacts the business of banking 11[in India];

Explanation: Any company which is engaged in the manufacture of goods or carries on any trade and which accepts deposits of money from the public merely for the purpose of financing its business as such manufacturer or trader shall not be deemed to transact the business of banking within the meaning of this clause;

12[(ca) "banking policy" means any policy which is specified from time to time by the Reserve Bank in the interest of the banking system or in the interest of monetary stability or sound economic growth, having due regard to the interests of the depositors, the volume of deposits and other resources of the bank and the need for equitable allocation and the efficient use of these deposits and resources;]

13[(CC) "branch" or "branch office", in relation to a banking company, means any branch or branch office, whether called a pay office or sub-pay office or by any other name, at which deposits are received, cheques cashed or moneys lent, and for the purposes of section 35 includes any place of business where any other form of business referred to in sub-section (1) of section 6 is transacted;]

14[(d) "company" means any company as defined in section 3 of the Companies Act, 1956 (1 of 1956); and includes a foreign company within the meaning of section 591 of that Act;]

15[(da) "corresponding new bank" means a corresponding new bank constituted under section 3 of the Banking Companies

(Acquisition and Transfer of Undertakings) Act, 1970 (5 of 1970), or under section 3 of the Banking Companies (Acquisition and Transfer of Undertakings) Act, 1980 (40 of 1980);]

(e) 16[* * *]

(f) "demand liabilities" means liabilities which must be met on demand, and "time liabilities" means liabilities which are not demand liabilities;

17[(ff) "Deposit Insurance Corporation" means the Deposit Insurance Corporation established under section 3 of the Deposit Insurance Corporation Act, 1961 (47 of 1961);]

15[(ffa) "Development Bank" means the Industrial Development Bank of India established under section 3 of the Industrial Development Bank of India Act, 1964 (18 of 1964);

(ffb) "Exim Bank" means Export-Import Bank of India established under section 3 of the Export-Import Bank of India Act, 1981 (28 of 1981);]

18[(ffc) "Reconstruction Bank" means the Industrial Reconstruction Bank of India established under section 3 of the Industrial Reconstruction Bank of India Act, 1984 (62 of 1984);]

19[(ffd) "National Housing Bank" means the National Housing Bank established under section 3 of the National Housing Bank Act, 1987;]

(g) "gold" includes gold in the form of coin, whether legal tender or not, or in the form of bullion or ingot, whether refined or not;

12[(gg) "managing agent" includes-

(i) secretaries and treasurers,

(ii) where the managing agent is a company, any director of such company, and any member thereof who holds substantial interest in such company,

(iii) where the managing agent is a firm, any partner of such firm;]

14[(h) "managing director", in relation to a banking company, means a Director who,by virtue of agreement with the banking company or of a resolution passed by the banking company in general meeting or by its Board of Directors or, by virtue of its memorandum or articles of association, is entrusted with the management of the whole, or substantially the whole of the affairs of the company, and includes a Director occupying the position of a Managing Director, by whatever name called:]

20[PROVIDED that the Managing Director shall exercise his powers subject to the superintendence, control and direction of the Board of Directors;]

21[(ha) "National Bank" means the National Bank for Agriculture and Rural Development established under section 3 of the National Bank for Agriculture and Rural Development Act, 1981 (61 of 1981);]

(i) 22[* * *1

(j) "prescribed" means prescribed by rules made under this Act;

21[(ja) "regional rural bank" means a regional rural bank established under section 3 of the Regional Rural Banks Act, 1976 (21 of 1976);]

(k) 23[* * *]

10[(l) "Reserve Bank" means the Reserve Bank of India constituted under section 3 of the Reserve Bank of India Act, 1934 (2 of 1934);]

(m) 24[* * *]

(n) "secured loan or advances" means a loan or advance made on the security of assets the market value of which is not at any time less than the amount of such loan or advance; and "unsecured loan or advance" means a loan or advance not so secured;

27[(ni) "Small Industries Bank" means the Small Industries Development Bank of India established under s. 3 of the Small Industries Development Bank of India Act, 1989;]

12[(na) "small-scale industrial concern" means an industrial concern in which the investment in plant and machinery is not in excess of seven and a half lakh of rupees or such higher amount, not exceeding twenty lakhs of rupees, as the Central Government may, by notification in the Official Gazette, specify in this behalf, having regard to the trends in industrial development and other relevant factors;]

15[(nb) "Sponsor Bank" has the meaning assigned to it in the Regional Rural Banks Act, 1976 (21 of 1976);

(nc) "State Bank of India" means the State Bank of India constituted under section 3 of the State Bank of India Act, 1955 (23 of 1955);]

26[(nd)] "subsidiary bank" has the meaning assigned to it in the State Bank of India (Subsidiary Banks) Act, 1959 (38 of 1959);

27[(ne)] "substantial interest:- (i) in relation to a company, means the holding of a beneficial interest by an individual or his spouse or minor child, whether singly or taken together in the shares thereof, the amount paid-up on which exceeds five lakhs of rupees or ten per cent of the paid-up capital of the company, whichever is less; (ii) in relation to a firm, means the beneficial interest held therein by an individual or his spouse or minor child, whether singly or taken together, which represents more than ten per cent of the total capital subscribed by all the partners of the said firm;

28[(o) all other words and expressions used herein but not defined and defined in the Companies Act, 1956 (1 of 1956), shall have the meanings respectively assigned to them in that Act.]

(2) 29[* * *]

28[5A. Act to override memorandum, articles, etc.

Save as otherwise expressly provided in this Act,

(a) the provisions of this Act shall have effect notwithstanding anything to the contrary contained in the memorandum or articles of a banking company, or in any agreement executed by it, or in any resolution passed by the banking company in general meeting or by its Board of Directors, whether the same be registered, executed or passed, as the case may be, before or after the commencement of the Banking Companies (Amendment) Act, 1959 (33 of 1959); and

(b) any provision contained in the memorandum, articles, agreement or resolution aforesaid shall, to the extent to which it is repugnant to the provisions of. this Act, become or be void, as the case may be.

BANKING REGULATION ACT, 1949

BUSINESS OF BANKING COMPANIES

6. Form and business in which banking companies may engage

(1) In addition to the business of banking, a banking company may engage in any one or more of the following forms of business, namely,-

(a) the borrowing, raising, or taking up of money; the lending or advancing of money either upon or without security; and drawing, making, accepting, discounting, buying, selling, collecting and dealing in bills of exchange, hundies, promissory notes, coupons, drafts, bill of lading, railway receipts, warrants, debentures, certificates, scrips and other instruments, and securities whether transferable or negotiable or not; the granting and issuing of letters of credit, travellers' cheques and circular notes; the buying, selling and dealing in bullion and specie; the buying and selling of foreign exchange including foreign bank notes; the acquiring, holding, issuing on commission, underwriting and dealing in stock, funds, shares, debentures, debenture stock, bonds, obligations, securities and investments of all kinds; the purchasing and selling of bonds, scrips or other forms of securities on behalf of constituents or others; the negotiating of loan and advances; the receiving of all kinds of bonds, scrips or valuables on deposit or for safe custody or otherwise; the providing of safe deposit vaults; the collecting and transmitting of money and securities;

(b) acting as agents for any government or local authority or any other person or persons; the carrying on of agency business of any description including the clearing and forwarding of goods, giving of receipts and discharges and otherwise acting as an attorney on behalf of customers, but excluding the business of a 30[Managing Agent or Secretary and Treasurer] of a company;

(c) contracting for public and private loans and negotiating and issuing the same;

(d) the effecting, insuring, guaranteeing, underwriting, participating in managing and carrying out of any issue, public or private, of State, municipal or other loans or of shares, stock, debentures or debenture stock of any company, corporation or association and the lending of money for the purpose of any such issue;

(e) carrying on and transacting every kind of guarantee and indemnity business;

(f) managing, selling and realising any property which may come into the possession of the company in satisfaction or part satisfaction of any of its claims;

(g) acquiring and holding and generally dealing with any property or any right, title or interest in any such property which may form the security or part of the security for any loans or advances or which may be connected with any such security;

(h) undertaking and executing trusts;

(i) undertaking the administration of estates as executor, trustee or otherwise;

(j) establishing and supporting or aiding in the establishment and support of associations, institutions, funds, trusts, and conveniences calculated to benefit employees or ex-employees of the company or the dependents or connections of such persons; granting pension and allowances and making payments towards insurance; subscribing to or guaranteeing moneys for charitable or benevolent object or for any exhibition or for any public, general or useful object;

(k) the acquisition, construction, maintenance and alteration of any building or works necessary or convenient for the purpose of the company;

(l) selling, improving, managing, developing, exchanging, leasing, mortgaging, disposing of or turning into account or otherwise dealing with all or any part of the property and rights of the company;

(m) doing all such other things as are incidental or conducive to the promotion or advancement of the business of the company;

(o) any other form of business which the Central Government may, by notification in the Official Gazette, specify as a form of business in which it is lawful for a banking company to engage.

(2) No banking company shall engage in any form of business other than those referred to in sub-section (1).

9[7. Use of words "bank", "banker", "banking" or "banking company"

(1) No company other than a banking company shall use as part of its name 15[or, in connection with its business] any

of the words "bank", "banker" or "banking" and no company shall carry on the business of banking in India unless it uses as part of its name at least one of such words.

(2) No firm, individual or group of individuals shall, for the purpose of carrying on any business, use as part of its or his name any of the words "bank", "banking" or "banking company".

(3) Nothing in this section shall apply to-

(a) a subsidiary of a banking company formed for one or more of the purposes mentioned in sub-section (1) of section 19, whose name indicates that it is a subsidiary of that banking company;

(b) any association of banks formed for the protection of their mutual interests and registered under section 25 of the Companies Act, 1956 (1 of 1956).]

8. Prohibition of trading

Notwithstanding anything contained in section 6 or in any contract, no banking company shall directly or indirectly deal in the buying or selling or bartering of goods, except in connection with the realization of security given to or held by it, or engage in any trade, or buy, sell or barter goods for others otherwise than in connection with bills of exchange received for collection or negotiation or with such of its business as is referred to in clause (i) of sub-section (1) of section 6:

10[PROVIDED that this section shall not apply to any such business as is specified in pursuance of clause (o) of sub-section (1) of section 6.]

Explanation: For the purposes of this section, "goods" means every kind of movable property, other than actionable claims, stock, shares, money, bullion and specie and all instruments referred to in clause (a) of sub-section (1) of section 6.

9. Disposal of non-banking assets

Notwithstanding anything contained in section 6, no banking company shall hold any immovable property howsoever acquired, except such as is required for its own use, for any period exceeding seven years from the acquisition thereof or from the commencement of this Act, whichever is later or any extension of such period as in this section provided, and such property shall be disposed of within such period or extended

period, as the case may be: PROVIDED that the banking company may, within the period of seven years as aforesaid, deal or trade in any such property for the purpose of facilitating the disposal thereof:

PROVIDED FURTHER that the Reserve Bank may in any particular case extend the aforesaid period of seven years by such period not exceeding five years where it is satisfied that such extension would be in the interests of the depositors of the banking company.

31[10. Prohibition of employment of Managing Agents and restrictions on certain forms of employment

(1) No banking company-

(a) shall employ or be managed by a Managing Agent; or

(b) shall employ or continue the employment of any person-

(i) who is, or at any time has been, adjudicated insolvent, or has suspended payment or has compounded, with his creditors, or who, is or has been, convicted by a criminal court of an offence involving moral turpitude; or

(ii) whose remuneration or part of whose remuneration takes the form of commission or of a share in the profits of the company:

14[PROVIDED that nothing contained in this sub-clause shall apply to the payment by a banking company of-

(a) any bonus in pursuance of a settlement or award arrived at or made under any law relating to industrial disputes or in accordance with any scheme framed by such banking company or in accordance with the usual practice prevailing in banking business;

(b) any commission to any broker (including guarantee broker), cashier-contractor, clearing and forwarding agent, auctioneer or any other person, employed by the banking company under a contract otherwise than as a regular member of the staff of the company; or]

(iii) whose remuneration is, in the opinion of the Reserve Bank, excessive; or

(c) shall be managed by any person-

14[(i) who is a Director of any other company not being-

(a) a subsidiary of the banking company, or

(b) a company registered under section 25 of the Companies Act, 1956 (1 of 1956):

PROVIDED that the prohibition in this sub-clause shall not apply in respect of any such Director for a temporary period not exceeding three months or such further period not exceeding nine months as the Reserve Bank may allow; or]

(ii) who is engaged in any other business or vocation; or

(iii) 9[whose term of office as a person managing the company is] for a period exceeding five years at any one time:

32[PROVIDED that the term of office of any such person may be renewed or extended by further periods not exceeding five years on each occasion subject to the condition that such renewal or extension shall not be sanctioned earlier than two years form the date on which it is to come into force:

PROVIDED ALSO that where the term of office of such person is for an indefinite period, such term, unless it otherwise comes to an end earlier, shall come to an end immediately on the expiry of five years from the date of his appointment or on the expiry of three months from the date of commencement of section 8 of the Banking Laws (Miscellaneous Provisions) Act, 1963 (55 of 1963), whichever is later:]

PROVIDED FURTHER that nothing in this clause shall apply to a Director, other than the Managing Director, of a banking company by reason only of his being such Director.

Explanation: For the purpose of sub-clause (iii) of clause (b), the expression "remuneration ", in relation to a persons employed or continued in employment, shall include salary, fees and perquisites but shall not include any allowances or other amounts paid to him for the purpose of reimbursing him in respect of the expenses actually incurred by him in the performance of his duties.

(2) In forming its opinion under sub-clause (iii) of clause (b) of sub-section (1), the Reserve Bank may have regard among other matters to the following:-

(i) the financial condition and history of the banking company, its size and area of operation, its resources, the volume of its business, and the trend of its earning capacity;

(ii) the number of its branches or offices;

(iii) the qualifications, age and experience of the person concerned;

(iv) the remuneration paid to other persons employed by the banking company or to any person occupying a similar position in any other banking company similarly situated; and

(v) the interests of its depositors.

(3) 33[***]

(4) 33[***]

(5) 33[***]

(6) Any decision or order of the Reserve Bank made under this section shall be final for all purposes.]

34[10A. Board of Directors to include persons with professional or other experience

(1) Notwithstanding anything contained in any other law for the time being in force, every banking company- (a) in existence on the commencement of section 3 of the Banking Laws (Amendment) Act, 1968, or (b) which comes into existence thereafter, shall comply with the requirements of this section: PROVIDED that nothing contained in this sub-section shall apply to a banking company referred to in clause (a) for a period of three months from such commencement.

(2) Not less than fifty-one per cent of the total number of members of the Board of Directors of a banking company shall consist of persons, who-

(a) shall have special knowledge or practical experience in respect of one or more of the following matters, namely,-

(i) accountancy,

(ii) agriculture and rural economy,

(iii) banking,

(iv) co-operation,

(v) economics,

(vi) finance,

(vii) law,

(viii) small-scale industry,

(ix) any other matter the special knowledge of, and practical experience, which would, in the opinion of the Reserve Bank, be useful to the banking company: PROVIDED that out of the aforesaid number of Directors, not less than two shall be persons having special knowledge or practical experience in respect of agriculture and rural economy, co-operation or small-scale industry; and

(b) shall not-

(1) have substantial interest in, or be connected with, whether as employee, manager or managing agent- (i) any company, not being a company registered under section 25 of the Companies Act, 1956 (1 of 1956), or (ii) any firm, which carries on any trade, commerce or industry and which, in either case, is not a small-scale industrial concern, or

(2) be proprietors of any trading, commercial or industrial concern, not being a small-scale industrial concern.

15[(2A) Notwithstanding anything to the contrary contained in the Companies Act, 1956 (1 of 1956), or in any other law for the time being in force,-

(i) no Director of a banking company, other than its Chairman or whole-time Director, by whatever name called, shall hold office continuously for a period exceeding eight years;

(ii) a Chairman or other whole-time Director of a banking company who has been removed from office as such Chairman, or whole-time Director, as the case may be, under the provisions of this Act shall also cease to be a Director of the banking company and shall also not be eligible to be appointed as a Director of such banking company, whether by election or co-option or otherwise, for a period of four years from the date of his ceasing to be the Chairman or whole-time Director, as the case may be.]

(3) If, in respect of any banking company, the requirements, as laid down in sub-section (2), are not fulfilled at any time, the Board of Directors of such banking company shall re-constitute such Board so as to ensure that the said requirements are fulfilled.

(4) If, for the purpose of re-constituting the Board under sub-section (3), it is necessary to retire any Director or Directors,

the Board may, by lots drawn in such manner as may be prescribed, decide which Director or Directors shall cease to hold office and such decision shall be binding on every Director of the Board.

(5) Where the Reserve Bank is of opinion that the composition of the Board of Directors of a banking company is such that it does not fulfil the requirements of sub-section (2), it may, after giving to such banking company a reasonable opportunity of being heard, by an order in writing, direct the banking company to so re-constitute its Board of Directors as to ensure that the said requirements are fulfilled and, if within two months from the date of receipt of that order, the banking company does not comply with the directions made by the Reserve Bank, that Bank may, after determining, by lots drawn in such manner as may be prescribed, the person who ought to be removed from the membership of the Board of Directors, remove such person from the office of the Director of such banking company and with a view to complying with provisions of sub-section (2), appoint a suitable person as a member of the Board of Directors in the place of the person so removed whereupon the person so appointed shall be deemed to have been duly elected by the banking company as its Director.

(6) Every appointment, removal or reconstitution duly made, and every election duly held, under this section shall be final and shall not be called into question in any court.

(7) Every Director elected or, as the case may be, appointed under this section shall hold office until the date up to which his predecessor would have held office, if the election had not been held, or, as the case may be, the appointment had not been made.

(8) No act or proceeding of the Board of Director of a banking company shall be invalid by reason only of any defect in the composition thereof or on the ground that it is subsequently discovered that any of its members did not fulfil the requirements of this section.

10B. Banking company to be managed by whole-time Chairman

35[(1) Notwithstanding anything contained in any law for the time being in force or in any contract to the contrary, every banking company in existence on the commencement of the Banking Regulation (Amendment) Act, 1994, or which comes into existence thereafter shall have one of its Directors, who may be appointed on a whole-time or a part-time basis as Chairman of its Board of Directors, and where he is appointed on a whole-time basis as Chairman of its Board of Directors, he shall be entrusted with the management of the whole of the affairs of the banking company: PROVIDED that the Chairman shall exercise his powers subject to the superintendence, control and direction of the Board of Directors.

(1A) Where a Chairman is appointed on a part-time basis-

(i) such appointment shall be with the previous approval of the Reserve Bank and be subject to such conditions as the Reserve Bank may specify while giving such approval:

(ii) the management of the whole of the affairs of such banking company shall be entrusted to a Managing Director who shall exercise his powers subject to the superintendence, control and direction of the Board of Directors.]

(2) 35[Every Chairman of the Board of Directors who is appointed on a whole-time basis and every Managing Director] of a banking company shall be in the whole-time employment to such company and shall hold office for such period, not exceeding five years, as the Board of Directors may fix, but shall subject to the provision of this section, be eligible for re-election or re-appointment:PROVIDED that nothing in this sub-section shall be construed as prohibiting a chairman from being a Director of a subsidiary of the banking company or a Director of a company registered cinder section 25 of the Companies Act, 1956 (1 of 1956).

(3) Every person holding office on the commencement of section 3 of the Banking Laws (Amendment) Act, 1968 (58 of 1968), as Managing Director of a banking company shall-

(a) if there is a Chairman of its Board of Directors, vacate office on such commencement, or

(b) if there is no Chairman of its Board of Directors, vacate office on the date on which the Chairman of its Board of Directors is elected or appointed in accordance with the provisions of this section.

(4) 35[Every Chairman who is appointed on a whole-time basis and every Managing Director of a banking company appointed under sub-section (1A)] shall be a person who has special knowledge and practical experience of-

(a) the working of a banking company or of the State Bank of India or any subsidiary bank or a financial institution, or

(b) financial, economic or business administration:

PROVIDED that a person shall be disqualified for being a 35[Chairman who is appointed on a whole-time basis or a Managing Director], if he-

(a) is a Director of any company other than a company referred to in the proviso to sub-section (2), or

(b) is a Partner of any firm which carries on any trade, business or industry, or

(c) has substantial interest in any other company or firm, or

(d) is a Director, Manager, Managing Agent, Partner or Proprietor of any trading, commercial or industrial concern, or

(e) is engaged in any other business or vocation.

(5) 35[A Chairman of the Board of Directors appointed on a whole-time basis or a Managing Director] of a banking company may, by writing under his hand addressed to the company, resign his office 36[* * *].

37[(5A) 35[A Chairman of the Board of Directors appointed on a whole-time basis or a Managing Director] whose term of office has come to an end, either by reason of his resignation or by reason of expiry of the period of this office, shall, subject to the approval of the Reserve Bank, continue in office until his successor assumes office.]

(6) Without prejudice to the provisions of section 36AA, where the Reserve Bank is of opinion that any person who is, or has been elected to be, the 35[Chairman of the Board of Directors who is appointed on a whole-time basis or the Managing-Director] of a banking company is not a fit and proper person to hold such office, it may, after giving to such person and to the banking company a reasonable opportunity of being heard, by order in writing, require the banking company to elect or appoint any other person as the 35[Chairman of the Board of Directors who is appointed on a whole-time basis or the

Managing-Director] and if, within a period of two months from the date of receipt of such order, the banking company fails to elect or appoint a suitable person as 35[Chairman of the Board of Directors who is appointed on a whole-time basis or the Managing Director], the Reserve Bank may, by order, remove the first-mentioned person from the office, of the 35[Chairman of the Board of Directors who is appointed on a whole-time basis or a Managing Director] of the banking company and appoint a suitable person in his place whereupon the person so appointed shall be deemed to have been duly elected or appointed, as the case may be, as the 35[Chairman of the Board of Directors who is appointed on a whole-time basis or the Managing Director] of such banking company and any person elected or appointed as Chairman under this sub-section shall hold office for the residue of the period of the person in whose place he has been so elected or appointed.

(7) The banking company and any person against whom an order of removal is made under sub-section (6) may, within thirty days from the date of communication to it or to him of the order, prefer an appeal to the Central Government and the decision of the Central Government thereon, and subject thereto, the order made by the Reserve Bank under sub-section (6), shall be final and shall not be called into question in any court.

(8) Notwithstanding anything contained in this section, the Reserve Bank may, if in its opinion it is necessary in the public interest so to do, permit the 35[Chairman of the Board of Directors who is appointed on a whole-time basis or a Managing Director] to undertake such part-time honorary work as is not likely to interfere with his duties as 35[such Chairman or Managing Director.]

(9) Notwithstanding anything contained in this section, where a person 35[appointed on a whole-time basis, as Chairman of the Board of Directors or Managing Director] dies or resigns or is by infirmity or otherwise rendered incapable of carrying out his duties or is absent on leave or other wise in circumstances not involving the vacation of his office, the banking company may, with the approval of the Reserve Bank, make suitable arrangements for carrying out the 35[duties of Chairman or Managing Director] for a total period not exceeding four months

7

Business of Banking Companies

Power of Reserve Bank to appoint Chairman of a banking company

(1) Where the office of the 35[Chairman of the Board of Directors appointed on a whole-times basis or the Managing Director] of a banking company is vacant, the Reserve Bank may, if it is of opinion that the continuation of such vacancy is likely to adversely affect the interests of the banking company, appoint a person eligible under sub-section (4) of section 10B to be so appointed, to be the 35[Chairman of the Board of Directors appointed on a whole-time basis or a Managing Director of the banking company and where the person so appointed is not a director of such banking company, he shall, so long as he holds the office of the 35[Chairman of the Board of Directors appointed on a whole-time basis or a Managing Director], be deemed to be a Director of the banking company.

(2) The 35[Chairman of the Board of Directors appointed on a whole-time basis or a Managing Director] so appointed by the Reserve Bank shall be in the whole-time employment of the banking company and shall hold office for such period not exceeding three years, as the Reserve Bank may specify, but shall, subject to other provisions of this Act, be eligible for re-appointment.

(3) The 35[Chairman of the Board of Directors who is appointed on a whole-time basis or a Managing Director] so appointed by the Reserve Bank shall draw from the banking company such pay and allowances as the Reserve Bank may determine and may be removed from office only by the Reserve Bank.

(4) Save as otherwise provided in this section, the provisions of section 10B shall, as far as may be, apply to the 35[Chairman of the Board of Directors appointed on a whole-time basis or a Managing Director] appointed by the Reserve Bank under sub-section (1) as they apply to a 35[Chairman of the Board of Directors appointed on a whole-time basis or the Managing Director] appointed by the banking company.]

10[10C. Chairman and certain Directors not to be required to hold qualification shares

35[A Chairman of the Board of Directors who is appointed on a whole-time basis or a Managing Director] of a banking company (by whomsoever appointed) and a director of a banking company (appointed by the Reserve Bank under section 10A) shall not be required to hold qualification shares in the banking company.]

10D. Provisions of sections 10A and 10B to override all other laws, contracts, etc.

Any appointment or removal of a 35[Director, Chairman of the Board of Directors who is appointed on a whole-time basis or Managing Director] in pursuance of section 10A or section 10B 10[or section 10BB] shall have effect and any such person shall not be entitled to claim any compensation for the loss or termination of office, notwithstanding anything contained in any law or in any contract, memorandum or articles or associations

11. Requirement as to minimum paid-up capital and reserves

(1) Notwithstanding anything contained in 38[section 149 of the Companies Act, 1956], no banking company in existence on the commencement of this Act, shall, after the expiry of three years from such commencement or of such further period not exceeding one year as the Reserve Bank, having regard to the interests of the depositors of the company, may think fit in any particular case to allow, carry on business 11[in India], and no other banking company shall, after the commencement of this Act, commence or carry on business 11[in India], 14[unless it complies with such of the requirements of this section as are applicable to it.]

14[(2) In the case of a banking company incorporated outside India-

(a) the aggregate value of its paid-up capital and reserves shall not be less than fifteen lakhs of rupees and if it has a place or places of business in the city of Bombay or Calcutta or both, twenty lakhs of rupees; and

(b) 39[the banking company shall deposit and keep deposited with the Reserve Bank either in cash or in the form of unencumbered approved securities, or partly in cash and partly in the form of such securities-

(i) an amount which shall not be less than the minimum required by clause (a); and

(ii) as soon as may be after the expiration of each 40[***] year, an amount calculated at twenty per cent of its profit for that year in respect of all business transacted through its branches in India, as disclosed in the profit and loss account prepared with reference to that year under section 29:]

PROVIDED that any such banking company may at any time replace-

(i) any securities so deposited by cash or by any other unencumbered approved securities or partly by cash and partly by other such securities, so however, that the total amount deposited is not affected;

(ii) any cash so deposited by unencumbered approved securities of an equal value.]

41[(2A) Notwithstanding anything contained in sub-section (2), the Central Government may, on the recommendation of the Reserve Bank, and having regard to the adequacy of the amounts already deposited and kept deposited by a banking company under sub-section (2), in relation to its deposit liabilities in India declare by order in writing that the provisions of sub-clause (ii) of clause (b) of sub-section (2) shall not apply to such banking company for such period as may be specified in the order.]

(3) In the case of any banking company to which the provisions of sub-section(2) do not apply, the aggregate value of its paid-up capital and reserves shall not be less than-

(i) if it has places of business in more than one State, five lakh of rupees, and if any such place or places of business is or are situated in the city of Bombay or Calcutta or both, ten lakhs of rupees;

(ii) if it has all its places of business in one State none of which is situated in the city of Bombay or Calcutta, one lakh of rupees in respect of its principal place of business, plus ten thousand rupees in respect of each of its other places of business, situated in the same district in which it has its principal place of business, plus twenty-five thousand rupees in respect of each place of business situated elsewhere in the State otherwise than in the same district:

PROVIDED that no banking company to which this clause applies shall be required to have paid-up capital and reserves exceeding an aggregate value of five lakhs of rupees:

PROVIDED FURTHER that no banking company to which this clause applies and which has only one place of business, shall be required to have paid-up capital and reserves exceeding an aggregate value of fifty thousand rupees:

41[PROVIDED FURTHER that in the case of every banking company to which this clause applies and which commences banking business for the first time after the commencement of the Banking Companies (Amendment) Act, 1962 (36 of 1962), the value of its paid-up capital shall not be less than five lakhs of rupees;]

(iii) if it has all its places of business in one State, or more of which is or are situated in the city of Bombay or Calcutta, five lakhs of rupees, plus twenty-five thousand rupees in respect of each place of business situated outside the city of Bombay or Calcutta, as the case may be:

PROVIDED that no banking company to which this clause applies shall be required to have paid-up capital and reserves exceeding an aggregate value of ten lakhs of rupees.

Explanation: For the purposes of this sub-section, a place of business situated 42[in a State] other than that in which the principal place of business of the banking company is situated shall, if it is not more than twenty-five miles distant from such principal place of business, be deemed to be situated within the same State as such principal place of business.

(4) Any amount deposited and kept deposited with the Reserve Bank under 43[*subsection (2) by any banking company incorporated 44[outside India] shall, in the event of the company ceasing for any reason to carry on banking business 11 [in

India], be an asset of the company on which the claims of all the creditors of the company 11[in India] shall be a first charge.

14[(5) For the purposes of this-section-

(a) "place of business" means any office, sub-office, sub-pay office and any place of business at which deposits are received, cheques cashed or moneys lent;

(b) "value" means the real or exchangeable value, and not, the nominal value which may be shown in the books of the banking company concerned.]

(6) If any dispute arises in computing the aggregate value of the paid-up capital and reserves of any banking company, a determination thereof by the Reserve Bank shall be final for the purposes of this section.

31[12. Regulation of paid-up capital, subscribed capital and authorised capital and voting rights of shareholders

(1) No banking company shall carry on business in India, unless it satisfies the following conditions, namely,-

(i) that the subscribed capital of the company is not less than one-half of the authorised capital and the paid-up capital is not less than one-half of the subscribed capital and that, if the capital is increased, it complies with the conditions prescribed in this clause, within such period not exceeding two years as the Reserve Bank may allow;

(ii) that the capital of the company consists of ordinary shares only or of ordinary shares or equity shares and such preferential shares as may have been issued prior to the lst day of July, 1944:

PROVIDED that nothing contained in this sub-section shall apply to any banking company incorporated before the 15th day of January, 1937.

(2) No person holding shares in a banking company shall, in respect of any shares held by him, exercise voting rights 28[on poll] 45[in excess of 46[ten per cent]] of the total voting rights of all the shareholders of the banking company.

(3) Notwithstanding anything contained in any law for the time being in force or in any contract or instrument no suit or other proceeding shall be maintained against any person registered as the holder of a share in a banking company on

the ground that the title to the said share vests in a person other than the registered holder:

PROVIDED that nothing contained in this sub-section shall bar a suit or other proceeding-

(a) by a transferee of the share on the ground that he has obtained from the registered holder a transfer of the share in accordance with any law relating to such transfer; or

(b) on behalf of a minor or a lunatic on the ground that the registered holder holds the shares on behalf of the minor or lunatic.

(4) Every Chairman, Managing Director or Chief Executive Officer by whatever name called of a banking company shall furnish to the Reserve Bank through that banking company returns containing full particulars of the extent and value of his holding of shares, whether directly or indirectly, in the banking company and of any change in the extent of such holding or any variation in the rights attaching thereto and such other information relating to those shares as the Reserve Bank may, by order, require and in such form and at such time as may be specified in the order.]

47[12A. Election of new Directors

(1) The Reserve Bank may, by order, require any banking company to call a general meeting of the shareholders of the company within such time, not less than two months from the date of the order, as may be specified in the order or within such further time as the Reserve Bank may allow in this behalf, to elect in accordance with the voting rights permissible under this Act fresh Directors, and the banking company shall be bound to comply with the order.

(2) Every Director elected under sub-section (1) shall hold office until the date up to which his predecessor would have held office, if the election had not been held.

(3) Any election duly held under this section shall not be called in question in any court.].

13. Restriction on commission, brokerage, discount, etc., on sale of shares

Notwithstanding anything to the contrary contained in 48[sections 76 and 79 of the Companies Act, 1956 (1 of 1956)1, no banking company shall pay out directly or indirectly by way of commission, brokerage, discount or remuneration in any form in respect of any shares issued by it, any amount exceeding in the aggregate two and one-half per cent of the paid-up value of the said shares.

14. Prohibition of charge on unpaid capital

No banking company shall create any charge upon any unpaid capital of the company, and any such charge shall be invalid.

28[14A. Prohibition of floating charge on assets

(1) Notwithstanding anything contained in section 6, no banking company shall create a floating charge on the undertaking or any property of the company or any part thereof, unless the creation of such floating charge is certified in writing by the Reserve Bank as not being detrimental to the interests of the depositors of such company.

(2) Any such charge created without obtaining the certificate of the Reserve Bank shall be invalid.

(3) Any banking company aggrieved by the refusal of certificate under sub-section (1) may, within ninety days from the date on which such refusal is communicated to it, appeal to the Central Government.

(4) The decision of the Central Government where an appeal has been preferred to it under sub-section (3) or of the Reserve Bank where no such appeal has been preferred shall be final.

15. Restrictions as to payment of dividend

49[(1)] No banking company shall pay any dividend on its shares until all its capitalised expenses (including preliminary expenses, organisation expenses, share selling commission, brokerage, amounts of losses incurred and any other item of expenditure not represented by tangible assets) have been completely written off.

28[(2) Notwithstanding anything to the contrary contained in sub-section (1) or in the Companies Act, 1956 (1 of 1956), a banking company may pay dividends on its shares without writing off-

(i) the depreciation, if any, in the value of its investments in approved securities in any case where such depreciation has not actually been capitalised or otherwise accounted for as a loss;

(ii) the depreciation, if any, in the value of its investments in shares, debentures or bonds (other than approved securities) in any case where adequate provision for such depreciation has been made to the satisfaction of the auditor of the banking company;

(iii) the bad debts, if any, in any case where adequate provision for such debts has been made to the satisfaction of the auditor of the banking company.]

31[16. Prohibition of common Directors

35[(1) No banking company incorporated in India shall have as a Director in its Board of Directors any person who is a Director of any other banking company.

(1A) No banking company referred to in sub-section (1) shall have in its Board of Directors more than three Directors who are Directors of companies which among themselves are entitled to exercise voting rights in excess of twenty per cent of the total voting rights of all the share-holders of that banking company.

(2) If immediately before commencement of the Banking Companies (Amendment) Act, 1956 (95 of 1956), any person holding office as a Director of a banking company is also a Director of companies which among themselves are entitled to exercise voting rights in excess of twenty per cent of the total voting rights of all the shareholders of the banking company, he shall, within such period from such commencement as the Reserve Bank may specify in this behalf-

(a) either resign his office as a Director of the banking company; or

(b) choose such number of companies as among themselves are not entitled to exercise voting rights in excess of twenty per cent of the total voting rights of all the shareholders of the banking company as companies in which he wishes to continue to hold the office of a Director and resign his office as a Director in the other companies.]

12[(3) Nothing in sub-section (1) shall apply to, or in relation to, any Director appointed by the Reserve Bank.]

14[17. Reserve Fund

(1) Every banking company incorporated in India shall create a reserve fund and 50[* **] shall, out of the balance of profit of each year, as disclosed in the profit and loss account prepared under section 29 and before any dividend is declared, transfer to the reserve fund a sum equivalent to not less than twenty per cent of such profit.

41[(1A) Notwithstanding anything contained in sub-section (1), the Central Government may, on the recommendation of the Reserve Bank and having regard to the adequacy of the paid-up, capital and reserves of a banking company in relation to its deposit liabilities, declare by order in writing that the provisions of sub-section (1) shall not apply to the banking company for such period as may be specified in the order:

PROVIDED that no such order shall be made unless, at the time it is made, the amount in the reserve fund under sub-section (1), together with the amount in the share premium account is not less than the paid-up capital of the banking company.]

(2) Where a banking company appropriates any sum from the reserve fund or the share premium account, it shall, within twenty-one days from the date of such appropriation, report the fact to the Reserve Bank, explaining the circumstances relating to such appropriation:

PROVIDED that the Reserve Bank may, in any particular case, extend the said period of twenty-one days by such period as it thinks fit or condone any delay in the making of such report.

51[18. Cash reserve

(1) Every banking company, not being a scheduled bank, shall maintain in India by way of cash reserve with itself or by way of balance in a current account with the Reserve Bank or by way of net balance in current accounts or in one or more of the aforesaid ways, a sum equivalent to at least three per cent of the total of its demand and time liabilities in India as on the last Friday of the second preceding fortnight and shall submit to the Reserve Bank before the twentieth day of every month a return showing the amount so held on alternate Fridays during a month with particulars of its demand and time

liabilities in India on such Friday or if any such Friday is a public holiday under the Negotiable Instruments Act, 1881 (26 of 1881), at the close of business on the preceding working day.

Explanation: In this section, and in section 24-

(a) "liabilities in India" shall not include-

(i) the paid-up capital or the reserves or any credit balance in the profit and loss account of the banking company,

(ii) any advance taken from the Reserve Bank or from the Development Bank or from the Exim Bank 52[or from the Reconstruction Bank] 19[or from the National Housing Bank] or from the National Bank 82[or from the Small Industries Bank] by the banking company;

(iii) in the case of a Regional Rural Bank, also any loan taken by such bank from its sponsor bank;

(b) "fortnight" shall means the period from Saturday to the second following Friday, both days inclusive;

(c) "net balance in current accounts" shall, in relation to a banking company, means the excess, if any, of the aggregate of the credit balance in current account maintained by that banking company with the State Bank of India or a subsidiary bank or a corresponding new bank over the aggregate of the credit balances in current account held by the said banks with such banking company;

(d) for the purpose of computation of liabilities, the aggregate of the liabilities of banking company to the State Bank of India, a subsidiary bank, a corresponding new bank, a Regional Rural Bank, another banking company, a co-operative bank or any other financial institution notified by the Central Government in this behalf, shall be reduced by the aggregate of the liabilities of all such banks and institutions to the banking company;

(e) the expression "Co-operative Bank" shall have the meaning assigned to it in clause (cci) of section 56.

(2) The Reserve Bank may, for the purpose of this section and section 24, specify from time to time, with reference to any transaction or class of transactions, that such transaction or transactions shall be regarded as liability in India of a banking company and, if any question arises as to whether any transaction or class of transaction shall be regarded for the

purposes of this section and section 24 as liability in India of a banking Company, the decision of the Reserve Bank thereon shall be final.]

19. Restriction on nature of subsidiary companies

10[(1) A banking company shall not form any subsidiary company except a subsidiary company formed for one or more of the following purposes, namely.-

(a) the undertaking of any business which, under clause (a) to (o) of sub-section (1) of section 6, is permissible for a banking company to undertake, or

(b) with the previous permission in writing of the Reserve Bank, the carrying on of the business of banking exclusively outside India, or

(c) the undertaking of such other business, which the Reserve Bank may, with the prior approval of the Central Government, consider to be conducive to the spread of banking in India or to be otherwise useful or necessary in the public interest.

Explanation: For the purpose of section 8, a banking company shall not be deemed, by reason of its forming or having a subsidiary company, to be engaged indirectly, in the business carried on by such subsidiary company.]

(2) Save as provided in sub-section (1), no banking company shall hold shares in any company, whether as pledgee, mortgagee or absolute owner, of an amount exceeding thirty per cent of the paid-up share capital of that company or thirty per cent of its own paid-up share capital under reserves, whichever is less: PROVIDED that any banking company which is on the date of the commencement of this Act holding any shares in contravention of the provisions of this sub-section shall not be liable to any penalty therefor if it reports the matter without delay to the Reserve Bank and if it brings its holding of shares into conformity with the said provisions within such period, not exceeding two years, as the Reserve Bank may think fit to allow.

(3) Save as provided in sub-section (1) and notwithstanding anything contained in sub-section (2), a banking company shall not, after the expiry of one year from the date of the commencement of this Act, hold shares, whether as pledge,

mortgagee or absolute owner, in any company in the management of which any Managing Director or Manager of the banking company is in any manner concerned or interested.

53[20. Restrictions on loans and advances

(1) Notwithstanding anything to the contrary contained in section 77 of the Companies Act, 1956 (1 of 1956), no banking company shall-

(a) grant any loans or advances on the security of its own shares, or

(b) enter into any commitment for granting any loan or advance to or on behalf of-

(i) any of its Directors,

(ii) any firm in which any of its Directors is interested as Partner, Manager, Employee or Guarantor, or

(iii) any company (not being a subsidiary of the banking company or a company registered under section 25 of the Companies Act, 1956 (1 of 1956), or a government company, of which 15[or the subsidiary or the holding company of which] any of the Directors of the banking company is a Director, Managing Agent, Manager, Employee or Guarantor or in which he holds substantial interest, or

(iv) any individual in respect of whom any of its Directors is a partner or guarantor

(2) Where any loan or advance granted by a banking company is such that a commitment for granting it could not have been made if clause (b) of sub-section (1) had been in force on the date on which the loan or advance was made or is granted by a banking company after the commencement of section 5 of the Banking Laws (Amendment) Act, 1968 (58 of 1968), but in pursuance of a commitment entered into before such commencement, steps shall be taken to recover the amounts due to the banking company on account of the loan or advance together with interest, if any, due thereon within the period stipulated at the time of the grant of the loan or advance, or where no such period has been stipulated, before the expiry of one year from the commencement of the said section 5:

PROVIDED that the Reserve Bank may, in any case, on an application in writing made to it by the banking company

in this behalf, extend the period for the recovery of the loan or advance until such date; not being a date beyond the period of three years from the commencement of the said section 5, and subject to such terms and conditions, as the Reserve Bank may deem fit: PROVIDED FURTHER that this sub-section shall not apply if and when the Director concerned vacates the office of the Director of the banking company, whether by death, retirement, resignation or otherwise.

(3) No loan or advance, referred to in sub-section (2), or any part thereof shall be remitted without the previous approval of the Reserve Bank, and any remission without such approval shall be void and of on effect.

(4) Where any loan or advance referred to in sub-section (2), payable by any person, has not been repaid to the banking company within the period specified in that sub-section, then, such person shall, if he is a Director of such banking company on the date of the expiry of the said period, be deemed to have vacated his office as such on the said date.

Explanation: In this section-

(a) "loan or advance" shall not include any transaction which the Reserve Bank may, having regard to the nature of the transaction, the period within which, and the manner and circumstances in which, any amount due on account of the transaction is likely to be realised, the interest of the depositors and other relevant considerations, specify by general or special order as not being a loan or advance for the purpose of this section;

(b) "Director" includes a member of any board or committee in India constituted by a banking company for the purpose of managing, or for the purpose of advising it in regard to the management of, all or any of its affairs.

(5) If any question arises whether any transaction is a loan or advance for the purposes of this section, it shall be referred to the Reserve Bank, whose decision thereon shall be final.]

54[20A. Restrictions on power to remit debts

(1) Notwithstanding anything to the contrary contained in section 293 of the Companies Act, 1956 (1 of 1956), a banking company shall not, except with the prior approval of the Reserve

Bank, remit in whole or in part any debt due to it by- (a) any of its Directors, or (b) any firm or company in which any of its Directors is interested as Director, Partner, Managing Agent or Guarantor, or (c) any individual if any of its Directors, is his Partner or Guarantor.

(2) Any remission made in contravention of the provisions of sub-section(1)shall be void and of no affect.]

21. Power of Reserve Bank to control advances by banking companies

(1) Where the Reserve Bank is satisfied that it is necessary or expedient in the public interest 86[or in the interests of depositors] 12[or banking policy] so to do, it may determine the policy in relation to advances to be followed by banking companies generally or by any banking company in particular, and when the policy has been so determined, all banking companies or the banking company concerned, as the case may be, shall be bound to follow the policy as so determined.

(2) Without prejudice to the generality of the power vested in the Reserve Bank under sub-section (1), the Reserve Bank may give directions to banking companies, either generally or to any banking company or group of banking companies in particulars, 9[as to-

(a) the purposes for which advances may or may not be made;

(b) the margins to be maintained in respect of secured advances;

(c) the maximum amount of advances or other financial accommodation which, having regard to the paid-up capital, reserves and deposits of a banking company and other relevant considerations, may be made by that banking company to any one company, firm, association to persons or individual;

(d) the maximum amount up to which, having regard to the considerations referred to in clause (c), guarantees may be given by a banking company on behalf of any one company, firm, association of persons or individual; and

(e) the rate of interest and other terms and conditions on which advances or other financial accommodation may be made or guarantees may be given.]

54[(3) Every banking company shall be bound to comply with any directions given to it under this section.]

15[21A. Rate of interest charged by banking companies not to be subject to scrutiny by courts

Notwithstanding anything contained in the Usurious Loans Act, 1918 (10 of 1918), or any other law relating to indebtedness in force in any State, a transaction between a banking company and its debtor shall not be reopened by any court on the ground that the rate of interest charged by the banking company in respect of such transaction is excessive.]

22. Licensing of banking companies

14[(1) Save as hereinafter provided, no company shall carry on banking business in India unless it holds a licence issued in that behalf by the Reserve Bank and any such licence may be issued subject to such conditions as the Reserve Bank may think fit to impose.].

(2) Every banking company in existence on the commencement of this Act, before the expiry of six months from such commencement, and every other company before commencing banking business 11 [in India], shall apply in writing to the Reserve Bank for a licence under this section:

PROVIDED that in the case of a banking company in existence on the commencement of this Act, nothing in sub-section (1) shall be deemed to prohibit the company from carrying on banking business until it is granted a licence in pursuance of 55[this section] or is by notice in writing informed by the Reserve Bank that a licence cannot be granted to it:

PROVIDED FURTHER that the Reserve Bank shall not give a notice as aforesaid to be a banking company in existence on the commencement of this Act before the expiry of the three years referred to in sub-section (1) of section 11 or of such further period as the Reserve Bank may under that sub-section think fit to allow.

(3) Before granting any licence under this section, the Reserve Bank may require to be satisfied by an inspection of the books of the company or otherwise that 56[***] the following conditions are fulfilled, namely:-

14[(a) that the company is or will be in a position to pay its present or future depositors in full as their claims accrue;

(b) that the affairs of the company are not being, or are not likely to be, conducted in a manner detrimental to the interests of its present or future depositors;]

10[(c) that the general character of the proposed management of the company will not be prejudicial to the public interest of its present or future depositors;

(d) that the company has adequate capital structure and earning prospects;

(e) that the public interest will be served by the grant of a licence to the company to carry on banking business in India;

(f) that having regard to the banking facilities available in the proposed principal area of operations of the company, the potential scope for expansion of banks already in existence in the area and other relevant factors the grant of the licence would not be prejudicial to the operation and consolidation of the banking system consistent with monetary stability and economic growth;

(g) any other condition, the fulfillment of which would, in the opinion of the Reserve Bank, be necessary to ensure that the carrying on of banking business in India by the company will not be prejudicial to the public interest or the interests of the depositors.]

15[(3A) Before granting any licence under this section to a company incorporated outside India, the Reserve Bank may require to be satisfied by an inspection of the books of the company or otherwise that the conditions specified in sub-section (3) are fulfilled and that the carrying on of banking business by such company in India will be in the public interest and that the government or law of the country in which it is incorporated does not discriminate in any way against banking companies registered in India and that the company complies with all the provisions of this Act applicable to banking companies incorporated outside India.]

14[(4) The Reserve Bank may cancel a licence granted to a banking company under this section:

(i) if the company ceases to carry on banking business in India; or

(ii) if the company at any time fails to comply with any of the conditions imposed upon it under sub-section (1); or

(iii) if at any time, any of the conditions referred to in sub-section (3) 15 [and sub-section (3A)] is not fulfilled:

PROVIDED that before cancelling a licence under clause (ii) or clause (iii) of this sub-section on the ground that the banking company has failed to comply with or has failed to fulfil any of the conditions referred to therein, the Reserve Bank, unless it is of opinion that the delay will be prejudicial to the interests of the companys depositors or the public, shall grant to the company on such terms as it may specify, and opportunity of taking the necessary steps for complying with or fulfilling such condition.

(5) Any banking company aggrieved by the decision of the Reserve Bank cancelling a licence under this section may, within thirty days from the date on which such decision is communicated to it, appeal to the Central Government.

(6) The decision of the Central Government where an appeal has been preferred to it under sub-section (5) or of the Reserve Bank where no such appeal has been preferred shall be final.]

14[23. Restrictions on opening of new, and transfer of existing, places of business

(1) Without obtaining the prior permissions of the Reserve Bank-

(a) no banking company shall open a new place of business in India or change otherwise than within the same city, town or village, the location of an existing place of business situated in India; and

(b) no banking company incorporated in India shall open a new place of business outside India or change, otherwise than within the same city, town or village in any country or area outside India, the location of an existing place of business situated in that country or area:

PROVIDED that nothing in this sub-section shall apply to the opening for a period not exceeding one month of a temporary place of business within a city, town or village or the environs thereof within which the banking company already has a place of business, for the purpose of affording banking facilities to the public on the occasion of an exhibition, a conference or a mela or any other like occasion.

(2) Before granting any permission under this section, the Reserve Bank may require to be satisfied by an inspection under section 35 or otherwise as to the financial condition and history of the company, the general character of its management, the adequacy of its capital structure and earning prospects and that public interest will be served by the opening or, as the case may be, change of location, of the place of business.

(3) The Reserve Bank may grant permission under sub-section (1) subject to such conditions as it may think fit to impose either generally or with reference to any particular case.

(4) Where, in the opinion of the Reserve Bank, a banking company has, at any time, failed to comply with any of the conditions imposed on it under this section, the Reserve Bank may, by order in writing and after affording reasonable opportunity to the banking company for showing cause against the action proposed to be taken against it, revoke any permission granted under this section.

57[(4A) Any Regional Rural Bank requiring the permission of the Reserve Bank under this section shall forward its application to the Reserve Bank through the National Bank which shall give its comments on the merits of the application and send it to the Reserve Bank:

PROVIDED that the Regional Rural Bank shall also send an advance copy of the application directly to the Reserve Bank.]

(5) For the purposes of this section "place of business" includes any sub-office, pay office, sub-pay office and any place of business at which deposits are received, cheques cashed or moneys lent.]

8

The Relationship between Banker and Customer

It is probably necessary to appreciate the nature of the relationship between a banker and his customer in order to understand the problems which would be encountered if steps were to be taken to protect the proceeds of benefit payments credited to a bank account from attachment on service of an arrestment. The banker/customer relationship was settled as long ago as 1848 in England by the

House of Lords in the case of Foley v Hill. The position has also been examined in Scotland and the following is an extract from The Laws of Scotland, Stair Memorial Encyclopaedia, Vol. 2, Banking and Financial Institutions paragraph 1168:- Relationship one of creditor and debtor. In Scotland the banker/customer relationship was described by Lord MacKay in Royal Bank of Scotland v Skinner 1931 SLT 382 at 384, OH. "After some fluctuation of opinion, it is now well settled that the relationship of customer and banker is neither a relation of principal and agent nor a relation of a fiduciary nature, trust, or the like, but a simple relation-it may be one sided, or it may be two-sided-of creditor-debtor. The banker is not, in the general case, the custodian of money. When money is paid in, despite the popular belief, it is simply consumed by the banker, who gives an obligation of equivalent amount". That statement accurately reflects the position under English Law as decided in Foley v Hill above. Where the customer has more than one account (one in debit and one in credit) and the banker has an exercisable right of set-off between the accounts, it is the net balance (if any) which the bank is liable to repay to the customer.

In the circumstances once money, whether representing the proceeds of a benefit payment or any other source, is credited to a bank account it simply becomes a debt due by the bank to the account holder and it is not necessary to identify the source of the funds credited to the account.

The decision in the case of Devaynes v Noble, (Clayton's Case) (1816) established the principle that the first credit to a bank account is reduced/extinguished by the first debit and consequently over a series of transactions between a bank and its customer the balance standing to the credit of an account is composed of the most recent credit/s to the account.

What is Attached by an Arrestment?

When an arrestment is served on a bank it is the bank's obligation to account to its customer for any credit balance due by the bank to that customer which is attached, not the actual money standing to the credit of a particular account.

Consequently the obligation extends to all sums due by the bank (including accounts held in different branches of the bank) to the customer and there is no need for the pursuing creditor to specify which account or which actual money held in the bank's books he is seeking to attach. (This is very different to the position of a Third Party Debt Order in England & Wales where it is necessary to specify the branch of the bank, the account name and number and for the creditor to pay a statutory fee of £55 to the bank to process the Order.)

If the above principle were to be changed in line with the desire of Citizens Advice Scotland ("CAS") if would be necessary for primary legislation to be passed to overturn the existing common law position. This would result in all credits to a bank account requiring clear identification as to their origin and a calculation being made as to what constitutes the balance of an account. A simple example may illustrate the potential problems which would be encountered.

Following the principle established in Clayton's Case only £50 of the creditor balance of £150.00 is made up from the Benefit payments. If the proposal put forward by CAS were to be accepted it would become necessary in every case where an arrestment is received by a bank for that bank to carry out a calculation as above to ascertain how much of the outstanding balance is attached. If in addition to the above account there is a second account where the same customer is due the bank say £100 by way of overdraft, the bank would be entitled to exercise its right of set-off thereby reducing the creditor balance to £50. Based on the rule in Clayton's Case it would appear that the resultant £50 would be attached by the arrestment as it would not represent the proceeds of the benefit payments but further clarification may be required.

What Happens where an Account is Overdrawn?

Where a credit representing a benefits payment is received for the credit of an overdrawn account it will immediately reduce/repay the amount overdrawn. That reflects the debtor-creditor relationship that exists between banker and customer. Whether the customer will be able to withdraw a sum equivalent to the amount received for the credit of the account will depend on whether there is a fluctuating overdraft facility in existence for the account or whether the debt stands for reduction only.

SUMMARY

All funds paid into a bank account become the property of the bank subject to the customer's right to demand repayment of any debt due by the bank. Any change would be a major shift in long established banking principles and could impact on all manner of banking products and arrangements. Considerable research would require to be undertaken to ascertain the potential unintended results. It is safe to assume that there would be considerable opposition to any change to banking law in this respect in view of the additional work which it would entail for banks in Scotland. Any change could also affect a bank's views on whether to bank such customers as it would make banking in Scotland more complex than in England & Wales. Apart from the particular circumstances envisaged by CAS it is difficult to see what advantages would accrue to any other customer of a bank. In any event, as it is the intention to introduce a minimum protected sum for all personal customers of £304 or higher, a customer receiving benefits payments will be protected to that extent. In addition, someone finding themselves in a situation where they have multiple debts would better to enter into a debt arrangement scheme or at least agree weekly/monthly repayments with his/her principal creditors in order to avoid the possibility of them serving arrestments or using other forms of diligence in an effort to obtain repayment.

It appears that CAS may not be addressing the real source of the problem. Trying to protect benefits from the effects of diligence may not result in a debtor's obligations being reduced and if not, recovery action in one form or another will continue. For the banking industry to function smoothly for the benefit of all customers, whether personal, commercial or corporate, simplicity and certainty for all is essential otherwise the costs of undertaking complex calculations for certain classes of customers could result in these costs being passed on to the customer base as a whole.

WOLFGANG WIEGAND*

Legal Aspects of the Bank-Customer Relationship in Electronic Banking**

PRELIMINARY REMARKS ON TOPIC AND TITLE

Electronic Banking has become the major topic in banking during the last decade of the past century. The reason is obvious. E-Banking is a part of E-Commerce, which is both one of the most significant products of the I(nformation) T(echnology) and one of its moving factors. Altogether, they are elements of what has become commonly known as 'Globalisation'. It is therefore a challenging task for any lawyer to speak or write about E-Banking. It is even more fascinating if this is combined with the bank-customer relationship. For the following reasons it may be also dangerous (especially in front of such an audience) to 'discuss legal aspects of the bank-customer relationship in E-Banking':

The bank-customer relationship is already a very complex and difficult item. The difficulties multiply if the relationship is combined with the technology of Electronic Banking.

1 Notwithstanding the fact that all over the world quite a lot has been written about E-Banking, the whole issue reminds me of medieval cartography. Cartographers did not like to concede that certain areas had not yet been 'discovered'. Therefore, instead of printing 'terra incognita' into the white spots, they put in 'ubi sunt hones'. It is my impression that in E-Banking today we have many spots 'where the lions are'.

It is for that reason that I will approach my topic step by step: First, I will deal with the legal aspects of the bank-customer relationship, then I will discuss some legal aspects of E-Banking and in a third step I will try to give a combined view of the legal aspects of the bank-customer relationship and E-Banking.

LEGAL ASPECTS

A. Structure and Variety of Bank Services

What we all thought to be true has been confirmed: Bank services are offered in a broad spectrum that is broadening every day. I do not think it is necessary to reiterate what has been mentioned by several contributors, especially by Mr. Breuer.

I would rather draw your attention to the fact that the variety of services has to be taken into account when we discuss the legal concept of the bank-customer relationship. This is one of the reasons why we cannot speak about the bank-customer relationship. There is another reason. One must not only differentiate according to the type of services rendered by the bank, but also take into consideration that corresponding to the different types of services there are different types of customers.

B. The Corresponding Variety of Customers

Looking at the counterpart of the bank, the different types of transactions are reflected by different types of persons contracting with the bank. There is not a uniform type of customer. Rather, there are many different types of customers pursuing different interests with different levels of competence and ability to do business. For the purpose of this paper and for reasons I will return to later I will use only two categories, customers that are clients and customers that are consumers.

I call 'clients' all those people who deal with banks at arm's length, who are able to protect and to further their interests. These people may use the consultancy services of banks, they may accept advice but they deal on the same level and as equals with the banks. This is true for the more or less wealthy people that are taken care of by the banks under the title of Private Banking or other comparable terms. On the other end of the spectrum we have the so-called Retail Banking where millions of people do their daily transactions like paying their mortgage interests or the rent for their homes, their insurance premiums and receiving their salaries and from time to time making some small investment. All these people are certainly consumers. They have neither the choice nor the chance to negotiate anything with the bank. They use the services under the terms of the general conditions of the bank whether they may accept these conditions for services rendered or not. The motto is 'take it or leave it'. For those people consumer protection rules have been developed worldwide, not restricted to the bank-customer relationship but of special import and significance in this legal relationship. And here is the genuine field of E-Banking. Before I return to that in a more specific way I will shortly deal with the legal concept of the bank-customer relationship as a whole.

C. The Legal Framework

The Simple Pattern 'One Transaction-One Contract'?

Looking at the variety of services rendered and the corresponding variety of clients it goes without saying that the legal feature of the bank-customer relationship should reflect these differences. That is true and simple if there is just one transaction or one type of service. If someone cashes a check or changes some money at the counter, these are simple transactions following the pattern 'one transaction-one contract'. But most people have a more complex relationship to their bank. In all these relations, the bank account is the centre and the basis for most of the services mentioned above. The combination of those services like payments, orders, small or major investments in the capital market or even asset management results in several different kinds of contracts or, as many authors say, a 'bundle of contracts'."

The Construct of the 'General Banking Contract'

Looking at this situation, the question has been raised by some authors whether there is a link or a common ground to all these contracts. In Germany, legal scholars have developed the figure of the 'General Banking Contract' {'Allgemeiner Bankvertragf as a so-called 'frame' or 'basic contract' for all sort of bank-customer relationships. On a high academic level there is an ongoing debate whether such a contract exists or cannot exist for dogmatic reasons. Whereas prominent authors deny the necessity and even the possibility of such a construct, I myself have taken the position that this is not a Prince-Hamlet-question 'to be or not to be'. In my view, it is rather a question of the most pragmatic way of organising the bank-customer relationship ('Geschäftsverbindung').

Looking at the results, there is namely one point that might be of some importance. Following the concept of the General Banking Contract, the General Contract Conditions are automatically applied in any additional business-contact between the bank and the customer, even before it comes to the conclusion of another additional contract, which is a substantial advantage for the bank.

Regarding all other points, there are no real differences between the results of both concepts, for the following reason: Under the prevailing doctrine in Germany, Switzerland and Austria mutual obligations of both parties exist from the first moment of business-contact between them. These obligations include inter alia duties of information, disclosure or as the case may be even warning.

Therefore, as a result, the legal situation of both the bank and the customer is quite the same as under the General Banking Contract.

D. The Regulatory Environment

Whereas the debate about the General Banking Contract is rather of academic nature and with little impact on bank-practice and, in addition, to a certain extent 'typically German', I will now turn to a really important point, an aspect all systems have in common and which is of higher significance for the modern banking law: The multilateral influence of various kinds of legislation and soft law on the bank-customer relationship." Due to this regulatory environment there are extreme restraints on the traditional concept of contractual freedom. These restraints stem from a network of regulations starting with traditional supervisory and prudential regulations, which are nowadays interlinked with provisions of criminal and administrative law. While the traditional prudential regulations were based on the principle of customer and creditor protection, the most influential and heavy restrictions stem now from the internationally accepted common goal to fight organised crime and money laundering. These regulations interfere in all phases of the bank-customer relationship.

The traditional 'know your customer-rule' was based on typical bank business experience and aims, adopted by the banks in their own interest, whereas now the 'know your customer-principle' mixes up with the banker's duty to identify the customer and to verify the purpose of the business, to clarify the origin of the money and so on.

Based on this system, there is a feedback to the traditional prudential regulations and supervisory rules because the supervisory authorities, such as the Swiss Federal Banking Commission, now assume that the banks' controlling duties also comprise identification rules as described before. As a consequence, one can say that this is a change of paradigms: Banks take part in an international system of mutual control including their own supervision, the bank-customer relationship as a private law contract is overlapped and partly overruled by public law provisions (in continental terminology), not only restricting the freedom of contract but also-as many observers believe-destroying the confidence between bank and customer, which is considered the most important element of this relation.

In addition to these public law rules, the traditional pattern of contract law has been put aside or amended to a great extent by consumer protection rules. Their importance and the impact on contract law is increasing nearly day by day for two interrelated reasons. One reason has already been touched upon earlier. In my division of customers into clients and consumers, I have mentioned that traditionally wealthy people investing money with banks have to fulfil the conditions to be considered as a client.

Development of case law and consumer protection rules as well as many legal authors have together caused a tendency to consider even those people as consumers. This means that they need protection as well in a way to be discussed later on. A second reason for the increasing influence of consumer law is that consumer protection is spreading into more and more fields of law. One of those fields is E-Commerce and E-Banking, to which we will turn now.

LEGAL ASPECTS OF ELECTRONIC BANKING

E-Banking as a Part of E-Commerce

E-Banking is a special form of E-Commerce. Since E-Commerce has spread all over the world, many institutions have started to draw up regulations or proposals for international rules on E-Commerce. In 1996, UNCITRAL established a model law on E-Commerce" and the European Union has set up a framework of regulations, the Directive 97/7/EC on the protection of consumers in respect to distance contracts, the Directive 2000/31/EC on certain legal aspects of information society services, in particular Electronic Commerce, in the internal market (Directive on Electronic Commerce) and the proposed Directive on financial services.

The Directive on distance contracts is focussing on consumers' protection, as the title already indicates. This directive is applicable to E-Commerce, but not to financial services, which are expressly exempted by Art. 3. Nevertheless, the directive is important for the understanding of the consumer protection concept in distant market transaction. Moreover, the gap will be filled by the-already mentioned-proposal of the commission for the financial services Directive, which includes an amendment of the Directive 97/7/EC and adapts its regulations to the special situation of electronic financial transactions. The E-Commerce Directive, however, is applicable to financial services right now. Although the main goal of this directive is to further 'the development of E-Commerce within the information society', it contains substantial protection rules. They all have one thing in common, and that is true not only for the regulations of the European Union:" To protect people concluding distance contracts by the use of modern technology. The directive of the European Union pursues that aim by a two-step-method. On a first level the Directive on Electronic Commerce constitutes information duties which have to be fulfilled by the provider of services with respect to every customer. Art. 5 'General information to be provided' reads:

'I. In addition to other information requirements established by Community law, Member States shall ensure that the service provider shall render easily, directly and permanently accessible to the recipients of the service and competent authorities, at least the following information:

(a) the name of the service provider;

(b) the geographic address at which the service provider is established;

(c) the details of the service provider, including his electronic mail address, which allow him to be contacted rapidly and communicated within a direct and effective manner;

(d) where the service provider is registered in a trade or similar public register, the trade register in which the service provider is entered and his registration number, or equivalent means of identification in that register;

(e) where the activity is subject to an authorisation scheme, the particulars of the relevant supervisory authority;

(f) as concerns the regulated professions:

- any professional body or similar institution with which the service provider is registered,
- the professional title and the Member State where it has been granted,
- a reference to the applicable professional rules in the Member State of establishment and the means to access them;

(g) where the service provider undertakes an activity that is subject to VAT, the identification number referred to in Article 22(1) of the sixth Council Directive 77/388/ EEC of 17 May 1977 on the harmonisation of the laws of the Member States relating to turnover taxes-Common system of value added tax: uniform basis of assessment (29).

2. In addition to other information requirements established by Community law, Member States shall at least ensure that, where information society services refer to prices, these are to be indicated clearly and unambiguously and, in particular, must indicate whether they are inclusive of tax and delivery costs.' In a second step an additional duty of information is established by Art.

'Information to be provided

1. In addition to other information requirements established by Community law, Member States shall ensure, except when otherwise agreed by parties who

are not consumers, that at least the following information is given by the service provider clearly, comprehensibly and unambiguously and prior to the order being placed by the recipient of the service:

(a) the different technical steps to follow to conclude the contract;

(b) whether or not the concluded contract will be filed by the service provider and whether it will be accessible;

(c) the technical means for identifying and correcting input errors prior to the placing of the order;

(d) the languages offered for the conclusion of the contract.

2. Member States shall ensure that, except when otherwise agreed by parties who are not consumers, the service provider indicates any relevant codes of conduct to which he subscribes and information on how those codes can be consulted electronically.

3. Contract terms and general conditions provided to the recipient must be made available in a way that allows him to store and reproduce them.

4. Paragraphs 1 and 2 shall not apply to contracts concluded exclusively by exchange of electronic mail or by equivalent individual communications.' The scope of application of this provision is restricted by two exemptions made by the Directive:

Paragraph 4 states that 'Paragraphs 1 and 2 shall not apply to contracts concluded exclusively by exchange of electronic mail or by equivalent individual communications'. This exception is of high theoretical and practical importance because it is based on a principal distinction made by the Directive and the implementing legislation.

Communications that allow direct, immediate and individual contact between the parties are considered to be and, therefore, treated like declarations between persons present which, obviously, is a circumstance crucial for the conclusion of the contract. Consequently, I will return to that when discussing the formation of contract.

The second exception is made 'when otherwise agreed by parties who are not consumers' (Paragraph 1). This exemption is fundamental not only for the E-Commerce Directive but also for the EU legislation and moreover for wide parts of legislation around the world.

Most of the rules made in favour of the consumer are imperative and, thus, restrain the autonomy of the contracting parties. Only a segment of population, the group of non-consumers, has (and enjoys) still the freedom of contract as it was conceptualised by the great continental codifications of the 19 th and 20''' century.

By agreement with the service provider, these non-consumers can waive their obligation to inform as provided by Paragraph 1 and 2.

For Switzerland cf. note 20, draft for a new art. 4 paragraph 2 of the Code of Obligations; for Germany the draft of a law concerning the revision of the Civil Code (Regierungsentwurf eines Gesetzes zur Modernisierung des Schuldrechts vom 9.5.2001); for England the Consumer Protection (Distance Selling) Regulations 2000 No. 2334. At this stage, 1will not discuss this information itself, which is all related to the specific technology used by the parties, but give a little thought to the purpose and the concept behind that. Both Art. 5 and Art. 10 start with the phrase 'in addition to other information requirements established by community law'. That means that the information duties in this Directive are an 'overhead' to already existing duties based on other directives. And indeed, these duties are specifically designed with respect to the method and means of communications. Nevertheless, the duties constituted by these directives and others are based on a general concept, which is normally called the information model or the principle of transparency.

I think it is not necessary to discuss this in detail, but I have to repeat the rationale behind the concept. On one hand, the idea is that one of the contracting partners has an advantage of knowledge, which must be compensated by information to give the other side the chance to decide 'en connaissance de cause'. It is for that reason that all the information duties have to be fulfilled before the potential contract-partner makes his decision ('prior to the order being placed'). We have to keep that in mind, because I will return to the information duty in the next section.

In addition to these information duties, the E-Commerce Directive of the European Union, but also the respective laws or suggested regulations in other countries, for example the proposal for Switzerland, include regulations regarding the conclusion of contract. In this regard, all regulations refer to the technique of the digital signature and its application to the formation of contract. This includes two totally different aspects: One is the question of formal requirements of the contract, the other one is the problem of safety of communication.

To solve the form problem, attempts have been made all over the world to substitute the traditional requirements by adequate electronic means. For a long time, the digital signature was considered the solution, because it can be regarded as equivalent substitute for the traditional hand signing of a contractual document.

Therefore, the EU and many other countries and paragraphs I and 2, but not for 3 and the General Contract Conditions; for that see below institutions drafted regulations focusing on the digital signature based on the public/private key technology.

However, the transformation into a practically manageable tool turned out to be more difficult than expected.

Whereas this is a general problem of E-Commerce, the safety aspect, although also a general problem, is of paramount importance-which brings me to the bank-specific aspects of E-Commerce.

Specific Problems of E-Banking

What is addressed generally with regard to E-Commerce under the title of safety of communication and data protection is a specific problem of banking law since bank secrecy is one of the most crucial and important problems of bank business. This is more or less true for all countries, but obviously in a special way for Switzerland.

Therefore, the question arises how the requirements of protection of bank secrecy can be complied with in electronic transactions. Putting aside the technical means which make it possible to protect the customer (although we have learned from Professor Hoeren that nothing is safe), we have to discuss whether banks have to take care of that problem by formulating respective clauses in their contract conditions. I will return to that point in the third section. On the other hand, banks have the duty-for reasons already discussed-to identify their customers. How that can be done in an electronic way and without endangering the bank secrecy is currently one of the most discussed problems, by banks as well as by supervisory authorities, in many European countries.

I will deal with that in the next section, where I will discuss how the legal aspects, of which I have given a very superficial overview, are interlinked and interrelated or, in other words, their interaction.

ACCUMULATION AND INTERACTION OF DUTIES IN THE ELECTRONIC BANK-CUSTOMER RELATIONSHIP

The Pre-Contractual Phase

Accumulation of Duties of Disclosure and Information

If one puts both the duties in the pre-contractual phase of the bank-customer contract" and those of E-Banking together, it results in an accumulation of duties. Based on general contract law, the bank has the duty to inform the customer about the structure and risk of the intended transaction and, moreover, under several jurisdictions it is expressly stated by statutory law or developed by case law that the bank has the duty to elaborate a profile of the customer. Based on that profile, the bank has to assess whether the customer has the financial means and the necessary knowledge for the intended transaction.

In addition to those traditional information and disclosure duties, the banks now have under the E-Commerce regulation the duty to supply the information that has been mentioned earlier.

Firstly, the information to be provided under Art. 5 of the E-Commerce rule, which meanwhile has been transformed into national laws in many jurisdictions of the EU or shall be integrated into them, for example into Swiss law by the proposal for an E-Commerce act.

Secondly, and still before the conclusion of the contract, the information required by Art. 10 of the E-Commerce Directive must be added, i.e.:

'(a) the different technical steps to follow to conclude the contract;

(b) whether or not the concluded contract will be filed by the service provider and whether it will be accessible;

(c) the technical means for identifying and correcting input errors prior to the placing of the order;'

This looks complicated, and it is. Satisfaction of these obligations would be easy if persons talked face-to-face, but it is quite difficult to manage all this by electronic means and to do it in a way that the obligations are really fulfilled. Therefore, it comes not as a surprise that the consequences of not performing these duties are disputed. In Germany for instance, the first Proposal of the draft law concerning the revision of the German Civil Code stated in § 305b Paragraph 5 'Non-performance of one of the duties mentioned above has no influence on the effectiveness of the contract.'

This paragraph however has been cancelled in the course of the revision of § 312e Paragraph 3, which reads in the actual Proposal 'Further-reaching duties of information based on other provisions are not concerned'.

In Switzerland, the legislator believes that it is more adequate to put these duties in the framework of unfair competition, which is only at first glance a better solution.

Besides the nature of those duties, their content and the way to comply with the requirements of Art. 5 and 10 is problematic. How can the bank, for example, provide 'the technical means for identifying and correcting input errors prior to placing the order'? And more generally, the crucial point is that the bank must have evidence that all the information has been given and, moreover, that it has been given 'clearly, comprehensibly and unambiguously'; and, in addition to that, for example the jurisprudence of the Swiss Supreme Court is going so far as to claim that the service provider has to check whether the customer really understood the information.

Duty to Give Advice or Warnings?

As earlier referred, it is common ground that banks have duties of information, disclosure and advice. It makes no sense to discuss here in detail how this obligation can be fulfilled with respect to the specific situation of E-Commerce and E-Banking. However, I will give just one Preliminary draft of a law concerning the revision of the German Civil Code (Diskussionsentwurf des Schuldrechtmodernisierungsgesetzes des Bundesministeriums der Justiz vom 4. August 2000).

'This e-mail message is confidential and may contain legally privileged information. If you are not the intended recipient you should not read, copy, distribute, disclose or otherwise use the information in this e-mail. Please also telephone or fax us immediately and delete the message from your system. | > mail may be susceptible to data corruption, interception and unauthorised amendment, and we do not accept liability for any such corruption, interception or amendment or the consequences thereof What I have quoted from this law firm's e-mail cover sounds like information, but it also includes a warning. This leads to the general question, whether the duties of the banks using electronic means are restricted to simple information or must be extended further to warning and advice. It is plain from case law and legal writing that the borderline between all three duties is small and cannot be drawn exactly.

Therefore most authors believe that under certain circumstances banks have the duty to warn the customer if specific risks come into play. This concept has been developed with regard to financial risks, but it is only a special feature of the general duty of loyalty all parties owe each other in the pre-contractual stadium.

Therefore, these duties comprise the risks caused by the use of the new technology.

Such a risk, in our case, might be the endangerment of the bank secrecy. Therefore, a bank offering financial services by electronic means has to decide whether already at this early stage the customer's attention should be drawn to the bank secrecy topic or if that may be done in a later phase of the bank-customer relationship in connection with the conclusion of the contract. This, however, will be discussed below in a more detailed manner. From here it is just a step to the next point. The question arises, whether the banks should give advice to the customer, and this is again asked in a double sense. It is not disputed that banks have a duty to give advice in the pre-contractual relationship, but only to what extent. With E-Banking, there is a second aspect of this duty. The advice should be given for the use of the technology as provided by Art. 5 and 10 of the E-Commerce Directive.

The content itself is comparable to a user's manual or instructions that come with products, but the advice must be given before the conclusion of the contract.

Taking a look at homepages and directories for E-Banking, one will already find advice to safe and proper use of electronic means.

Customer's Obligations

On the other hand, it goes without saying that the customer, too, has obligations in this pre-contractual phase of the business relations. Besides the well-known duty of loyalty and the duty to provide the bank with the necessary information as to his identity, purposes of the transactions, etc., an additional duty of the customer arises when using modern technologies. He has to comply with the advice and information given by the bank to make proper use of the means. This is of special relevance for the formation of a contract, which I will turn to now.

Conclusion of Contract

First, we must be aware of the two different situations to deal with: The easy one is where the customer already has a bank account or has otherwise done business with the bank. Under these circumstances, it is only a transformation from normal banking to E-Banking. Therefore, everything that has been said about the bank-customer relations, the 'know your customer-principle' and the mutual obligations are not new for this relationship. But everything concerning the special aspects of E-Banking must be taken into consideration at a certain moment which is usually when the customer asks the banker 'Could we do that by E-Banking?' or vice versa when he is asked (as it happens to everyone of us from time to time) 'Why don't you use the much easier way of E-Banking?' Then all the information described above must be given to the customer, and, at present, certainly a warning must be given concerning bank secrecy and data protection.

Most of the banks try to comply with these prerequisites by an agreement on the General Contract Conditions for E-Banking. Before I discuss this in more detail, I would like to take a look at the second and much more complicated situation. It is the problem of opening an account by electronic means without having been a customer to that bank before.

In this situation we have to deal with two problems. One has already been touched upon just before, but not addressed. It is the question of how we handle the declaration of will in electronic means. When I have said that the banks in transforming existing bank relations into E-Banking asked the customer to agree to the special conditions of E-Banking contracts, then this is an amendment of that contract, which has to be done by exchange of declarations of will. Again, this is easier in a pre-existing relation. Of course, it is beyond doubt that declarations of will can be exchanged by electronic means. Disputes have, however, arisen in two areas. One is whether and how the prerequisites of form can be fulfilled by using electronic means, the other one is how the traditional model of exchange of offer and accept works in this field.

It is my understanding that most jurisdictions take the position that advertisement and things alike do not constitute an offer.

An exception is made by Swiss Code of Obligation, Art. 7 § 3, which reads: 'The display of goods with an indication of their price is, however, as a rule considered to be an offer.' The proposal for the Swiss law on Electronic Commerce will extend this to services presented in an electronic way.

Therefore, already today in anticipation of that situation Swiss Banks on their homepages expressly point out that services presented cannot be considered as a binding offer. It is questionable how and to what extent this will work in practice.

Even more questionable is the way of the Directive on Electronic Commerce: Its Art. 11 deals with 'placing of the order' and provides as follows:

1. Member States shall ensure, except when otherwise agreed by parties who are not consumers, that in

cases where the recipient of the service places his order through technological means, the following principles apply:

- the service provider has to acknowledge the receipt of the recipient's order without undue delay and by electronic means,
- the order and the acknowledgement of receipt are deemed to be received when the parties to whom they are addressed are able to access them.

2. Member States shall ensure that, except when otherwise agreed by parties who are not consumers, the service provider makes available to the recipient of the service appropriate, effective and accessible technical means allowing him to identify and correct input errors, prior to the placing of the order.
3. Paragraph 1, first indent, and paragraph 2 shall not apply to contracts concluded exclusively by exchange of electronic mail or by equivalent individual communications.'

This provision is the result of a compromise. The idea is that the conclusion of the contract follows the rules of the respective jurisdiction. Therefore, it is and shall be a question of national contract law to decide what is the offer and the acceptance and at which moment the conclusion of the contract must be fixed. Notwithstanding this, the provision imposes an additional obligation to inform the user of the service immediately about the receipt of his order. The reason is twofold. First, it aims at the consumer's protection. He shall be, as soon as it reasonably can be done or expected, informed whether the order has been received and accepted; furthermore, as with all EU regulations, the equal treatment of consumers should be granted. Nevertheless, the doubts and differences are numerous: The effect ofthat 'acknowledgement' depends on the concept of the applicable national law. In German or Austrian law, the 'acknowledgement' may have only the function of a confirmation of receipt or a confirmation of the (foregoing) conclusion of the contract ('Bestätigungsschreiben')."

But it may well be that this declaration must be understood as the acceptance of the order and, therefore, marks the conclusion of the contract. It is for this reason that, again, the sanctions of the violation of this additional duty is in the same way disputed as the consequences of the violation of the specific E-Commerce information duties.

Notwithstanding the unclear function of the 'acknowledgement', Art. 11 contains further points that are important for E-Commerce law and obviously for the E-Banking business.

Paragraph 1 and 2 repeat and confirm the limitations of application already made by and discussed in connection with Art. 5:

Non-consumers can waive the application of Art. 11, which, furthermore, is not applied at all if 'contracts concluded exclusively by exchange of electronic mail or by equivalent individual communications' (Paragraph 3) are concerned.

Kramer Ernst A" Schweigen auf kaufmännische Bestätigungsschreiben und rechtsgeschäftlicher Vertrauensgrundsatz, in: recht (1990). p. 99 ss. The second exemption does not comprise Paragraph 1, second indent. This exception of the exception (which in my view also should have been made for the first exemption) is plain from the content of this indent:

'-the order and the acknowledgement of receipt are deemed to be received when the parties to whom they are addressed are able to access them' (Paragraph 1). It is obvious that this is not an isolated provision created with regard to the purpose of Art. 11. Instead, it contains a general principle concerning the receipt of a declaration of will when the declaration is transmitted by electronic means. It transforms and-at the same time-confirms the concept codified in Germany (§ 130 of the Civil Code) and adopted by doctrine in Switzerland and Austria.

It goes without saying that this indent-as its wording 'offer and acknowledgement' indicates-has to be applied to all 'electronic' declarations of will. This is certainly true for the EU countries, but also accepted in other jurisdictions.

Opening of a New Account

Whereas conclusion of contract and compliance with form requirements are problems to be solved in any E-Commerce transaction, there are special and additional problems when a bank account shall be opened. These problems have just been indicated by using the word 'identity', and I need not reiterate what I have said about identification of the customer.

In all countries, under the described restraints of public law, it is still difficult, if not impossible, to open an account by electronic means. As far as Switzerland is concerned, the Swiss Federal Bank Commission has edited minimal standards for Internet banks."

General Contract Conditions

As the last step of the conclusion of the contracts most banks want to have included in the contractual relation the General Contract Conditions and, in addition to that, the special contract conditions for E-Banking. By doing so, they try to resolve some of the problems described above, as bank secrecy, the proper use of technology and the obligations of the customer to give special care to the PIN code and comparable sensitive items. Therefore, the issue of General Contract Conditions has two aspects. The first is, how they can be integrated into the contract, and the second is, whether at all and if so, to what degree, the used clauses are valid.

As to the first point, the national rules of contract law apply and I do not dare in front of Norbert Horn, one of the 'Gurus' of the General Contract Condition law, discuss that in detail. I would rather draw the attention to the fact that, beside those national rules, an additional obligation is established in the EC Directive. This obligation can be complied with before concluding the contract or after it had been concluded, and it is formulated as follows: 'Contract terms and general condition provided to the recipient must be made available in a way that allows him to store and reproduce them'.

And again, the consequences of not complying with this provision are questionable. In my view, the violation of this duty has no effect on the validity of the contract and the included General Contract Terms if the requirements for their incorporation as provided by national law have been fulfilled. For that situation, I consider the application of the rules of unfair competition as an adequate sanction.

Performance Phase

Traditional and New Duties of the Bank

When rendering the services bank and customer have agreed upon, the bank has traditional duties, especially the due diligence and, as far as German, Swiss and Austrian law is concerned, fiduciary obligations. In addition to these traditional duties, the bank has to comply with duties such as protection of the bank secrecy and the data of the customer, which have already been mentioned in connection with the pre-contractual phase, but nevertheless have to be fulfilled in the performance phase as well. Their extent depends on the law applicable in the respective case. Furthermore, there are duties of information with respect to the technology. The bank has to inform the customer about foreseeable system failures, interruptions by scheduled maintenance services and so on. Corresponding to that, the customer has the obligation to inform the bank immediately if he might have lost his code, pin or other sensitive items. Both obligations aim at the avoidance of upcoming risks.

But many of the risks of the modern technology are unforeseeable, some are unavoidable. Therefore one of the main issues of the discussion about E-Banking is how the liability problem can be solved by a just allocation of risks.

The Allocation of Risk and the General and Special Contract Conditions

Nearly all financial institutions try to transfer the risk to the customer by a combined use of General Contract Conditions and special E-Net or E-Banking conditions. I will discuss some of the clauses regarding non-performance of the main contractual obligation as well as the duty of information. When I discuss those clauses-selected from major banks forms-it is not my intention to measure whether a specific national law or the jurisprudence of the respective courts would accept those clauses by applying the current standards of control of general terms of contracts and the national contract law. I would rather discuss whether under the perspective of reasonable distribution of risk such clauses are acceptable.

There are two types of clauses: One group is expressly conceived as exclusion of liability, whereas another group of rules could be characterised as regarding the distribution of risk.

(i) Common in General Bank Conditions is the following clause: 'The [Bank] accepts no guarantee whatsoever that the data transmitted by it via the Internet is correct and complete. In particular, information relating to accounts and safekeeping accounts (balances, statements, transactions etc.) as well as information which is generally available, such as stock market and foreign currency rates, is deemed to be provisional and not binding. Data via the Internet does not represent a binding offer unless it is expressly denoted as a binding offer.'

'The bank assumes no responsibility whatsoever for the accuracy and the completeness of data which it transmits. In particular, information regarding accounts (balances, statements, transactions) and generally available information, such as stock market prices and foreign exchange rates, is to be regarded as provisional and non-binding and further the bank accepts no liability whatsoever for losses incurred by the customer or its authorized representatives as a result of transmission errors, technical faults, lost connections, malfunction or illegal tempering with telecommunication systems.'

On the other hand 'the customer and his authorized representatives are obligated to keep the password as well as the authorization codes [...] secret and to prevent their misuse by unauthorized persons. In particular, after it has been changed, the password must not be written down or stored unprotected on the customer's computer. The customer bears the consequences of all risk arising from the disclosure of his authorization characteristics or those of his authorized representatives.'

The last clause sounds reasonable and allocates the risk where it lies. The first two clauses are unacceptable for two different reasons. The first clause contains a manifest violation of the duties of the bank. If a bank offers services including prices or figures of a statement, it is its contractual obligation to provide correct data to the customer. If the bank does not want to be bound by the figures transmitted by the Internet it should not offer Internet banking. It is nothing else than a venire contra factum proprium to persuade the customers to use E-Banking and to state at the same time that all declarations given by electronic means are not reliable or binding (but only for the bank)!

The same is true in another way for the second clause. It is not acceptable to agree mutually on the use of Internet technology but to transfer the consequences of any transmission failure to the customer. Even worse is the clause that can be found in some of the conditions excluding the liability of the bank for any failure of their intern IT-system or interruption of availability due to maintenance or other comparable reasons. In my view there can be no doubt that more reasonable and just distributions of risk will be enforced not only by courts which have already started to do so, but also by the market which will not accept such distribution of risk-an aspect I will return to at the end.

(ii) The second group of clauses is not formulated as an exclusion of liability but advice or warning in the sense described above. Those clauses concern the information the customer should be given due to the duties of disclosure and information as described above. I give three examples:

- 'Particular importance was attached to security in the development of Internet Banking. A multi-stage security system which utilizes, amongst other things, cryptographic procedures of a very high standard, was developed in order to protect the customer. As a result of the encryption it is fundamentally impossible for any unauthorized person to view confidential customer account data. Nevertheless, it is not possible to guarantee total security both for the [Bank] as well as the customer even with all the state of the art security precautions. The user acknowledges that his computer in particular represents the weak link in Internet Banking. [...]'
- 'The customer acknowledges the following risks in particular: Insufficient system knowledge and inadequate security precautions can make unauthorized access easier (e.g. insufficient estimate of the space needed for saving data on the hard disk, file transfers, screen display etc.). The customer is responsible for obtaining precise information on the necessary security precautions.

No one can rule out the possibility of the customer's Internet provider creating a traffic characteristic, i.e. this provider has the facility to find out when the customer has been in contact with whom.

There is the risk of a third party obtaining access to the customer's computer unnoticed whilst the customer is using the Internet.

When using the Internet there is the risk of computer viruses being spread to the computer. So-called virus scanners can assist the customer in his security precautions.

It is important for the customer to only work with software from a reliable source.'

'The customer acknowledges that the data is transported via an open network, the Internet, to which everyone has access. Data is therefore regularly transmitted across national borders without being monitored. This also applies to a data transfer when sender and recipient are located in Switzerland. Although the individual data packages are transmitted in encrypted form, sender and recipient in each case however remain unencrypted. This information can also be read by third parties. It is therefore possible for a third party to draw conclusions about the existence of a bank relationship.'

Again: It is not my intention to discuss in detail which would be the reaction of national courts or which particular sentence could not be accepted. Instead 1 would like to emphasise that these clauses are different from those excluding liability. The banks try to separate the risk spheres by describing the risk and using the formula 'the customer acknowledges'. In my view most of the information given is correct and helpful. I doubt, however, whether this information is clear enough to meet the standards established by legal scholars and courts (at least in Europe) with regard to the obligation of information, disclosure and especially warning. Thus, for example in Switzerland, additional advice should be given that the customer, by accepting the conditions, renounces protection of the bank secrecy when the data is sent across national border. The same is true with the general description of the risk of using the Internet. Nevertheless, clauses of this kind are arguable and the extents to which they are acceptable depends on a general assessment of the just distribution of risk. Regarding this just distribution it is necessary and helpful to consider the question in a wider context.

A Distant View

The feature we are looking at is no surprise for everyone who is familiar with legal history. It is a well known and often described tendency when the kinds of production change, new technologies come into play and new products enter into the market.

Though it would be tempting to discuss this in a detailed manner I restrict myself to a few remarks. The first concerns the legislature for the Austrian Civil Code in the beginning of the 19 th century.

The question of what degree of negligence would be necessary but also sufficient for liability was a major issue. It was argued that a strict concept of negligence would be an impediment for the development of economy and business and, therefore, could not be acceptable for the new code. A hundred years later a New York judge held:

'We must have factories, machinery, dams, canals and railroads. They are demanded by the manifold wants of mankind and lie at the basis of all our civilization. If Ihave any of these upon my lands, and they are not a nuisance and are not so managed as to become such, I am not responsible for any damage they accidentally and unavoidably do my neighbour. He receives his compensation for such damage by the general good, in which he shares, and the right which he has to place the same thing upon his land.'

And even going further, the Supreme Court of the State of New York decided 1911:

> *'It would be quite as logical and effective to argue that this legislation only reverses the laws of nature, for in everything within the sphere of human activity the risks which are inherent and unavoidable must fall upon those who are exposed to them... The Constitution,... in substance and effect, forbids that a citizen shall be penalized or subjected to liability unless he has violated some law or has been guilty of some fault.'*

However, due to the change of the assessment of industrial interests and social protection nobody would share the view of the New York judges. They, nevertheless, show that it is not outrageous, even not unusual, that within a period of change the producer of risk as well as the society, which believes in the profit, that the new technology of new products will bring to the common wealth, consider it as 'normal' to allocate the risk to the individual suffering the damage. To phrase it in another way: Under those specific circumstances the principle casum sentit dominus or in common law 'the losses lie where they fall' is accepted as a natural rule and not overruled by liability provisions that transfer the risk to the producer of that risk. Having this in mind it is easier to understand the rationale of the General Contract Conditions and their special E-Banking Conditions when banks offer Electronic Banking to their customers. Notwithstanding that background, the banks will not be able to further the electronic technique of banking without reconsidering their attitude with regard to the allocation of risk. This leads to some final remarks.

SUMMARY AND PERSPECTIVE

When E-Banking or generally E-Commerce entered into the market a change of paradigm seemed to have started. Meanwhile hopes have been set back and prognoses were corrected. The reasons for this more realistic view are manifold and cannot be discussed in detail in this context. It is plain that the development in the technology industry and the respective market is one of the reasons, but not the only one. Changing assessment of the future in development of the different branches of the bank industry and the extremely high costs for information technology have forced the banks to reconsider their strategy. Notwithstanding this change of view, E-Banking will play an important role in the bank business. The legal framework is about to be constructed by the legislators, jurisprudence and legal theory. I have tried to show that many of the traditional concepts of contract law can be applied without any problem to this form of banking, amended and supported by the new regulations that have been established all over the world, in Europe by the European Union and the implementing national legislation as well as corresponding proposals in other countries like Switzerland or Eastern Europe. On the other hand, it is necessary to find a balanced distribution of risk, i.e. to avoid that the risk is totally transferred to the customer but also to avoid customer protection that suffocates the whole E-Banking. If this is accomplished, the future of E-Banking hasjust begun.

NEGOTIABLE INSTRUMENTS ACT, 1981

The Negotiable Instruments Act was passed in 1881. Some provisions of the Act have become redundant due to passage of time, change in methods of doing business and technology changes. However, the basic principles of the Act are still valid and the Act has stood test of time. The Act extends to the whole of India. There is no doubt that the Act is to regulate commercial transactions and was drafted to suit requirements of business conditions then prevailing.

The instrument is mainly an instrument of credit readily convertible into money and easily passable from one hand to another.

LOCAL USAGE PREVAILS UNLESS EXCLUDED-The Act does not affect any local usage relating to any instrument in an oriental language. However, the local usage can be excluded by any words in the body of the instrument, which indicate an intention that the legal relations of the parties will be governed by provisions of Negotiable Instruments Act and not by local usage. [section 1].--Thus, unless specifically excluded, local usage prevails, if the instrument is in regional language.

BILL OF EXCHANGE AND PROMISSORY NOTES EXCLUDED FROM INFORMATION TECHNOLOGY ACT-Section (1)(4)(a) of Information Technology Act provides that the Act will not apply to Bill of Exchange and Promissory Notes. Thus, a Bill of Exchange or Promissory Note cannot be made by electronic means. However, cheque is covered under of Information Technology Act and hence can be made and / or sent by electronic means.

CHANGES MADE BY AMENDMENT ACT, 2002-(a) Definition of 'cheque' and related provisions in respect of cheque amended to facilitate electronic submission and/or electronic clearance of cheque. Corresponding changes were also made in Information Technology Act. (b) Bouncing of cheque-Provisions amended * Provision for imprisonment upto 2 years against present one year * Period for issuing notice to drawer increased from 15 days to 30 days * Government Nominee Directors excluded from liability * Court empowered to take cognizance of offence even if complaint filed beyond one month * Summary trial procedure permitted for imposing punishment upto one year and fine even exceeding Rs 5,000 * Summons can be issued by speed post or courier service * Summons refused will be deemed to have been served * Evidence of complainant through affidavit permitted * Bank's slip or memo indicating dishonour of cheque will be prima facie evidence unless contrary proved * Offence can be compounded.--The amendments have been made effective from 6-2-2003.

Transferee can get better title than transferor-Normal principle is that a person cannot transfer better title to property that he himself has. For example, if a person steals a car and sells the same, the buyer does not get any legal title to the car as the transferor himself had no title to the car. The real owner of car can anytime obtain possession from the buyer, even if the buyer had purchased the car in good faith and even if he had no idea that the seller had no title to the car. This provision is no doubt sound, but would make free negotiability of instrument difficult, as it would be difficult to verify title of transferor in many cases. Hence, it is provided that if a person acquires 'Negotiable Instrument' in good faith and without knowledge of defect in title of the transferor, the transferee can get better title to the negotiable instrument, even if the title of transferor was defective. This is really to ensure free negotiability of instrument so that persons can deal in the instrument without any fear.

DIFFERENCE BETWEEN NEGOTIATION AND TRANSFER/ASSIGNMENT-Difference between "Negotiation' and assignment/transfer is that in case of negotiation, the transferee can get title better than transferor, which can never happen in assignment/transfer.

STATUTORY DEFINITION OF NEGOTIABLE INSTRUMENT-A "negotiable instrument" means a promissory note, bill of exchange or cheque payable either to order or to bearer. Explanation (i): A promissory note, bill of exchange or cheque is payable to order which is expressed to be so payable or which is expressed to be payable to a particular person, and does not contain words prohibiting transfer or indicating an intention that it shall not be transferable. Explanation (ii): A promissory note, bill of exchange or cheque is payable to bearer which is expressed to be so payable or on which the only or last endorsement is an endorsement in blank. Explanation (iii): Where a promissory note, bill of exchange or cheque, either originally or by endorsement, is expressed to be payable to the order of a specified person, and not to him or his order, it is nevertheless payable to him or his order at his option. [section 13(1)].--A negotiable instrument may be made payable to two or more payees jointly, or it may be made payable in the alternative to one of two, or one or some of several payees. [section 13(2)].

Promissory Note-A "promissory note" is an instrument in writing (not being a bank-note or a currency-note) containing an unconditional undertaking, signed by the maker, to pay a certain sum of money only to, or to the order of, a certain person, or to the bearer of the instrument. [Section 4].

Bill of Exchange-As per statutory definition, "bill of exchange" is an instrument in writing containing an unconditional order, signed by the maker, directing a certain person to pay a certain sum of money only to, or to the order of, a certain person or to the bearer of the instrument. [Para 1 of section 5]. A cheque is a special type of Bill of Exchange. It is drawn on banker and is required to be made payable on demand.

DRAWER, DRAWEE AND PAYEE-The maker of a bill of exchange or cheque is called the "drawer"; the person thereby directed to pay is called the "drawee" [section 7 para 1].--The person named in the instrument, to whom, or to whose order the money is by the instrument directed to be paid, is called the "payee" [section 7 para 5].--However, a drawer and payee can be one person as he can order to pay the amount to himself.

AT SIGHT, ON PRESENTMENT, AFTER SIGHT-In a promissory note or bill of exchange the expressions "at sight" and "on presentment" mean 'on demand'. The expression "after sight" means, in a promissory note, after presentment for sight, and, in a bill of exchange, after acceptance, or noting for non-acceptance, or protest for non-acceptance. [section 21].--Thus, in case of document 'after sight', the countdown starts only after document is 'sighted' by the concerned party.

Stamp duty on Negotiable Instrument-A negotiable instrument is required to be stamped. Stamp duty on Bill of Exchange and Promissory Note is a Union Subject. Hence, stamp duty is same all over India.

Hundi-a local instrument-Hundi is an indigenous instrument similar to Negotiable Instrument. The term is derived from Sanskrit word 'hund' which means 'to collect'. If it is drawn in local language, it is governed by local usage and customs.

Provisions in respect of Cheques-A "cheque" is a bill of exchange drawn on a specified banker and not expressed to be payable otherwise than on demand. 'Cheque' includes electronic image of a truncated cheque and a cheque in electronic form. [section 6]. The definition is amended by Amendment Act, 2002, making provision for electronic submission and clearance of cheque. The cheque is one form of Bill of Exchange. It is addressed to Banker. It cannot be made payable after some days. It must be made payable 'on demand'.

Crossing of Cheque-The Act makes specific provisions for crossing of cheques.

CHEQUE CROSSED GENERALLY-Where a cheque bears across its face an addition of the words "and company" or any abbreviation thereof, between two parallel transverse lines, or of two parallel transverse lines simply, either with or without the words "not negotiable", that addition shall be deemed a crossing, and the cheque shall be deemed to be crossed generally. [section 123]

CHEQUE CROSSED SPECIALLY-Where a cheque bears across its face an addition of the name of a banker, either with or without the words "not negotiable", that addition shall be deemed a crossing, and the cheque shall be deemed to be crossed specially, and to be crossed to that banker. [section 124].

PAYMENT OF CHEQUE CROSSED GENERALLY OR SPECIALLY-Where a cheque is crossed generally, the banker on whom it is drawn shall not pay it otherwise than to a banker. Where a cheque is crossed specially, the banker on whom it is drawn shall not pay it otherwise than to the banker to whom it is crossed, or his agent for collection. [section 126].

CHEQUE BEARING "NOT- NEGOTIABLE"-A person taking a cheque crossed generally or specially, bearing in either case the words "not negotiable", shall not have, and shall not be capable of giving, a better title to the cheque than that which the person form whom he took it had. [section 130]. Thus, mere writing words 'Not negotiable' does not mean that the cheque is not transferable. It is still transferable, but the transferee cannot get title better than what transferor had.

Electronic Cheque-Provisions of electronic cheque has been made by Amendment Act, 2002. As per Explanation I(a) to section 6, 'A cheque in the electronic form' means a cheque which contains the exact mirror image of a paper cheque, and is generated, written and signed by a secure system ensuring the minimum safety standards with the use of digital signature (with or without biometrics signature) and asymmetric crypto system.

Truncated Cheque-Provisions of electronic cheque has been made by Amendment Act, 2002. As per Explanation I(b) to section 6, 'A truncated cheque' means a cheque which is truncated during the clearing cycle, either by the clearing house during the course of a clearing cycle, either by the clearing house or by the bank whether paying or receiving payment, immediately on generation of an electronic image for transmission, substituting the further physical movement of the cheque in writing.

Penalty in case of dishonour of cheques for insufficiency of funds-If a cheque is dishonoured even when presented before expiry of 6 months, the payee or holder in due course is required to give notice to drawer of cheque within 30 days from receiving information from bank.. The drawer should make payment within 15 days of receipt of notice. If he does not pay within 15 days, the payee has to lodge a complaint with Metropolitan Magistrate or Judicial Magistrate of First Class, against drawer within one month from the last day on which drawer should have paid the amount. The penalty can be upto two years imprisonment or fine upto twice the amount of cheque or both. The offense can be tried summarily. Notice can be sent to drawer by speed post or courier. Offense is compoundable.

It must be noted that even if penalty is imposed on drawer, he is still liable to make payment of the cheque which was dishonoured. Thus, the fine/imprisonment is in addition to his liability to make payment of the cheque.

Return of cheque should be for insufficiency of funds-The offence takes place only when cheque is dishonoured for insufficiency of funds or where the amount exceeds the arrangement. Section 146 of NI Act only provides that once complainant produces bank's slip or memo having official mark that the cheque is dishonoured, the Court will presume dishonour of the cheque, unless and until such fact is disproved.

Calculation of date of maturity of Bill of Exchange-If the instrument is not payable on demand, calculation of date of maturity is important. An instrument not payable on demand is entitled to get 3 days grace period.

Presentment of Negotiable Instrument-The Negotiable Instrument is required to be presented for payment to the person who is liable to pay. Further, in case of Bill of Exchange payable 'after sight', it has to be presented for acceptance by drawee. 'Acceptance' means that drawee agrees to pay the amount as shown in the Bill. This is required as the maker of bill (drawer) is asking drawee to pay certain amount to payee. The drawee may refuse the payment as he has not signed the Bill and has not accepted the liability.

In case of Promissory Note, such acceptance is not required, as the maker who has signed the note himself is liable to make payment. However, if the promissory note is payable certain days 'after sight' [say 30 days after sight], it will have to be presented for 'sight'.

If the instrument uses the expressions "on demand", "at sight" or "on presentment", the amount is payable on demand. In such case, presentment for acceptance is not required. The Negotiable Instrument will be directly presented for payment.

Acceptance and payment for honour and drawee in need-Provisions for acceptance and payment for honour have been made in case when the negotiable instrument is dishonoured. Bill is accepted for honour when it is dishonoured when presenting for acceptance, while payment for dishonour is made when Bill is dishonoured when presented for payment.

Negotiation of Instrument-The most salient feature of the instrument is that it is negotiable. Negotiation does not mean a mere transfer. After negotiation, the holder in due course can get a better title even if title of transferor was defective. If the instrument is 'to order', it can be negotiated by making endorsement. If the instrument is 'to bearer', it can be negotiated by delivery. As per definition of 'delivery', such delivery is valid only if made by party making, accepting or indorsing the instrument or by a person authorised by him.

An instrument can be negotiated any number of times. As per section 118(e), endorsements appearing on the negotiable instrument are presumed to have been made in the order in which they appear on the instrument, unless contrary is proved. [There is no mandatory provision to put date while signing, though advisable to do so]. Section 118(d) provides that there is presumption that the instrument was negotiated before its maturity, unless contrary is proved. As per section 60, Bill can be negotiated even after date of maturity by persons other than maker, drawee or acceptor after maturity. However, person getting such instrument is not 'holder in due course' and does not enjoy protections available to 'holder in due course'.

Liability of parties-Basic liability of payment is as follows- (a) Maker in case of Promissory Note or Cheque and (b) Drawer of Bill till it is accepted by drawee and acceptor after the Bill is accepted. They are liable as 'principal debtors' and other parties to instrument are liable as sureties for maker, drawer or acceptor, as the case may be. When document is endorsed number of times, each prior party is liable to each subsequent party as principal debtor. In case of dishonour, notice is required to be given to drawer and all earlier endorsees.

PRESUMPTIONS AS TO NEGOTIABLE INSTRUMENTS- Until the contrary is proved, the following presumptions shall be made:-(a) of consideration-that every negotiable instrument was made or drawn for consideration, and that every such instrument, when it has been accepted, indorsed, negotiated or transferred, was accepted, indorsed, negotiated or transferred for consideration;--(b) as to date-that every negotiable instrument bearing a date was made or drawn on such date;--(c) as to time of acceptance-that every accepted bill of exchange was accepted within a reasonable time after its date and before its maturity;--(d) as to time of transfer--that every transfer of a negotiable instrument was made before its maturity;--(e) as to order of indorsements-that the indorsements appearing upon a negotiable instrument were made in the order in which they appear thereon; (f) as to stamps-that a lost promissory note, bill of exchange or cheque was duly stamped;--(g) that holder is a holder in due course-that the holder of a negotiable instrument is a holder in due course: provided that, where the instrument has been obtained from its lawful owner, or from any person in lawful custody thereof, by means of an offence or fraud, or has been obtained from the maker or acceptor thereof by means of an offence or fraud, or for unlawful consideration, the burden of proving that the holder in due course lies upon him. [section 118]

The main purpose for which the Act was designed was to ensure information about all deals concerning land so that correct land records could be maintained. The Act is used for proper recording of transactions relating to other immovable property also. The Act provides for registration of other documents also, which can give these documents more authenticity. Registering authorities have been provided in all the districts for this purpose.

Note that this registration is entirely different from registration of charge done by Registrar of Companies under Companies Act. If the charge relates to immovable property, registration with Registrar (appointed by State Government) under Registration Act and registration under Companies Act with ROC are both required.

Documents of which registration is compulsory-Registration of documents relating to immovable property is compulsory. Registration of will is optional.

Documents not requiring registration-Some documents though related to immovable property are not required to be registered. These are given in section 17(2) of the Act.

Time of presentation for registration-Document should be submitted for registration within 4 months from date of execution [section 23]. Decree or order of Court can be submitted within four months from the day it becomes final. If document is executed by several persons at different times, it may be presented for registration within 4 months from date of each execution [section 24]. If a document is executed abroad by some of the parties, it can be presented for registration within four months after its arrival in India [section 26].

RE-REGISTRATION-If a person finds that a document has been filed for registration by a person who is not empowered to do so, he can present the document for re-registration within 4 months from the date he became aware of the fact that registration of document is invalid [section 23A].

Where document should be registered-Document relating to immovable property should be registered in the office of Sub-Registrar of sub-district within which the whole or some portion of property is situated [section 28]. Other document can be registered in the office of Sub-Registrar where all persons executing the document desire it to be registered [section 29]. A Registrar can accept a document which is registerable with sub-registrar who is subordinate to him [section 30(1)]. Document should be presented for registration at the office of Registrar/Sub-Registrar. However, in special case, the officer may attend residence of any person to accept a document or will [section 31].

All persons executing document must appear before Registrar-All persons executing the document or their representatives, assigns or agents holding power of attorney must appear before registering officer [section 34(1)]. They have to admit execution and sign the document in presence of Registrar, as required under section 58(1)(a). Appearance may be simultaneous or at different times [section 34(2)]. If some of the persons are unable to appear within 4 months, further time upto additional 4 months can be given on payment of fine upto 10 times the proper registration fee [proviso to section 34(1)].

If document relates to transfer of ownership of immovable property, passport size photograph and finger prints of each buyer and seller of such property shall be affixed to document. [proviso to section 32A]. The Registrar is required to ensure that these are endorsed on the document.

Registration by Registering Officer-If the Registering Officer is satisfied about identity of persons and if they admit about execution of documents, and after registration fees are paid, the registering officer will register the document [section 35(1)]. He will make necessary entries in the Register maintained by him.

Certification of registration-After all formalities are complete, the Registering Officer will endorse the document with word 'Registered', and sign the same. The endorsement will be copied in Register. After registration, the document will be returned to the person who presented the document [section 61].

Effective date of document-A document takes effect from its date of execution and not from date of registration. However, if the document states that it will be effective from a particular date, it will be effective from that date [section 47].

Document registered has priority over oral agreement-Any non-testamentary document registered under the Act takes effect against any oral agreement relating to the property. The only exceptions are: (a) If possession of property (movable or immovable) is delivered on basis of such oral agreement and such delivery of possession is valid transfer under any law (b) Mortgage by deposit of title deeds takes effect against any mortgage deed subsequently executed and registered which relates to same property [section 48].

Effect of non-registration-If a document which is required to be registered under section 17 or under provisions of Transfer of Property Act, 1882 is not registered, the effect is that such un-registered document * does not affect any immovable property comprised therein * cannot be received as evidence of any transaction affecting such property.---Thus, the document becomes redundant and useless for all practical purposes. It can be accepted as evidence in

9

Modern Commerce, Modern Banking and e-Commerce

The aim of this chapter is to use historical insights from modern commerce as entry points to examine the macro-level phenomena associated with electronic commerce. Commerce in its modern form first appeared in early 13th century Italy where conducive political conditions existed. Trade facilitated the exchange of goods, thereby enhancing the efficiency of processes between production and consumption. Even more important was its role in raising the level of human capital, promoting the spread of ideas and information, changing people's attitudes and behaviour. Some modern business practices and institutions which evolved with modern commerce are bookkeeping, modern banking, commodities market, putting out systems (or outsourcing as we know it now), insurance, stock exchange, and venture capital.

The current historical context favorable to e-commerce is globalization. The emergence of network organizations helped to establish some of the practices supporting business-to-business electronic commerce. E-commerce holds the potential to reduce time and transaction costs. However, the historical perspective suggests that the most profound implications of e-commerce are likely to be at the macro-level or socio-institutional level. Some implications can already be seen while others are still developing. We are witnessing the impacts of e-commerce on older business practices, and business models while there are likely implications for business cycles. Such a perspective can provide pointers for future research. Lessons from history suggest a need to pay due attention to intervention at the socio-institutional level to reap the benefits of this form of commerce.

INTRODUCTION

E-commerce is a commercial activity dealing directly with the trading of goods and services and with other related business activities, in which the electronic communication medium plays a central role. These activities include the communication of information, the management of payment, the negotiating and trading of financial instruments, and the management of transport. As an economic activity, e-commerce represents an inter-play of physical, human and societal resources. Physical resources include natural resources, technologies and physical infrastructure.

Human resources refer to human labour, knowledge and skill in their broadest sense.

Societal resources include resources residing in moral and ethical systems, institutions, culture, language, social harmony and community spirit. EC operates within the constraints of these three resources while, at the same time, influencing and moulding them. These three resources have much in common with the human, physical and natural capital identified by the World Bank (2000) in a model used to investigate growth and development.

This paper aims to contribute to a meaningful and well-informed examination of the macro-level phenomena associated with EC, and why economists and policy-makers should pay due attention to them. It further aims to show that solid theoretical and conceptual frameworks for guiding research into e-commerce can be found based on a study of the history of modern commerce. I assume that history is indispensable in shaping our understanding of the present and our quest for enlightenment on the future is rooted in understanding of the past and the present. Insights from the past are meant to serve as entry points for studying the on-going e-commerce.

WHAT CAN WE LEARN FROM HISTORY OF MODERN COMMERCE

Commerce increases the efficiency of the processes between production and consumption. This relation may be termed the first order effect. However, historical hindsight shows the importance of societal context and of the contributions made by commerce to the formation of socio-economic institutions and business practices. These contributions may be termed the higher order effects whose consequences are more far-reaching for societal development. This paper, given its scope, will not consider the even greater effects of commerce on political, cultural, intellectual, and philosophical dimensions, as evidenced during the Renaissance. It will confine itself to applying insights from history to the study the EC's impact on socio-economic institutions and other macro-level phenomena. The use of history to inform inquiry into the societal effects of technology-related innovations is a rewarding approach adopted by many researchers, e.g. Drucker (1965), Rosenberg (1976), Freeman (1987) and Shapiro and Varian (1999).

SOCIETAL CONTEXT

Thirteenth Century Italy witnessed a community of traders active within a greater society undergoing profound cultural, economic, social and political transformation (Braudel 1985). The political freedom in Italy was conducive to lively commerce and innovations, and the subsequent societal conditions ushered in the Renaissance (Hale 1993; Roberts 1996; Finer 1997). The Italian experience is an illustrative case study of how trade and business operated on the basis of existing technology and culture and within the constraints of political conditions. Traders conduct their business on the principle of making a profit in the process of buying and selling goods. The first order effect of their activities directly promoted efficiency between production and consumption, and indirectly promoted the utilization of resources. Scholars of economic history, however, recognized that the economic repercussions of trading activities went well beyond efficiency in the use of resources in the trading activities themselves (Bauer 2000).

These activities resulted in much more than markets for specific products. They helped to create commercial institutions and practices and raise the level of human capital, which proved to be of great utility to the entire economy in the ensuing era of rapid industrialization (Price 1989). These repercussions or higher order effects result in immense social implication when viewed from a broader and longer term perspective (Bauer 2000). This phenomenon is also observed to be present in the history of technology (Malone and Rockart 1991).

Electronic Commerce in Today's Context

With the benefits of insight from the history of modern commerce, one can study the historical context of EC, and its first and higher order effects. Globalization is the current historical context favouring EC. The emergence of network organizations has helped establish some of the practices supporting business-to-business (B2B) electronic commerce.

The first order effect of e-commerce is the reduction of time and transaction cost, thereby promoting efficiency in the link between production and consumption. Some of the higher order effects already exist; some are still in development while others represent potential institutional changes. This paper discusses the following effects:

1. The release of labour and capital resources from intermediary activities into the production of goods and services, thereby exerting a deflationary effect.
2. The stimulation and fulfillment of an increasingly widespread demand brought on by the wider market open to EC, thereby encouraging expansion in industry and global trade.
3. An increase in inter-dependency among business firms that also creates a demand for rating agencies.
4. Challenges to the logic and assumptions of traditional business models by new business models.
5. The stimulation of businesses to engage in areas hitherto alien to them, thus promising an enhancement of innovative processes.
6. A transformation of the banking sector.

Emergent trends confirm the historical experience that the far-reaching consequences of e-commerce are likely to be at the level of social institutions. History also suggests a need to pay due attention to intervention of socio-institutional structure to reap the benefits of EC.

My approach involves some affinity with that taken by Choi et al. (1997). They correctly observe that electronic commerce goes beyond the mere adoption of new Internet technology for conducting traditional business practices. "Electronic commerce operates in a new electronic marketplace where the very players, products and processes are fundamentally changed." (Choi et al., 1997, p. 463.) The approach in this paper is different from Choi et al. in that their emphasis is at the micro level such as copyright protection, product choice, and discriminatory pricing while my emphasis is more on the macro level where I look at the effects of e-commerce on existing business institutions and on the formation of new business institutions and practices. My overlap with them lies in the areas of electronic payment systems and business and policy implications of EC.

By its very nature, a new institution does not emerge like Minerva from Jove's forehead. Typically, it is the outcome of countless modifications of earlier practices, made as a result of practical experience. Successful formation of institutions is not merely an armchair exercise. The nature of such a social process implies that we can observe the impacts of e-commerce at macro level only after a time lapse.

INSIGHTS FROM ECONOMIC HISTORY

The beginning of the last millennium saw an interesting change in Europe. Towns were gradually being transformed from bishops' seats of administration and fortified havens into vital centres of economic life. They also came to play an important role in political development (Lopez 1976; Finer 1997). When the kingship was powerful, a coherent political system was in effective operation. Where it was weak, the kingdom dissolved into a collection of petty principalities, free cities, and even city republics. Italy was perhaps the most extreme example of the disintegration of such political arrangement. This change proved favorable for cities like Venice, Florence, and Genoa which bloomed and grew to become economic and cultural engines. These cities drove and expressed new aspirations and ways of thinking directed to material purposes and created new social behaviours. Venice was a great commercial centre, and it was here that banking for the first time separated itself from the changing of money (Roberts 1996). Indeed, the word "bank" derives from the Italian "banco," the small table or bench on which the banker kept his accounts of deposits and loans (Sylla 2004). Florence was the focus of the most intense and influential cultural activity in the whole of Europe. From 1350 to 1450, more scholars, artists, scientists, architects, and poets lived and worked in Italy than anywhere else in the western world. Many of them came from other countries to participate and contribute to that great unplanned historical phenomenon known later as the Renaissance. "Europe went, as it were, to school there." (Roberts 1996, p.193.)

Against this background of intellectual vitality, flourishing commerce brought with it a chain of institutional innovations. The Bill of Exchange appeared in the 13th century along with the first bankers. Limited liability was known in Florence in 1408, and marine insurance was available before that (Roberts 1996). Double entry bookkeeping evolved to meet the needs of merchants (Bodie and Merton 1998). By 1500, Italians invented new credit instruments for the financing of international commerce. The forerunners of present-day manufacturers were the merchants who adopted and refined the Verlagswesen or the putting out system (Heaton 1948; Braudel 1968; Clough and Cole 1968). The Amsterdam stock exchange was established in the early 17th century (Braudel 1968). The 19th century saw the regular market being replaced by continuous trading, purchase by sample, the rise of shop-keeping, and replacement of fairs by produce exchanges or bourses. While commerce exerted tremendous effects on the wider society, it could only operate within the societal framework.

For example, it was dependent on what transport technology was available and it functioned within the commercial policies of governments. The development of commerce was both a cause and a consequence of industrialization (Birnie 1952). Capitalism was conceived and took shape in the womb of trade.

The contribution of traders to the establishment of banks is well documented (Summer 1971; Clough and Cole 1968). "Banks began when men saw from experience that there was not sufficient money in specie for great commerce and great enterprise." (Summer 1971, p.200.) In Europe, banks were established in centres of great foreign commerce such as Venice, Amsterdam, Hamburg, and Nuremberg. Financial instruments such as letter of credits and bills of exchange were introduced to meet the needs of commerce. It was "merchant capital which created markets, financed manufactures, floated the American colonial economies, and launched banking and insurance"

(Grassby 1970, p.106). Even today, we still see the role of traders as modest providers of credit to peasants and farmers in developing countries. In emerging economies, the activities of traders promote not only the more efficient deployment of available resources, but also the growth of resources (Bauer 1991).

Opportunities for exchange provide scope for division of labour and the emergence of different crafts and skills. It may be argued that traders play a role in helping to transform a subsistence economy to an exchange economy. Trading activities are thus productive both statically and dynamically. Traders were risk-takers who, under the right conditions, underwent a metamorphosis to become financial and industrial capitalists. The instruments of capitalism were invented in the course of turning the wheels of commerce. Two examples are limited liability and the putting out system. The practice of limiting the liability of passive partners made it easier for companies to attract investors to participate in new business ventures. It provided an efficient means for entrepreneurs to pool together public financial resources by selling them shares on the stock exchange. Limited liability is an instrument for sharing risks and profits that proved crucial in the growth of capitalism. It is certainly a very important financial innovation, and has been used by some history students of financial systems to explain the differences between the bank-based financial systems typified by German-style universal banking and market-based financial systems of the Anglo-American variety (Forsyth and Verdier 2003). Countries that adopted early limited liability tended to have commercial banking specializing in short-term lending, as well as securities markets specializing in financing longer-term capital needs of companies. In countries without a long history of commercial development and an original accumulation of capital available, capital scarcity created a demand by firms for long-term loans from banks to take advantage of new, large-scale production technologies. Universal banks appeared in such countries to satisfy the demand for long-term financing that otherwise would not be met.

The putting out system was an organizational device used by merchants who identified and seized new economic opportunities beyond their role as buyers and sellers. The system was known to be in full swing in Italy and some other parts of Europe by the 13th and 14th centuries (Braudel 1968; Clough and Cole 1968). Under the system, a Verleger or wealthy merchant put out work. He provided the artisans with the raw materials and part of the wages, the remainder being paid on the delivery of the product which he then sold. Its distinct features were that work was done on a large scale by hired labour, that the workers did not own the raw materials and often not even the tools, and that the merchant controlled the whole process from start to finish. This form of outsourcing marked the dawn of industrial capitalism.

Contacts through traders are prime agents in the spread and exchange of new ideas, behaviour, and production methods- a fact in contemporary business, in modern commerce, and in commerce during the dawn of human civilisation (Day 1928). Early trade opened the first slender means of communication (Mangat 1969). In the 13th and early 14th century the most widely copied and read book in Italy was Marco Polo's, where practical information on markets were mixed with the romance of travel (Lopez 1976). The spread of ideas and information was further promoted by others who travel with traders with the explicit purpose of propagating their faith. Islam was introduced to Southeast Asia as a historical upshot of the commercial activities of the Arab traders. External commercial contacts often first suggest the very possibility of change, including economic improvement (Bauer 2000, p.8). The Mongolian conqueror Genghis Khan and his successors instructed their spies to travel with merchants on the trade routes to collect information about their victims (Fairbank and Reischauer 1979).

LEARNING FROM HISTORY OF MODERN COMMERCE

Globalization is the most important economic, political and cultural phenomenon of our time (Micklethwait and Wooldridge 2000). It is a process of social change, characterised by the globalization of markets, a shift towards an economy based on knowledge and information, and the growing importance of technology in everyday life (Castells 2000a, 2000b). The advent of network organizations provided some of the practices supporting B2B electronic commerce, such as supply chain management, just-in-time sourcing, lean production, and inter-

organizational information systems. Network organizations are now common both within and across national borders. Together with trade, capital and investment flow, and migration, network organizations represent one of the defining features of globalization. In the absence of such features, e-commerce as we know it would be very much restricted.

For example, if carmakers cannot import car components, there is not much future for Covisint, the e-procurement hub set up by major carmakers. "Indeed, well-designed trade policies can accelerate the development of electronic commerce, for instance, by removing some of the uncertainty that hangs over it today" (OECD 2000, p.92). Globalization spurs competition and hence innovation. It speeds up the diffusion of new technology through trade and investment. In its turn, by reducing the cost of communications, IT helps to globalize production and capital markets. E-commerce holds the potential to reduce time and transaction cost, thereby promoting the efficiency in the link between production and consumption. The data available so far suggest a picture of remarkable cost-savings and improved efficiency for firms participating in B2B electronic commerce.

For society as a whole, e-commerce constitutes a strong price-deflationary activity because raising prices is harder when your customers can instantly compare them with everyone else's. From a historical perspective, the more interesting and important aspects of e-commerce are likely to be in its higher order effects. Six of such effects are discussed in the sub-sections that follow. Some already occurred while others are still evolving.

Deflationary and Other Macro-Economic Effects

Electronic markets affect the consumer purchase process in two ways (Turban et al. 2000). The first involves the digitization of market mechanisms, reducing customers' search costs in terms of money, time, and effort needed to gather information on price, quality, and product features. The second involves the digitization of information products and their distribution. These cost structure of these products is increasing returns and minimal reproduction costs. "Digitization also eliminates the need for sellers to maintain an inventory that

must be physically shipped to the consumer. A digitized market can be especially efficient when electronic payment methods will become more widely used." (Turban et al 2000: 437.) As labour and capital resources are released as a result of e-commerce and channeled into the production of other goods and services, their overall supply would go up, thereby exerting a downward pressure on prices.

Wallis and North (1986) measured the size of transaction costs that go through the market in the U.S. economy, such as costs associated with banking, insurance, finance, wholesale, and retail trade; or in terms of occupation, such as lawyers and accountants. They found that in 1970, more than 45 percent of national income was devoted to transactions. This percentage was an increase from about 25 percent a century earlier. The importance of transaction activities to American business applies to global business too. Modern international business exhibits a high degree of diversification in its production, production processes, and markets. "Inter alia, this is revealed by the increasing role of transaction-related business activities. ... In case of single market firm competing in perfect markets, transaction costs are zero. As firms become multi-activity and markets become imperfect, transaction costs assume a greater significance, and, in some cases, the proficiency of transaction-driven activities may determine the success or failure of an enterprise." (Dunning 1993, p. 5).

The conclusion to draw from this discussion is significant. Though e-commerce would not reduce transaction costs to zero, it would nevertheless reduce them significantly. Given the pervasive role of transactions, one important aspect of e-commerce is that it will improve the efficiency of all parts of the economy. Some studies tried to quantify the impact of e-commerce at the macro-economic level. For example, the Australian Department of Communication, Information Technology and Arts (1999) estimated that the net impact could be a 2.7 percent increase in the level of national output. Ancther study suggests that the rise of B2B e-commerce will, in the long run, increase the level of GDP by 5 percent (Goldman Sachs 2000). These studies are based on a number of quite restrictive assumptions and their results should thus be read with caution. Figures of these types and anecdotal evidences

are not convincing enough to persuade many economists who would prefer to see more evidence before pronouncing this trend permanent (Micklethwait and Wooldridge 2000). However, OECD reports broad agreement that at least in the United States, Australia, Denmark and Norway, changes in the growth rates of labour productivity are related to significant technological changes (OECD 2000a).

The development of the Internet and e-commerce could also modify some features of the current economic cycle. In one view, e-commerce facilitates more efficient stock management, leading to lower inventories as a ratio of sales and thereby modifying the stock building pattern. Since the late 1980s, inventories relative to sales fell sharply all over American manufacturing. The U.S. Department of Commerce (2000) calculates that this change saved American companies some $10 billion a year, with a cumulative amount of $115 billion since 1988. The downside is that without the buffer or reservoir role of stock, any downturn is transmitted more quickly through the whole system. The chairman of the U.S. Federal Reserve Bank, Alan Greenspan, told the Senate hearing in March 2001 that "The faster adjustment process does raise some warning flags. Firms appear to act in a far closer alignment than in previous decades. The result is not only a faster adjustment but one that is potentially more synchronized, compressing changes into an even shorter time frame."

Here we can see how e-business practice can have profound implications for the business cycle. Moreover, increased price competition in product markets may allow the economy to sustain more jobs without stoking inflation for a period of time. These features work to modify the usual process of inflation and thus the responsiveness of inflation to the business cycle (OECD 2000a). Another important development to follow is that by exposing firms to global competition, the Internet might also expedite progress towards implementing product market reforms (OECD 2000a, p.17).

Potential to Create New Markets

The wider market open to e-commerce could potentially stimulate and satisfy an increasingly widespread demand, thereby encouraging expansion in industry and foreign trade.

Peet (2000) expects a major winnowing of e-commerce firms down to a small number of giants, probably led by those best able to solve the fulfillment problem. This view applies well to companies competing with traditional retailers. But another possibility is just as significant: an opportunity for companies whose competitive edge is specialization. The global reach of the Internet means that the local neighborhood is not defined by physical geography but by specialty. "For goods and services that can be ordered and delivered over the network, the Internet is truly a global marketplace." (Choi et al 1997:501.) Companies which cannot possibly survive in a major city can do a brisk business serving a world market. New businesses in cyberspace would appear. An example is online publishing of books and journals that would be too expensive to publish in traditional form.

Opportunities exist for many smaller competitors providing special interest news and services. Where new businesses depend upon the postal services for fulfillment, the delivery cost is relatively high. The challenge is to develop the market and expand sales. As the volume of such business grows, fulfillment specialists and other services would arise to support them, reducing the delivery costs. With global B2B e-commerce, worldwide trade information is needed to help organizations improve their global sourcing, procurement, supply chain visibility, order commitment, transportation management, and collaboration capabilities. e-commerce means 24-hour, 365 days a year availability of services globally. It translates into a skewed advantage for global firms. It will improve the competitiveness of global firms and give customers greater convenience and flexibility. One common strategy to achieve global reach is through merger and acquisition. This strategy, however, may not be the preferred path of the more agile and successful corporations, given the high rates of debacles in cross border merger and acquisition (Micklethwait and Wooldridge 2000). How firms go about tackling this challenge will certainly be worth watching.

Inter-Dependency between Business Firms and Need for Rating Agencies

Competitive advantage is often gained by integrating supply chain activities at a lower cost than competitors (Kalakota and

Whinston 1997). Increased competition drives business firms to look for cost reduction and efficiency in co-ordination and integration of the supply chain. Isolated business activities such as marketing, material procurement and stock management, manufacturing, and distribution are reorganized to function in tandem. To maximize the efficiency of online procurement, companies must tie together their inventory control systems with web based exchanges. Online sales need to be linked to order entry systems and customer relationship management. What is important here is that the process of integration is not limited to an individual company, but across all firms in a supply chain-from supplier to customer (Kalakota and Whinston 1997). Such a trend deepens the co-ordination of processes and the integration of data. The upshot is that a business firm may be conceived as a node in a complex network of business activities. To borrow a term from Hanson (2000), networks can be perceived as a form of social technology.

EC increases inter-dependency among businesses. The level of integration currently seen among network organizations is gradually becoming more common among business organizations. Integration calls for a re-thinking of business ethics. It pays to play fair.

Trading in cyberspace involves risk. Uncertainty is associated with lack of relevant information that matters (Bodie and Merton 1998). It is similar to the risk early traders in nascent industrial societies faced when they began buying goods produced by strangers. Before the Industrial Revolution, they bought shoes from the shoemaker whom they knew directly or whom they knew from friends in the community. In the business environment brought on by the Industrial Revolution, they had no such direct knowledge, and brand emerged as an innovation to serve customers' need for identification when buying products made by "strangers".

There are interesting parallels in the new trading environment in cyberspace. For example, rating agencies are in demand to monitor and grade, on a regular basis, the quality of goods and services, and to rate the ability of buyers and sellers to meet their commitments. The electronic market supports an efficient use of information dispersed among economic agents. It provides a concrete example of a rational economic order, as described by Hayek (1945). He argues that the economic problem of society is a problem of the using knowledge not given to anyone in its totality. "The peculiar character of the problem of a rational economic order is determined precisely by the fact that the knowledge of the circumstances of which we must make use never exists in concentrated or integrated form, but solely as the dispersed bits of incomplete and contradictory knowledge which all the separate individuals possess. (Hayek 1945, p.519)" A related need is for some business party to guarantee or insure the quality of products customers are buying, e.g. in electronic auction. The seller needs to be guaranteed that the buyers will pay. A business opportunity is created for banks with global spread, to offer a service that parallels the letter of credit to some extent.

NEW BUSINESS MODELS AS INNOVATION

New business models are challenging the logic and assumptions of traditional models. Though investors and financial traders can argue about the value of Amazom.com, consensus exists in appreciating Amazon's business model as an organizational innovation. Businesses acting as intermediaries between supply and demand of B2B markets would become redundant while demands for services that facilitate the emergent e-commerce would grow.

One of the most important challenges facing organizations in the age of electronic commerce is the development of new business strategies and models. New business models challenge the logic and assumptions of traditional models. Referring to the first phase of electronic commerce, Keen (2001) recalls that the focus was on the technology as the driver: "Now companies are recognizing that this is about commerce: business models, process/technology integration, service, and relationships (Keen 2001, p.164)." This view is a manifestation that the new environment presents opportunities for some and threats for others. Indeed, inability to outgrow the dominant, outdated business design and thinking is often what leads to business failure (Kalakota and Robinson 2001).

The pressure is now on companies to function in a state of more or less constant transformation. Senior management must live with the challenges of earning revenues from well-tested practices while being prepared to experiment with new ideas which may undo these old practices. It is in essence a problem described as striking a balance between exploration and exploitation (March 1994). The last quarter of 1999 and early 2000 saw a lot of excitement in the capital market over dot.com companies. This excitement encouraged entrepreneurs to plunge into starting or expanding e-commerce companies even though investment analysts pointed out the pitfalls of burning money to increase market share. However, it is such investment climates that promote the emergence of new business models. From a longer term perspective, society would benefit even though individual investors may lose their shirts. To paraphrase March (1994):

Successful organizations build a 'can do' attitude that leads people to underestimate risk. Such attitude is likely to be prevalent in young, apparently successful high-growth firms where the environment conspires to induce investors to believe that they know the golden grail of investment. This risk underestimation is a way of inducing investment that may prove to be costly to the individuals concerned, but it may end up serving the larger society.

In the light of such developments, we reflect on the future shape of competitive strategy as part of new business models.

(a) In the world of EC, the barriers to entering business were lowered significantly. New entrants do not need to invest as much time and capital to run their business as did their counterparts in the so-called old economy. They quickly become threats to the incumbents. This change is especially true in information-related or information-intensive businesses e.g. e-publishers. Moreover competition to a company also comes from firms in other sectors; for example, telephone companies can offer services that would encroach in the traditional business of banks as financial intermediaries.

(b) Critical and demanding customers in the home market were seen as an essential factor in sharpening the claws of competition among companies (Porter 1990). With EC, especially so for information related products that can be marketed through the Internet, it is not always relevant to refer to the term home market, because the market is global.

(c) The behaviour of the capital market in the last quarters of 1999 and 2000, and the response of firms to that behaviour reflect the significant influence of the financial market upon business strategy. Given that companies rely more and more on equity capital for funding (OECD 2000b), top managers must be shrewd in formulating their strategy and presenting it in such a way as to boost investors' confidence, or at least to retain it. The relationship between capital market and e-business is a key consideration in such strategy formulation and presentation. This consideration is not easy given the nature of capital market, with all its sentiments, unpredictability, irrationality, and discipline.

(d) The emphasis on competition and lock-in found in Porter (1980) must be balanced with the language of co-operation, trust, mutual benefit, and openness. An OECD report (1999) spoke of the emergence of openness as a strategy, with many of the most successful e-commerce ventures granting their customers unparalleled access to their inner workings, databases, and personnel. Companies are entering a new ecology of business which demands new business models and new ways of thinking and acting.

(e) The traditional focus on the individual firm as the competitive unit shifted to the entire supply chain (Gattorna and Walters 1996). Three factors contributed:

1. Customers are demanding more varied, often individualized value from the supply chain.
2. New information technology makes it possible to obtain an overview of the entire supply chain and to use it to meet the demand.
3. The emergence of global markets and global sourcing stretched these supply chains over inter-continental distances. The time lags at this global scale make the efficient management of these long chains all the more critical.

Timmers (2000) classifies 11 business models that are currently found in the electronic commerce. Some of these models are the e-version of the traditional forms of running a business, while the rest go far beyond the traditional approaches. The innovative ones opt for value chain integration, and seek ways to add value through information management and rich functionality. "Creating these new business models is feasible only because of the openness and connectivity of the Internet. A consequence of the same open nature of the Internet is that it may be rather difficult to keep the details of a business model hidden. The possibility is not excluded, however, of protecting the intellectual property of a business model by legal means. For example, Priceline.com acquired a U.S. patent in August 1998 for its reverse auction business model (Timmers 2000: 45)." The story of Abuzz, documented by Kanter (2001), can be read as a story in exploring successful business models.

New Business Environment

The new business environment ushered in by e-commerce also stimulates businesses to engage in areas hitherto alien to them. As mentioned earlier, telephone companies can become financial companies by allowing customers to pay for goods and services by putting the charge on their bill. With the advent of Wireless Application Protocol (WAP) technology, mobile phones can provide customers with direct access to the Internet. Mobile online shoppers would use their WAP phones to make purchases without a credit card.

The new environment promotes innovation in two ways:

1. e-commerce increases efficiency in the innovative process.
2. By the integrated nature of technological innovations.

Increased Efficiency in the Innovative Process

On the supply side, technology increases the range of choices. On the demand side, adoption patterns are always responsive in ensuring the successful diffusion of the technological potential. "In many markets the constraining force on technological advancement is not the ability to produce new goods but uncertainty about consumer demand and the rate at which it will eventuate." (Roberts 2000: 31.)

Two types of management error result from this demand uncertainty:

1. managers launch high-technology failures and
2. managers fail to launch products that would have been successful (Eliashberg, Lilien, and Rao 1997).

The first represents supply for which there is no latent demand, while the latter represents latent demand for which there is no supply. In some instances, such as in the automobile industry, this gap is narrowed by the supplier and the buyer working together in the development of new products. Buyers and suppliers in the industry use computer-aided design technologies across firm boundaries to co-design components (Bensaou 1999). In other industries, these difficulties can be partly overcome with closer links to a wider market. One of the strengths of Internet-based e-commerce is that it is based on a global network accessible to all, easy to use, inexpensive and capable of communicating product information to potential customers in over 160 countries worldwide (Barjis & Chong 2000). However, more openness is needed to narrow the gap separating supply and demand. This pattern is also noticed by an OECD (1999) study on the economic and social impact of electronic commerce.

The open strategy of many of the most successful e-commerce ventures led to a shift in the role of customers, who are increasingly involved as partners in product design. What we are in fact witnessing is the penetration of market governance (Williamson 1975) into the whole web of demand and supply. Data capturing experiences and results of using products can be collected and processed to correct flaws in the design, production, and transport stages, a sort of learning by using (Rosenberg 1994). For example, garages in various parts of the world can access the web network designed for them by Nissan and Renault. After repairing and maintaining a Nissan or Renault car, the mechanics use the website to key in the details of the replaced components and of the car, thus providing feedback that the car makers can use to improve the design of their new models. Perhaps it is time to coin a new term to replace the term supply chain, defined by Christopher (1998) as the network of organizations that are involved, through upstream and downstream linkages, in different processes and activities that produce value in the form of products and services in the hands of ultimate consumers. I would suggest the term web of supply and demand and innovation, which is more akin to the dynamic supply webs notion defined by Kumar and Christiaanse(1999) than to Christopher's supply chain. My formulation nevertheless differs from Kumar and Christiaanse because it explicitly includes the role of web-based e-commerce in reducing wastage and uncertainty in the innovation process.

The Integrated Nature of Technological Innovations

The second effect comes from the integrated nature of technological innovations (Rosenberg 1976; Sahal 1981). As e-commerce evolves it is likely to follow the 'reverse product cycle', in which process efficiency gains are followed by quality improvements to existing products and then the creation of new products. "Typically it is in this final stage that significant economic growth occurs. E-commerce has the potential to be a platform from which significant new products emerge, many of which will be digital and online. New products have a tendency to beget more new products and processes in a virtuous spiral ..." (OECD 1999: 23.)

IMPACT ON BANKS

Commerce in our age inevitably involves monetary transaction. It would thus come as no surprise that e-commerce could affect banking in a very fundamental way, and would be affected by the ways banks respond to the new demands. For example, it will further undermine the power of bank branches (Lawrence et al 1998). E-commerce created a demand for low cost facility for micro payments (Choi et al 1997). There has been a report of the business opportunity for credit card companies and banks to act as information intermediaries in such a way that allows on-line customers to hide their identities from e-retailers (The Economist Dec 9 th 2000).

Some other areas in which banks can develop e-commerce products are (Wenninger 2000):

protection for e-commerce participants against fraud arising from the misrepresentation of identities, assistance for small businesses to enter into EC, electronic billing services, offering firms the technology for business-to-business electronic commerce. In short, e-commerce may pay an active role in transforming banks.

CONCLUDING REMARKS

Studying electronic commerce from the perspective of history allows us to glean new meanings and implications by looking at old facts. Business and management-oriented books are right in pointing out that doing business electronically is not merely buying and selling on the Internet. They argue that business itself is largely a process of information gathering, processing and distribution. Digitising the process makes operations more efficient and would yield higher returns for the firms. My approach looks beyond this. It is alert to changes in the areas of institutions, and the likely implications of e-commerce on business practices, business models, and business cycles. Such perspective can give some pointers for future research. For example, accounting theory as we know it is inadequate in coping with the demands of e-business, and research in this area is likely be both challenging and rewarding.

In what ways would widespread adoption of supply chain management affect the volatility of commodities market? Another example is the prospect of the eroding tax base of governments as a result of wide-spread e-business practices; this outcome would result in serious social and political consequences. Electronic commerce is closely connected with changes in what Freeman (1987) calls techno economic paradigm. This type of change is characterized by its effects on the input cost structure and the conditions of production and distribution for almost every branch of the economy. Productivity gains are realized throughout the economy as a result of a process of learning, adaptation, incremental innovation and institutional change. It has been suggested that for a society to reap the full benefits of a technology, there must be a match between the technological system and the socio-institutional setup (Perez 1983). If the problems of institutional adaptation can be overcome, such techno-economic transformations offer opportunities for new employment-generating investment and labor-saving productivity gains. "These opportunities arise both in the provision of new and improved consumer goods and services, and in the provision of a new range of capital equipment for all sectors of the economy" (Freeman 1987, p.57).

This view is broadly echoed by the OECD (1999) which sees e-commerce as an economic phenomenon and part of the broader process of social change. "As both a product and manifestation of such transformations, electronic commerce is being shaped by, and increasingly will help to shape, modern society as a whole. Societal factors will thus have a profound influence on its future development. They will also merit attention from a public policy standpoint, both to establish the social conditions that allow electronic commerce to reach its full economic potential and to ensure that its benefits are realised by society as a whole" (OECD 1999, 143). This significant shift in the way business is conducted is happening within the new historical context of globalization. Electronic commerce is enabled by, but at the same time enhancing The process of social institutional adaptation on such scale and scope is neither simple nor straightforward.

The emergence of new business practices and institutions involves a restructuring of many interests, and it is contingent on a variety of complex societal conditions. To paraphrase Putterman and Rueschemeyer (1992): Historically, the formation of business institutions represents social innovations of immense significance, based on political, economic, and cultural resources and guided by trial and error in the pursuit of large-scale economic interests. In the process of promoting electronic commerce, key players should tap into existing societal resources and, more importantly, should contribute to the reservoir of societal resources. This paper aims to contribute to an appreciation of the importance of such process by reviewing the history of modern commerce and to suggest a possible profile of anticipation based on the evolving present.

Bibliography

Ariel Buira: *Challenges to the World Bank and IMF: Developing Country Perspectives*, London, Anthem Press, 2003.

Bandow, Doug, and Ian Vasquez: *Perpetuating Poverty: The World Bank, the IMF, and the Developing World*, Washington, DC: Cato Institute, 1994.

Edwards, S.: *Capital Controls, Exchange Rate and Monetary Policy in the World Economy,* Cambridge, Cambridge University Press, 1995.

Guhan, S.: *The World Bank's Lending in South Asia*, Washington, Brookings Institution, 1995.

Lawrence H. White: *The Theory of Monetary Institutions*, Oxford, Blackwell, 1999.

Magliveras, Konstantinos D. *Banks, Fraud and Crime*, Lloyd's of London Press, London, 2000.

Paul, Kegan : *Money and the Mechanism of Exchange,* Oxford, London, 1890.

Ranade, Sudhanshu: *Rural Banking Adrift*, Bombay, Jaico Publishing House, 1984.

Robert Z. Aliber: *The International Market for Foreign Exchange*, New York, Praeger, 1969.

Seligman, E. R. A. : *Currency Inflation and Public Debts,* New York, 1922.

Summner, Prof. : *History of American Currency,* MacMillan, New York, 1874.

Vines, David and Christopher Gilbert: *The IMF and its Critics: Reform of the Global Financial Architecture*, Cambridge, Cambridge University Press, 2004.

Wolfe, J.N.: *Value, Capital and Growth,* Chicago, Edinburgh University Press. 1968.

Index